PROGRAM TRANSLATION FUNDAMENTALS

METHODS AND ISSUES

COMPUTER SOFTWARE ENGINEERING SERIES
ISSN 0888-2088

1. *Fundamentals of Data Structures**
   Ellis Horowitz and **Sartaj Sahni**
2. *Fundamentals of Computer Algorithms**
   Ellis Horowitz and **Sartaj Sahni**
3. *Graph Algorithms**
   Shimon Even
4. *Foundations of Computer Science**
   M. S. Carberry, H. M. Khalil, J. F. Leathrum, and **J. S. Levy**
5. *Assemblers, Compilers, and Program Translation**
   Peter Calingaert
6. *Computers and Social Controversy**
   Tom Logsdon
7. *Computer Systems Architecture**
   Jean-Loup Baer
8. *Structured BASIC and Beyond**
   Wayne Amsbury
9. *Jewels of Formal Language Theory**
   Arto Salomaa
10. *The Nature of Computation: An Introduction to Computer Science**
    Ira Pohl and **Alan Shaw**
11. *Pascal: An Introduction to Methodical Programming, Second Edition**
    W. A. Findlay and **D. A. Watt**
12. *Principles of Database Systems, Second Edition**
    Jeffrey Ullman
13. *Computers in Number Theory**
    Donald Spencer
14. *Learning BASIC Step by Step**
    Vern McDermott and **Diana Fisher**
15. *Paradigms* and *Programming with Pascal**
    Derick Wood
16. *Pascal for FORTRAN Programmers**
    Ronald Perrott and **Donald C. S. Allison**
17. *Advanced BASIC Step by Step**
    Vern McDermott and **Diana Fisher**
18. *Fundamentals of Programming Languages, Second Edition**
    Ellis Horowitz
19. *Learning Pascal Step by Step**
    Vern McDermott, Andrew Young, and **Diana Fisher**
20. *Fundamentals of Data Structures in Pascal, Second Edition**
    Ellis Horowitz and **Sartaj Sahni**
21. *Programming Languages: A Grand Tour, Third Edition**
    Ellis Horowitz
22. *Program Translation Fundamentals: Methods and Issues*
    Peter Calingaert

*These previously published books are in the *Computer Software Engineering Series* but they are not numbered within the volume itself. All future volumes in the *Computer Software Engineering Series* will be numbered.

PROGRAM TRANSLATION FUNDAMENTALS
METHODS AND ISSUES

PETER CALINGAERT

*University of North Carolina
at Chapel Hill*

COMPUTER SCIENCE PRESS

Computer Science Press, Inc.
1803 Research Boulevard
Rockville, Maryland 20850

1 2 3 4 5 6   Printing   Year   93 92 91 90 89 88

Library of Congress Cataloging-in-Publication Data

Calingaert, Peter
        Program Translation Fundamentals.

        (Computer software engineering series, ISSN 0888–2088 ; 22)
        Bibliography: p.
        Includes index.
        1. Translators (Computer programs)   I. Title. II. Series.
QA76.76.T83C35   1987   005.4′5   87–17856
ISBN 0–88175–096–4

PREFACE

This book is the successor to my *Assemblers, Compilers, and Program Translation*. Like its predecessor, it is devoted to computer programs that translate other computer programs. They are known as **translation programs** or **translators**. The book is intended primarily for use as a one-semester text in a first course on translators. Although designed for advanced undergraduate or beginning graduate students, it is suitable also for self-study by programmers and other computer professionals.

Of the many students and practitioners of computer science, few will ever be called upon to build a compiler, or other complex translator. For that reason, I believe that compiler construction should not be the focus of a first course in translators. The book presents instead a unified treatment of principles, methods, and issues of translation. These are discussed in the context of many different types of translators, not only compilers.

Although few readers will ever need to build a translator, some knowledge of translators is indispensable. There are many reasons. All programmers, except perhaps those who code in raw decimal for a pocket computer, use translators all the time. The efficacy with which they use a computer system is enhanced by an understanding of the translators that serve as intermediaries in expressing their instructions to the system.

Moreover, two important areas of both practical and theoretical interest are more easily accessible to persons with knowledge of translators than to those without. It is obvious that the study and design of programming languages are dependent upon understanding how programs written in those languages can be translated. It is perhaps less evident that some knowledge of translators is helpful in the study of operating systems. One reason is that issues of binding time, which are often clearer in the context of translation, are important in control programs too. Another is that many of the demands upon an operating system, particularly in storage management, are direct consequences of source-language requests and translator function. A third reason is that the translation mechanisms of generation and interpretation are widely used in control programs.

Furthermore, many computer professionals will design application systems. The user of such a system specifies requirements by what is in effect an application language. In designing both that language and its translator, the application system designer must be able to determine which translation techniques are appropriate and must be able to use them effectively.

Finally, the increasingly widespread use of microcomputers, with their sometimes limited programming support, has enlarged the need for translators. More importantly, perhaps, it has enlarged the population of potential translator writers. The emphasis here is usually on simple translators to run on the microcomputer itself, although the use of a more powerful computer to generate code for the microcomputer may be a suitable alternative.

Construed narrowly, the term "translator" denotes a program that transforms the representation of an algorithm from one language to another. It generates an output program to correspond to an input program. The content of the input program is by and large preserved, but its encoding is changed. Often the input encoding is more oriented to human communication and less to machine communication than is the output encoding. Such translations are performed by assemblers and compilers. Macro processors and linkers, on the other hand, perform translations in which changing the encoding is secondary to other functions, text substitution by the former and resolution of symbolic references by the latter.

The narrow construction of "translators" excludes two types of programs, interpreters and loaders, but the book treats both. The result of interpretation is not to recast an algorithm, but rather to execute it. Yet many of the functions performed by interpreters are identical or similar to those of the translators that generate output programs. Moreover, interpretive and generative translators not uncommonly cooperate in the execution of a program. We often classify loaders as control programs, and so they are, but there are three reasons for studying them with translators. One is that they are often combined with linkers. A second is that the requirement to perform relocation constrains the form of the output produced by other translators. The third is that in performing relocation, the loader really is acting as a translator.

My readers are assumed to have some experience in programming both in an assembler language and in a machine-independent procedural language, such as PL/I, PASCAL, C, or MODULA–2. They need not be conversant, however, with the details of language syntax. In fact, the book expresses algorithms in a notation that is reminiscent of many languages, but with limited adherence to any particular syntax. Readers should also be familiar with the representation and manipulation of arrays, queues, stacks, and trees, and with the use of linked lists. Although readers should have studied the role of individual bits in representing both instructions and data in a machine, it is not expected that they have done so for more than one machine. In particular, readers are not assumed to be familiar with both direct-addressing and base-addressing machines, nor with both single-accumulator and multiple-accumulator architectures. Prior acquaintance with the theory of formal languages, although it cannot but help, is nowhere assumed.

Recent years have brought increased emphasis on functional and logic languages. Despite their growing importance, I believe that it is appropriate not to include them in a first book on translators. Coverage is therefore restricted to procedural languages.

Many books on translators treat only a few types, often compilers alone, or perhaps assemblers and loaders. They thus forgo the opportunity to note similarities and distinctions among different translators, to highlight important choices between translation techniques, or to show how various translators cooperate with each other. Instead, they offer depth at the cost of restricting the breadth of coverage. I believe strongly that more balanced coverage is preferable to early specialization.

Chapter 1 presents an overview of the objectives of translation, of the languages to be translated, and of the types of tools and translators. It offers a brief historical chronicle, and continues with a discussion of the role of program modules. The chapter concludes by asserting the important distinction between translator function and implementation.

Chapter 2 is about assembly without either macro or conditional processing. It presents the standard two-pass assembler, first in rudimentary form and then endowed with many of the commonly encountered optional features. One-pass assemblers are introduced here to accent the concept of binding time, which is used throughout the book as a theme, even when not mentioned explicitly.

Chapter 3 discusses several programming language matters: reusability, block structure, modes of module activation, linkage mechanisms, and parameter correspondence. The chapter offers a concise review of issues particularly important to translation, and may be omitted by readers who are thoroughly familiar with programming languages.

Chapter 4 deals with macro processing, treated generally as parametric substitution of text, but emphasizing the generation of source code for further translation. The coverage includes nested definitions and calls. Chapter 5 describes and compares the two major translation mechanisms, interpretation and generation. Conditional assembly, which depends on the notions of interpretation, is discussed afterwards, as is the combination of macro processing with assembly.

Chapter 6 discusses two functions important to many different types of translators, both generative and interpretive. These are lexical and syntactic analysis. Formal context-free grammars are introduced and two parsing methods presented. Operator precedence is the example of a bottom-up method, chosen for its efficiency in parsing expressions. Recursive descent is the example of a top-down method, chosen for its ease of implementation. The latter method is extended to lexical analysis, for which the table-driven implementation of a finite automaton is also described.

Chapter 7 begins with a miniature exposition of the compilation process. It continues by examining two data structures of major importance in compilation: intermediate code and symbol tables. A brief review of selected data structures, hashing functions, and overflow techniques appropriate to symbol tables is followed by a more thorough discussion of symbol tables for languages with block structure. Chapter 8 concludes the treatment of compiler design begun in Chapter 6 and continued in Chapter 7. It emphasizes semantic processing and the machine-dependent steps of storage allocation, target-code generation, code optimization, and error handling.

Chapter 9 addresses chiefly linkers and loaders, both separately and in combination. Although loaders are often studied in conjunction with assemblers, I have deferred the topic for three reasons. One is because compilers, too, produce programs that must be linked and loaded. A second is that deferring Chapter 9 allows more calendar time for the interesting programming assignments that can be based upon earlier chapters. A third reason is that relocating loaders, and particularly dynamic loading and dynamic linking, provide a natural transition to the study of operating systems.

Finally, Chapter 10 turns from individual translators and specific techniques to several issues of importance to program translation in general. These include the hardware and software environments within which the translators operate; the differences among translators; the judicious choice of translation techniques to effect various design trade-offs; the separate translation of modules; program portability; and the use of the computer to help write its own translators.

Some departures from the foregoing sequence are quite possible, particularly if an instructor is available to smooth over possible discontinuities. Linkers and loaders can be combined with assemblers; Chapter 9 can follow Chapter 2, and I have sometimes taught the material in that order. Instructors who prefer to treat first the matters common to all translators can cover Chapters 3 and 6 immediately after Chapter 1. Chapters 7 and 8, on the other hand, depend in varying degrees on the earlier chapters and cannot easily be advanced.

The instructor who prefers a more leisurely pace, or who wishes to cover most of the material in a quarter rather than a semester, can omit one or more topics without loss of continuity. The most suitable candidates for omission are nesting in macros (4.5 and 4.6), the combination of macro processing with assembly (5.4), character recognition (6.3.3), lexical ambiguity (6.3.4), block-structured symbol tables (7.4.4) or all of symbol tables (7.4), code optimization

(8.4), error handling (8.5), linkage using a transfer vector (9.2.3), dynamic loading (9.2.6), dynamic linking (9.2.7), translator organization (10.3.4), and translator generators (10.6). Although the omission of one-pass assemblers (2.3) may tempt the instructor, I recommend against it strongly. Not to explore fully the resolution of forward references is educationally unsound.

One academic quarter is enough to cover the entire book with graduate or advanced undergraduate students. With selected graduate students, we have been able to cover almost the entire text in half a semester, but without assigning any programming.

Each chapter concludes with suggestions for further study and a set of exercises. The suggested readings are not comprehensive, but rather selected to extend or complement my presentation. Full citations are given in the Bibliography, which also lists many works not specifically suggested. These are chiefly journal articles and conference papers that the reader can use as an initial guide to further exploration of translators.

The exercises fall into two categories. More than 150 review questions appear at the end of the chapters. They are intended to be answered without writing. A few questions merely test the readers' recall. Most, however, require thoughtful analysis. There are also more than 100 problems to be worked. They emphasize synthesis rather than analysis. Some are finger exercises to provide drill in specific translation techniques. Others present extensions of the text. A few challenge readers to apply their understanding to unfamiliar situations. Most of the exercises are original and class-tested. I have adapted a few particularly fine problems from other sources.

The coverage of the different translators necessarily varies, and is deeper for the simpler translators than it is for compilers. The book discusses algorithms and data structures in enough detail to permit the reader to implement a working assembler, macro processor, interpreter, linker, or loader. The reader should not expect, however, to be able to implement a full compiler on the basis of this book alone.

I am grateful to the many readers who have continued to use *Assemblers, Compilers, and Program Translation*, despite its advancing age. Some sections of that book are as appropriate today as when it was first published, and I have not hesitated to incorporate them. But the present book reflects my analyzing *de novo* the fundamental issues of program translation and how to present them. My analysis was aided by Edward J. Miranda, to whom I am indebted for a careful analysis of the strengths and weaknesses of the earlier book. Peter J. Brown scrutinized the proposal for the present book, and offered much valuable advice. I have tried to follow most of it.

One result of the redesign has been the deletion of a few topics, the expansion of a few, and the addition of others. Almost all of Chapter 10, in particular, is new material. Modernization is evident in the examples, the suggestions for further study, and the bibliography. Some of the passages from the earlier book appear almost *verbatim*, but most appear with varying degrees of rewriting. Another result has been considerable reorganization, especially of the second half of the book.

The manuscript was tested in a class taught by Richard T. Snodgrass, who offered many valuable suggestions for improvement. Rick's students, most of whom participated anonymously in this test, were a big help. Juan Valiente, who assisted in teaching the course, prepared new solutions to some of the problems. In translating the earlier book into Chinese, Fangwei Pu prepared solutions to almost all of its exercises. He also suggested several revisions.

Hala Abdalla found an important substantive error in my original treatment of operator precedence. Harvey Cohen not only pinpointed the most obscure passage in the earlier book, but also informed me of some important computer developments that I had ignored. Bharat Jayaraman and I had several extremely valuable discussions of programming languages and translation. Gyorgy Revesz published an improvement to one of my macro processing algorithms that led to an informative correspondence. To these scholars, too, I am grateful for their interest and contributions.

Peter Calingaert

CONTENTS

3   Program Modules

4   Macro Processing

5   Interpretation and Generation

8 Compilation

9 Linking and Loading

10 General Issues

Chapter 1

Overview

1.1 OBJECTIVES OF TRANSLATION

A translator permits the programmer to express an algorithm in a language other than that of the machine that is to execute the algorithm. Why should the programmer select a language other than machine language? After all, so doing commits the programmer to the costs incurred in performing translation. Programming in machine language would obviate these costs. Nevertheless, the machine-language programmer is rare. The reason is that machine language is very ill-designed for human communication. This is not the fault of the machine designers. The purpose of machine language is to express algorithms in a form in which the machine can interpret them efficiently. Because automatic computers use two-state storage and switching devices almost exclusively, sequences of binary digits provide the most natural form for expressing instructions. Sequences of binary digits prove very unnatural, however, for humans to construct or to understand. Hence, programmers prefer to express algorithms in a different form.

But it is more than personal preference that mandates the use of more expressive languages than those whose sentences are merely strings of zeros and ones. The greater ease of expression in other languages confers important benefits. One is increased accuracy of programming. Errors are easier to avoid and to detect when the symbol set is larger than {0,1}, and when the program text is shorter. Another benefit is increased programmer productivity: what can be written more easily can be written more rapidly. A particularly important benefit is that the programmer need no longer be intimately familiar with the computer that will execute the program. Let a language be available that expresses concepts in terms related not to the computer, but rather to the problem that the user is trying to solve. Then we can place the power of the computer at the disposal of workers who are not computer experts.

Moreover, if the language is independent of the computer, we can transport programs between computers that have different machine languages. This leads to further increase in programmer productivity and to the advantages of exchanging programs. The cost, for any number of programs, includes the construction and use of a single translator for each desired machine language.

The input to a translation program is expressed in a **source** language. The result of performing the translation may be the execution of the required algorithm on a machine whose language, the **host** language, is other than the source. Alternatively, the translator may produce as output a representation of the algorithm in a **target** language. That target language is often the machine language of some computer, which is then able to execute the algorithm. Sometimes a nonmachine language is chosen as target. Typically, this language is itself the source language for a second translator, which then yields the desired result. If the target language is machine language, the translator output is often called **machine code**.

1.2 SOURCE LANGUAGES

Categories. Source languages differ widely, and in various respects. The following classifications may appear simplistic to some readers, but will help us in delineating the scope of this book.

Some languages are intended to allow the programmer to address a wide variety of problems and applications; we refer to them as **general-purpose**. Other languages are more focussed in their intended use. These **special-purpose** languages differ widely in their areas of application. Examples include RPG for report generation, GPSS for event-driven simulation, LOTUS 1–2–3 for spreadsheet manipulation, and SAS for statistical analysis.

Some languages emphasize the specification of a solution *procedure*. Others emphasize the *requirements* for a solution rather than the procedure to be used to arrive at the solution. This leads to a classification of languages into two groups, **procedural** and **declarative**. Most of the widely used general-purpose languages are procedural, as are some special-purpose languages. Recent activity in programming-language design has focussed primarily on declarative languages.

Nonprocedural Languages. There are perhaps two major classes of declarative languages. **Functional** languages, also called "applicative languages", are based on the specification of value. Leading examples are LISP and APL, although both of these (except so-called "pure" LISP) have procedural elements as well. **Logic** languages are based on predicate logic, equational logic, or set theory. The best-known example is PROLOG. Functional and logic programming languages often resemble mathematical notation.

Many special-purpose languages also are nonprocedural and express a result that the computer is to accomplish. Examples include specifications of report writing and of file sorting. The former specifications include descriptions of data fields and report formats; the latter include descriptions of data records, keys, and desired sequences. In some operating systems, the command language is another nonprocedural source language. We can view all of these languages as constituting another class of declarative languages.

Procedural Languages. Procedural languages differ in the degree to which they reflect the structure of the target machine. Those in one group are intended to be **machine-dependent**. They are designed to permit the programmer to control machine operation in detail. They necessarily reflect the machine structure explicitly, and are known as **assembler** languages. Usually, a given assembler language is intended for use with a single machine design. Assembler language differs from the binary machine language chiefly in that operations and their operands can be expressed symbolically, without concern for actual encodings or numeric addresses.

Representation of an algorithm without reference to a particular machine is considered to be at a higher level of abstraction than
are assembler languages. The most common designation for languages that express algorithms in such a manner is "higher-level".
Sometimes they are called "user-oriented" to distinguish them from
the "machine-oriented" assembler languages. We shall use instead
the more appropriate phrase **machine-independent** languages.

Machine-independent procedural languages are characterized
by more powerful primitive operations and more powerful control
structures than are available in machine language or in assembler
language. An example of a primitive operation might be reading a
record from a file specified only by name; another is exponentiation.
Typical control structures include repetition of a group of instructions until a specified condition holds. A few of these languages
are designed to resemble a natural language, such as English, more
closely than could an assembler language. Among the best known
languages in this category are ADA, ALGOL68, APL*, BASIC, C,
COBOL, FORTRAN, MODULA–2, PASCAL, and PL/I.

Choice of Languages. Procedural special-purpose languages present
no translation requirements other than those of procedural general-
purpose languages. Declarative special-purpose languages often have
idiosyncratic features. The translator must, of course, handle these
properly. Discussing them here, however, would add much more
bulk than illumination to our introductory treatment. Moreover,
readers are more likely to be familiar with one or more general-
purpose languages than with special-purpose languages.

Declarative languages are now undergoing intense investiga-
tion. New languages and new approaches to their translation appear frequently. The field is exciting, and holds great potential.
Most programming, however, is still done in procedural languages.
These include not only the assembler languages but a substantial
majority of the important machine-independent languages. It is appropriate, therefore, for an introductory treatment not to encom-
pass declarative languages. We shall therefore restrict our coverage to procedural languages, both machine-dependent and machine-
independent.

---

*to the extent that it is procedural rather than declarative

1.3 TRANSLATION MECHANISMS

In translating an algorithm, the translator must both analyze and synthesize. This holds whether the translation results in direct execution on the host machine or in a target-language program for later execution on the target machine. The translator must analyze the source-language representation of the algorithm to determine what actions are ultimately to be performed. It must also synthesize those actions, either into direct performance or into a target-language representation.

Analysis of source language incorporates three stages: lexical, syntactic, and semantic. **Lexical** analysis is the determination of what symbols of the language are represented by the characters in the source-language text. For many machine-independent languages, lexical analysis would classify "*pressure*" as an identifier, "13" as an integer, "(" and "<=" as special symbols, "'LANGUAGE'" as a character string, and ".314159E+01" as a so-called "real" number. Examination of the text to identify and classify symbols is known as **scanning**, and lexical analyzers are therefore often called **scanners**.

Syntactic analysis is the determination of the structure of the source-language program. If the source language is an assembler language with a fixed format for each instruction, this analysis could be trivial. The symbol in columns 10–14 might, for example, always specify the operation code of the machine-language instruction to be performed. If the format is not so constrained, or if the source language is more complex, syntactic analysis poses more of a challenge. Lexical analysis of the program fragment "$a + b * c$" would establish that it comprises three identifiers separated by two special symbols. It would probably also determine that the special symbols represent binary operations. The major task in syntactic analysis of the fragment would be to determine whether the operation represented by "+" was to be performed before or after that represented by "*". In making the determination, the syntactic analyzer would apply a specification of the rules for constructing symbol strings of the programming language. This set of rules is known as a **grammar** for the language. Application of a grammar to determining syntactic structure is known as **parsing**, and syntactic analyzers are therefore often called **parsers**.

Semantic analysis determines the source-language program's *meaning* in the sense that it identifies the actions specified by the program. For the string "$a + b * c$" semantic analysis would determine what particular actions are specified by "+" and by "*". For reasons we shall discuss later, translators often perform semantic analysis in conjunction with syntactic analysis. Conceptually, it is nevertheless a different process.

The synthesis of action by the translation program involves one of two mechanisms. **Interpretation** is the direct performance of the actions identified in the process of analyzing the source-language program. For each possible action there exists a host-language subroutine to perform it. Interpretation requires the proper subroutine to be called at the right time with the appropriate parameters. **Generation** is the creation of target-language code to perform at a later time each action identified by analysis of the source-language program. Appropriate parameters assist in shaping the code sequence to be produced. Many people restrict the term "generation", using it only for source languages nearer the machine-oriented end of the spectrum. They apply "compilation" to those languages that are more user-oriented.

1.4 TYPES OF TRANSLATORS

Translators that synthesize actions by interpretation are called **interpreters**. Although we have been discussing translation *programs*, it is important to observe that interpreters may be made of hardware as well as software. In fact, every computer is an interpreter of its own machine language, because it translates machine-language instructions into actions. As a result, every sequence of program translations includes a hardware interpreter at the end, even if no interpretation by software occurs. For reasons that will become clear after we examine translation mechanisms further, interpretation is easier to perform than generation. Consequently, interpreters are usually easier to write than are generative translators. They tend, however, to result in much slower execution.

It would seem natural to designate as "generators" those programs that translate by generation. The term is indeed used, but it is customarily restricted to programs whose input is nonalgorithmic. Examples include report program generators (RPG) and sort generators. Of the generative translators from algorithmic source language, the most important are assemblers, compilers, linkers, and loaders. For the simplest **assembler**, the target language is machine language. Its source language has instructions in one-to-one correspondence with those of machine language, but with symbolic names for both operations and operands. The translator just converts each assembler-language instruction into the corresponding machine-language instruction, collecting those instructions into a program. Less elementary assemblers translate the program into a target-language form that permits us to combine the program with other programs before execution.

Many programs contain sequences of instructions that are repeated in either identical or nearly identical form. The repetitious writing of such sequences is obviated by the **macro processor**. This translator allows the user to define once a sequence of source-language code and then to refer to it by name each time it is to be translated. Each reference, which may use parameters to introduce controlled variation, results in the generation of source-language text for a subsequent translation. **Conditional** macro processors provide for the conditional performance of part of the translation.

The **compiler** translates from a machine-independent source language to a machine-oriented target language. Several target-language instructions usually result from each source-language instruction.

The **linker** takes as input independently translated programs whose original source-language representations include symbolic references to each other. Its task is to resolve these symbolic references and produce a single program. There is typically little difference between the linker's source and target languages. Other names for the linker are "binder", "consolidator", "librarian", and "linkage editor".

The **loader** takes a program produced by assembler, compiler, or linker. It places that program in a particular set of physical main storage locations. It also makes the changes necessary in the program to permit it to be executed when resident in those locations. The loader's target language is true machine language; its source language is nearly machine language.

Loading is intimately associated with the storage management function of operating systems, and is usually performed later than are assembly and compilation. Some actions in linking must be deferred until load time and others may be deferred until execution. It is therefore convenient to classify linkers and loaders as control programs. This they are, but they are translators as well and interact closely with assemblers and compilers. It is instructive to study linkers and loaders both in the operating system context and in the translator context.

1.5 HISTORICAL NOTES

The earliest computers, even those considered large at the time, executed single programs written in raw machine language. To keep track of storage use, the programmer customarily prepared by hand a "memory map" on which to write symbolic names for the variables whose values occupied the corresponding locations. Computers became larger and faster. When main storage reached a thousand words or so, the memory map became too unwieldy. Moreover, it was much easier to think of symbolic operation codes, such as LOAD and ADD, rather than the decimal or even binary numbers used to represent them in machine language. These needs led to the elementary symbolic assembler. Another early development was the **absolute** loader. This program would take a machine-language program, whether written directly by a programmer or produced by an assembler, read it into main storage, and transfer control to it.

Within a few years, two major new features appeared. One was designed for computers whose main storage was on magnetic drum, for which the maximum random access time greatly exceeded the minimum, by a factor of perhaps 50. The **optimizing** assembler assigned to data and instructions those storage addresses that would minimize execution time. Because the main storage media in current use present a uniform random access time, this feature is no longer needed. The second feature, provision of macro generation and conditional assembly, soon extended the power of assemblers. Unlike the optimizing assembler, this feature was not limited to a particular hardware design, and is still in widespread use.

A nearly parallel development was due to the rather limited instruction repertoires of early machines. Desirable instructions that had not been foreseen in the hardware design were expressed in a language different from the limited machine language or assembler language. Because the hardware was unable to interpret these new instructions, their interpretation was performed by programs, called **interpreters**. Among the most popular features provided by the early interpreters were three-address instruction formats and floating-point arithmetic operations.

Not only the floating-point arithmetic subroutines, but other subroutines, both arithmetic and nonarithmetic, constituted growing libraries of subroutines available to all users of a system. If the subroutines were written to be executed while occupying fixed locations in storage, then their use was highly constrained. This was because not more than one program can occupy a given storage location. Added to this was the problem that the user program that called the subroutines needed storage of its own. The conflicting storage requirements were resolved in the following manner. Both the system subroutines and the assembler output were produced in a form in which addresses were specified not absolutely, but only relative to the start of the program. A **relocating loader** would read the program into whatever storage locations were available, and then insert the correct absolute addresses that corresponded to the starting location chosen.

Before loading, another step became convenient. This was the linking of a user program to subroutines, or of separately written or translated user programs to each other. The result was a single program to be loaded. Symbolic names defined in one of the modules to be linked could be referenced in another module that had been prepared separately without access to the definition. Linkers provided the required resolution of intermodule symbolic references.

The poor execution efficiency of interpreters led to a desire to perform generative translation, yet without losing the extended source-language capabilities of existing interpreters. This most difficult of the language translation requirements was met by the compiler. In fact, the earliest successful compiler particularly stressed target-language efficiency to enhance its chances of adoption. For quite a few years compilers were limited to problem-oriented languages designed for restricted fields of application, usually either business or numeric calculation. Later, more widely applicable languages became available, and so did the corresponding compilers.

1.6 MODULAR DEVELOPMENT

In writing a large program, it is often convenient to manage the programming effort by dividing the program into subprograms or **modules**. These may be written more or less independently of each other and can often be translated separately and combined after translation. This approach is termed **modular development** of programs. The term "module" often has special meanings in discussions of software engineering. It may denote an assignment in the division of programming responsibility, or a unit in the subdivision of the functional specifications of a program. We shall use it here in a more limited sense to denote a program unit that can be translated independently of other units. Examples include a procedure in C, a user-defined function in APL, and a "control section" in IBM 370 assembler language.

Among the most important advantages of modular development are (1) the ability to design, code, and test different program components in parallel; and (2) the restriction of changes to only applicable modules rather than throughout the program. Because some program development costs rise faster than proportionally to the length of a program component, another benefit of modularization is reduction of these costs.

A source-language program contains three kinds of references. In assembler language, for example, **absolute** references include operation codes, numeric and string-valued constants, and fixed addresses. The values of absolute references are independent of which storage locations the resulting machine code will eventually occupy. **Relative** references include the addresses of instructions and of working storage. These are fixed only with respect to each other, and are normally stated relative to the address of the beginning of the module. Because the modules of a program are interdependent, identifiers declared in one module are often referenced within another. The use, within one module, of an identifier declared within another is called an **external** reference. Whether an external reference is in fact absolute or relative is not necessarily known at the time the module is translated.

Many compilers and most assemblers are designed to satisfy the desire to create programs by writing separate **source modules**. The very word "assembler" was adopted to emphasize the assembly of several source modules into a single program. Both compilers and such **module assemblers**, also called "routine" or "subprogram" assemblers (*cf.* Barron78), typically perform the first of three successive translation steps. They translate a source module into an **object module**.

Although the **object code** within an object module is similar to machine code, there are two differences. One is that external references have not been translated into machine language. The reason is that the modules in which they are defined are not available to the translator. The other difference is that relative references have not been translated into machine-language addresses. This is because it is not yet known which locations in the machine the program will occupy during execution.

To assist in subsequent steps of translation, the object module contains three tables in addition to the object code. One table lists identifiers declared within the module and intended to be referenced in other modules. A second lists all references within the module whose corresponding definitions are presumed to be in other modules. The third lists all relative references within the object code.

The second translation step is performed by the linker. It accepts two or more object modules as input and resolves the external references by comparing declarations in one module with references in the others. The linker produces as output a single module ready for loading, hence termed a **load module**. The load module is free* of external references and contains the complete program in **relocatable** code. This differs from machine code only in that relative references have not yet been translated. The load module contains a table of these relative references.

The third step in translation is the replacement of relative references by absolute addresses. This becomes possible when the actual

---

*This is an oversimplification. The module may still contain so-called **weak** external references that will actually not be made during the ensuing execution.

main storage locations to be occupied by the program during execution become known. A relocating loader reads the program into storage and adjusts the relative references to refer to those actual locations. The output from the loader is an **executable module** in machine language, ready for execution.

Figure 1.1 depicts the three standard translation steps in modular program development. If only a single source-language module containing no external references is translated, it can be loaded directly without intervention by the linker. In some programming systems the format of linker output is compatible enough with that of its input to permit the linking of a previously produced load module with some new object modules.

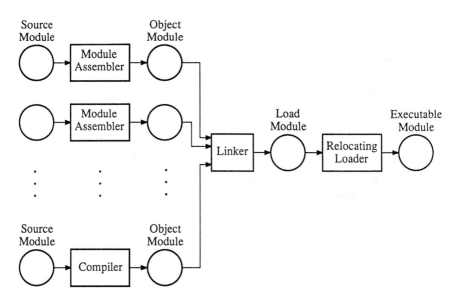

Figure 1.1   Module Translation Sequence

The functions of linking and loading are sometimes both performed by a single program, called a **linking loader**. This combining of the two functions is often a great convenience. It is important to realize, however, that they are distinct functions, each of which can be performed independently of the other.

Many systems have adopted standard naming conventions to assist the user in distinguishing among the various types of modules. In the IBM PC Disk Operating System, for example, a three-character file-name suffix (called the "extension") identifies the module type. Source modules have extensions that identify the particular source language (*e.g.*, ASM for assembler and PAS for PASCAL). Object modules have extension OBJ, relocatable modules have extension EXE, and executable modules have extension COM.

1.7 FUNCTION AND IMPLEMENTATION

In describing software, it is important to distinguish, as it is for hardware, among **architecture**, **implementation**, and **realization**.* The architecture, or **function**, of a program is *what* the program does, as specified in its external description. The implementation is *how* the program performs that function, how it is organized internally. The realization is the *embodiment* of that organization in the particular language in which it is written and on the particular machine on which it runs.

The realization of translators is intimately bound with techniques of programming, and depends upon the details of specific languages and machines. To avoid excessive dependence on those matters, we shall concentrate on function and implementation. The choice of function does not dictate the choice of implementation. As for most programs, there is more than one way to implement the desired function. Indeed, different philosophies of translator design emphasize characteristics that result in widely varying implementations. Among the characteristics that influence implementation, or are consequences of the implementation, are the following.

> Translation speed
> Translator size
> Simplicity
> Generality
> Ease of debugging in source language
> Target-language code speed
> Target-language code size

---

*Brooks75 [page 49] discusses the application to software engineering of this important insight due to Blaauw [Blaauw66, Blaauw70].

The various characteristics cannot in general be established independently; for example, efficiency of compiled code usually costs compiler time and space.

In the following chapters we shall examine both the functions of the principal types of translators, and the details of how generation and interpretation are performed. In discussing implementations, we shall not attempt to cover all possible approaches, but shall concentrate instead on typical forms of implementation. This will be particularly true for compilers. Because their function is the most complex of all the translators, compiler implementation shows the widest variety. There exist entire large books on compiler design; the material on compilers in this book is illustrative rather than exhaustive.

FOR FURTHER STUDY

A good overview of system software, considerably more detailed than this opening chapter, is Chapter 12 of Freeman75. For the early history of translators, good sources are Knuth62, Rosen64, Rosen67a, and Rosen69. Toy86 (Section 2.9) presents a historical survey through the 1970s, and follows the modern custom of classifying languages and their translators by "generation". Rosen69 also surveys the history of electronic digital computers. The original papers collected and introduced in Randell75 tell that of pre-electronic digital computers.

REVIEW QUESTIONS

1.1 A set of 96 symbols (*e.g.*, the ASCII "graphics" characters) is generally agreed to be better for writing programs than is the two-symbol set {0,1}. Is a larger symbol set always better than a smaller one?

1.2 Can we really transport programs between computers that have different machine languages?

1.3 Name an operating system command language that is procedural, and one that is not.

1.4 Is it always helpful to represent operands symbolically?

1.5 How closely does any program language you know resemble a natural language?

1.6 A microprogram-controlled computer is an interpreter of its own machine language; in fact, the interpreter is a program written in microcode. Is a hardwire-controlled computer also an interpreter of its own machine language?

1.7 Assume that each subroutine is written to occupy fixed locations in storage. Clearly, not more than one subroutine can occupy a given location at any one time. Repeated loading of subroutines that compete for the same location is inefficient. Suggest a better way to avoid potential conflicts in subroutine addresses.

1.8 Name the differences between *object* code and *machine* code.

1.9 How does a *load* module differ from an *object* module?

1.10 What program development costs rise faster than proportionally to the length of a program component?

Chapter 2

Assembly

The simplest assembler program is the **load-and-go assembler**. It accepts as input a program whose instructions are essentially in one-to-one correspondence with those of machine language, but with symbolic names used for operations and operands. It produces as output a machine-language program in main storage, ready to be executed. The translation is usually performed in a single pass over the input program text. The resulting machine-language program occupies storage locations that are fixed at the time of translation and cannot be changed afterwards. The program can call library subroutines, provided that they occupy other locations than those required by the program. Because there is no provision for combining separate subprograms translated in this manner, the load-and-go assembler forgoes the advantages of modular program development.

Module assemblers usually embody a two-pass translation. During the first pass, the assembler examines the assembler-language program and collects the symbolic names into a table. During the second pass, the assembler generates object code.

In this chapter we examine in some detail the function and implementation of those assemblers that provide neither macro processing nor conditional assembly. Those functions are presented in Chapters 4 and 5, respectively. Because of its importance, the standard two-pass assembler is presented in detail, followed by a briefer description of two one-pass assemblers. Before describing a full-function two-pass assembler, however, we concentrate on basic aspects of assembly by examining first a rudimentary assembler.

2.1 RUDIMENTARY TWO-PASS ASSEMBLER

2.1.1 Function

The program of Figure 2.1, although written in a hypothetical assembler language for a mythical computer, contains the basic elements that need to be translated into machine language. For ease of reference, each instruction is identified by a line number, which is *not* part of our program.* Each instruction in our language contains either an operation specification (lines 1–15) or a storage specification (lines 16–21). An operation specification is a symbolic operation code, which may be preceded by a label and must be followed by zero, one, or two operand specifications, as appropriate to the operation. A storage specification is a symbolic instruction to the assembler. In our assembler language, it must be preceded by a label and must be followed, if appropriate, by a constant. Labels and operand specifications are symbolic addresses; every operand specification must appear somewhere in the program as a label.

Our machine has a single accumulator and a main storage of unspecified size. Its 15 instructions are listed in Figure 2.2. The first column shows the assembler-language operation code and the second gives the machine-language equivalent (in decimal). The fourth column specifies the number of operands, and the last column describes the action that occurs when the instruction is executed. In that column "ACC", "OPD1", and "OPD2" refer to contents of the accumulator, of the first operand location, and of the second operand location, respectively. The length of each instruction in words is one greater than the number of its operands. Thus if the machine has 12-bit words, an ADD instruction is two words, or 24 bits, long. The table's third column, which is redundant, gives the instruction length. If our mythical computer had a fixed instruction length, we

---

*In some assembler languages, on the other hand, the line number is part of the program and may even be mandatory.

Line	Label	Operation	Operand 1	Operand 2
1.		COPY	ZERO	OLDER
2.		COPY	ONE	OLD
3.		READ	LIMIT	
4.		WRITE	OLD	
5.	CALCNEXT	LOAD	OLDER	
6.		ADD	OLD	
7.		STORE	NEW	
8.		SUB	LIMIT	
9.		BRPOS	FINAL	
10.		WRITE	NEW	
11.		COPY	OLD	OLDER
12.		COPY	NEW	OLD
13.		BR	CALCNEXT	
14.	FINAL	WRITE	LIMIT	
15.		STOP		
16.	ZERO	CONST	0	
17.	ONE	CONST	1	
18.	OLDER	SPACE		
19.	OLD	SPACE		
20.	NEW	SPACE		
21.	LIMIT	SPACE		

Figure 2.1   Sample Assembler-Language Program

could omit the third column. Because the number of operands would
also be fixed, we could also omit the fourth.

The storage specification SPACE reserves one word of storage
that presumably will eventually hold a number; there is no operand.
The storage specification CONST also reserves a word of storage; its
one operand is the value of a number to be placed in that word by
the assembler.

The instructions of the program are presented in four fields, and
might indeed be constrained to such a format on the input medium.
The label, if present, occupies the first field. The second field contains the symbolic operation code or storage specification, which will
henceforth be referred to simply as the **operation**. The third and
fourth fields hold the operand specifications, or simply **operands**, if
present.

Although it is not important to our discussion to understand
what the example program does, the foregoing specifications of the

Operation code Symbolic	Machine	Length	No. of operands	Action
ADD	02	2	1	ACC ← ACC + OPD1
BR	00	2	1	branch to OPD1
BRNEG	05	2	1	branch to OPD1 if ACC < 0
BRNONZ	09	2	1	branch to OPD1 if ACC ≠ 0
BRPOS	01	2	1	branch to OPD1 if ACC > 0
BRZERO	04	2	1	branch to OPD1 if ACC = 0
COPY	13	3	2	OPD2 ← OPD1
DIVIDE	10	2	1	ACC ← ACC ÷ OPD1
LOAD	03	2	1	ACC ← OPD1
MULT	14	2	1	ACC ← ACC × OPD1
READ	12	2	1	OPD1 ← input stream
STOP	11	1	0	stop execution
STORE	07	2	1	OPD1 ← ACC
SUB	06	2	1	ACC ← ACC − OPD1
WRITE	08	2	1	output stream ← OPD1

Figure 2.2 Instruction Set

machine and of its assembler language reveal the algorithm. The program uses the recursion relation $f_i = f_{i-1} + f_{i-2}$, implemented by the assignment NEW ← OLD+OLDER, to compute the so-called Fibonacci numbers (0, 1, 1, 2, 3, 5, 8, ..). The program prints all numbers beyond the zero, but not exceeding the positive integer limit read in on line 3 of the program, and then prints that limit. The astute reader will observe ways to improve the program. For example, we could rewrite the loop to require only one branch. Nevertheless, the forward branch is an important component of many longer assembler-language programs, and it has been left on purpose in this short example (at line 9).

Now that we have seen the elements of an assembler-language program, we can ask what functions the assembler must perform in translating it. Here are the major ones.

Replace symbolic addresses by numeric addresses.
Replace symbolic operation codes by machine operation codes.
Reserve storage for instructions and data.
Translate constants into machine representation.

The assignment of numeric addresses can be performed, except by a load-and-go assembler (which we are not now considering), without foreknowledge of what actual locations will eventually be occupied by the assembled program. It is necessary only to generate addresses relative to the start of the program. We shall assume that our assembler normally assigns addresses starting at 0. In translating line 1 of our example program, the resulting machine instruction will therefore be assigned address 0 and occupy three words, because COPY instructions are three words long. Hence the instruction corresponding to line 2 will be assigned address 3. Similarly, the READ instruction will be assigned address 6, the WRITE instruction of line 4 will be assigned address 8, and so on to the end of the program. But what addresses will be assigned to the operands named ZERO and OLDER? These addresses must be inserted in the machine-language representation of the first instruction.

2.1.2 Implementation

The assembler uses a counter to keep track of machine-language addresses. Because these addresses will ultimately specify locations in main storage, the counter is called the **location counter**, although "address counter" would be more accurate terminology. Before assembly, the location counter is initialized to zero. After each source line has been examined on the first pass, the location counter is incremented by the length of the machine-language code that will ultimately be generated to correspond to that source line.

When the assembler first reaches line 1 of the example program, it encounters the symbols ZERO and OLDER. It cannot replace those symbols by addresses, because they make **forward references** to source-language program lines not yet reached by the assembler. The most straightforward way to cope with the problem of forward references is to examine the entire program text once, before attempting to complete the translation. During that examination, the assembler determines the address that corresponds to each symbol, and places both the symbols and their addresses in a **symbol table**. This is possible because each symbol used in an operand field must also appear as a label. The address corresponding to a label is just the address of the first word of the machine-language code for the line starting with that label. Those addresses are supplied by the location counter. Creation of the symbol table requires one pass over the source text. During a second pass, the assembler uses the addresses collected in the symbol table to perform the translation. As each symbolic address is encountered in the second pass, the corresponding numeric address is substituted for it in the object code.

Two of the most common logical errors in assembler-language programming involve improper use of symbols. If a symbol appears in the operand field of some instruction, but nowhere in a label field, it is **undefined**. If a symbol appears in the label fields of more than one instruction, it is **multiply defined**. In building the symbol table on the first pass, the assembler must examine the label field of each instruction to permit it to associate the location counter value with each symbol. Multiply-defined symbols will be found on this pass. Undefined symbols, on the other hand, will not be found on the first pass unless the assembler also examines operand fields for symbols. Although this examination is not required for construction of the symbol table, normal practice is to perform it anyhow, because of its value in early detection of program errors.

There are many ways to organize a symbol table. Although the manner of implementing the symbol table is of considerable practical importance, it is not relevant to the present discussion. We shall simply treat the symbol table as a set of (symbol, address) pairs, and assume the existence of procedures for insertion, search, and retrieval. In the illustrations that follow, the set of pairs is represented by a linear list in the order in which the symbols are first encountered. Symbol table organization is discussed in Section 7.4.

The state of processing after line 3 has been scanned is shown in Figure 2.3. During processing of line 1, the symbols ZERO and OLDER were encountered and entered into the first two positions of the symbol table. The operation COPY was identified, and instruction length information from Figure 2.2 used to advance the location counter from 0 to 3. During processing of line 2, two more symbols were encountered and entered in the symbol table, and the location counter was advanced from 3 to 6. Line 3 yielded the fifth symbol, LIMIT, and caused incrementation of the location counter from 6 to 8. At this point the symbol table holds five symbols, none of which yet has an address. The location counter holds the address 8, and processing is ready to continue from line 4. Neither the line numbers nor the addresses shown in part (a) of the figure are actually part

Line	Address	Label	Operation	Operand 1	Operand 2
1.	0		COPY	ZERO	OLDER
2.	3		COPY	ONE	OLD
3.	6		READ	LIMIT	

(a) Source text scanned

Symbol	Address
ZERO	--
OLDER	--
ONE	--
OLD	--
LIMIT	--

Location: 8

Line: 4

(b) Symbol table   (c) Counters

Figure 2.3   First Pass after Scanning Line 3

of the source-language program. The addresses record the history of incrementation of the location counter; the line numbers permit easy reference. Clearly, the assembler needs not only a location counter, but also a **line counter** to keep track of which source line is being processed.

During processing of line 4 the symbol OLD is encountered for the second time. Because it is already in the symbol table, it is not entered again. During processing of line 5, the symbol CALCNEXT is encountered in the label field. It is entered into the symbol table, and the current location counter value, 10, is entered with it as its address. Figure 2.4 displays the state of the translation after line 9 has been processed.

The first pass continues in the same manner until line 14. There a label is encountered that is already in the symbol table, because it first appeared as an operand, on line 9. The symbol does not need to be entered again in the table, but its address, which has just become known, does. Each of lines 16–21 corresponds to one word of machine code, and the location counter is therefore incremented by one for each line. Each of these lines also includes a label, and the corresponding address for each is entered in the symbol table. Thus we see that the chief concerns of the first pass are to advance the location counter and build the symbol table. The state reached at the end of the first pass is depicted in Figure 2.5.

Line	Address	Label	Operation	Operand 1	Operand 2
1.	0		COPY	ZERO	OLDER
2.	3		COPY	ONE	OLD
3.	6		READ	LIMIT	
4.	8		WRITE	OLD	
5.	10	CALCNEXT	LOAD	OLDER	
6.	12		ADD	OLD	
7.	14		STORE	NEW	
8.	16		SUB	LIMIT	
9.	18		BRPOS	FINAL	

(a) Source text scanned

Symbol	Address
ZERO	--
OLDER	--
ONE	--
OLD	--
LIMIT	--
CALCNEXT	10
NEW	--
FINAL	--

Location: 20
Line: 10

(b) Symbol table   (c) Counters

Figure 2.4   First Pass after Scanning Line 9

The code generation is performed by our simple assembler during a second pass over the source text. Before starting the second pass, the line counter is reset to 1 and the location counter to 0. For each line of source code the assembler now produces a line of object code, which consists of the address, length, and text of the corresponding machine-language representation. The line and location counters are incremented as on the first pass. Line 1 is translated into 00 3 13 33 35 to indicate address 0, length 3 words, operation code 13, and operand addresses 33 and 35. The machine operation code is found in Figure 2.2. This operation code table is fixed for all assemblies, being defined by the assembler and machine languages, and is part of the assembler program. The numeric addresses are found in the address fields of the symbol table entries for ZERO and OLDER. The symbol table is different, of course, for each assembly and is built during the first pass.

Line	Address	Label	Operation	Operand 1	Operand 2
1.	0		COPY	ZERO	OLDER
2.	3		COPY	ONE	OLD
3.	6		READ	LIMIT	
4.	8		WRITE	OLD	
5.	10	CALCNEXT	LOAD	OLDER	
6.	12		ADD	OLD	
7.	14		STORE	NEW	
8.	16		SUB	LIMIT	
9.	18		BRPOS	FINAL	
10.	20		WRITE	NEW	
11.	22		COPY	OLD	OLDER
12.	25		COPY	NEW	OLD
13.	28		BR	CALCNEXT	
14.	30	FINAL	WRITE	LIMIT	
15.	32		STOP		
16.	33	ZERO	CONST	0	
17.	34	ONE	CONST	1	
18.	35	OLDER	SPACE		
19.	36	OLD	SPACE		
20.	37	NEW	SPACE		
21.	38	LIMIT	SPACE		

(a) Source text scanned

Symbol	Address
ZERO	33
OLDER	35
ONE	34
OLD	36
LIMIT	38
CALCNEXT	10
NEW	37
FINAL	30

Location: 39
Line: 22

(b) Symbol table   (c) Counters

Figure 2.5   Result of First Pass

Successive lines are translated in the same manner. When line 5 is reached, a label is found. How is it treated on the second pass? It is ignored, because nothing in the machine code corresponds to the label field, and the address is given by the location counter.

Hence the output corresponding to line 5 is 10 2 03 35. Lines 1–15, which contain operation specifications in the operation field, are all translated in this manner. Thus we see that the second pass uses the symbol table to generate the object program.

But what about lines 16–21? For these the content of the operation field is a storage specification. The corresponding machine code is not an instruction. In fact, CONST specifies that its operand is to be placed in one word of machine code and SPACE specifies only that one word of machine code is to be reserved. Thus the object code produced from source line 16 is 33 1 00 and that corresponding to line 17 is 34 1 01. The content of the word corresponding to line 18 is not specified, and anything can be generated. Using "XX" to represent an arbitrary value, we can write the object code corresponding to line 18 as 35 1 XX. Figure 2.6 presents the object code that corresponds to the entire source-language program.

Address	Length	Machine code
00	3	13 33 35
03	3	13 34 36
06	2	12 38
08	2	08 36
10	2	03 35
12	2	02 36
14	2	07 37
16	2	06 38
18	2	01 30
20	2	08 37
22	3	13 36 35
25	3	13 37 36
28	2	00 10
30	2	08 38
32	1	11
33	1	00
34	1	01
35	1	XX
36	1	XX
37	1	XX
38	1	XX

Figure 2.6 Object Code Generated on Second Pass

The object code will eventually be processed by the loader. We can think of the XX as a specification to the loader that the content of the location corresponding to address 35 does not need to have any specific value loaded. The loader can then just skip over that location. Some assemblers specify anyway a particular value for reserved storage locations, often zeros. There is no logical requirement to do so, however, and the user unfamiliar with his assembler is ill-advised to count on a particular value.

The specifications CONST and SPACE do not correspond to machine instructions. They are really directives to the assembler program. They are often called "pseudo-instructions" or "assembler instructions". We shall refer to them more accurately, however, as **assembler directives**. Of the two types of assembler directives in our example program, one results in the generation of machine code and the other in the reservation of storage. Later we shall see assembler directives that result in neither of these actions. The assembler directives are available to the assembler in a table. One organization provides a separate table that is usually searched before the operation code table is searched. Another is to include both machine operations and assembler directives in the same table. A field in the table entry then identifies the type to the assembler. Yet a third approach is to distinguish assembler directives from machine instructions syntactically, as in .ASCII v. ADD.

A few variations to the foregoing process are possible. Some of the translation can actually be performed during the first pass. Operation fields must be examined during the first pass to determine their effect on the location counter. The second-pass table lookup to determine the machine operation code can be obviated at a small cost. This is the production of intermediate text that holds machine operation code and instruction length in addition to source text. Another translation performable during the first pass is that of constants, e.g., from source-language decimal to machine-language binary. The translation of any symbolic addresses that refer backwards in the text, rather than forward, could be performed on the first pass. It is more convenient, however, to wait for the second pass and treat all symbolic addresses uniformly.

A minor variation is to assemble addresses relative to a starting address other than 0. The location counter is merely initialized to the desired address. If, for example, the value 200 is chosen, the symbol table would appear as in Figure 2.7. The object code corresponding to line 1 would be 200 3 13 233 235.

Symbol	Address
ZERO	233
OLDER	235
ONE	234
OLD	236
LIMIT	238
CALCNEXT	210
NEW	237
FINAL	230

Figure 2.7   Symbol Table with Starting Location 200

If it is known at assembly time that the program is to reside at location 200 for execution, then full object code with address and length need not be generated. The machine code alone will suffice. In this event the result of translation would be the following 39-word sequence.

```
13 233 235   13 234 236   12 238   08 236   03 235 02
236  07 237  06 238  01 230   08 237   13 236 235 13
237 236  00 210  08 238  11  00  01  XX   XX   XX XX
```

2.2 FULL TWO-PASS ASSEMBLER

2.2.1 Functions

Virtually all assembler languages incorporate more facilities for specifying machine function than does the rudimentary example presented in the previous section. We now examine the rich variety of functions that may be present. In Section 2.2.2 we discuss how each can be implemented.

Symbolic Instructions. We have already seen that the operation code may be represented symbolically. The symbol used is often called a **mnemonic operation code**, or simply a **mnemonic**, because it is usually selected for its mnemonic significance. Thus ADD and LOAD, or even A and L, are more likely to be used for instructions that add and load than are, say, XB5 and ZARF. Some assemblers can extend symbolic representation to other fields of the instruction, including specifications of such addressing modes as indexing and indirect addressing. One useful extension is the so-called **extended mnemonic**. This has the form of a symbolic operation code, but designates more information than just the machine operation code. The DEC PDP-11, for example, has a general-purpose operation code for branch on condition (x0000xxx) that is specialized to a particular condition by the four bits denoted x. The extended mnemonic BCC (branch on carry clear) specifies the complete operation code 10000110.

Symbolic Addresses. The programmer selects a symbol to refer to the location that an item will occupy when the program is executed. For an item that occupies more than one addressable location, the address of the first location is normally used. Suppose that a 4-byte integer-valued field named PRESSURE occupies storage locations known to the assembler as 1836–1839 in a byte-addressed machine. Then the address 1836 would be associated with the symbol PRESSURE. A common, but unfortunate, terminology is to refer to the address as the "value" of the symbol. In discussing an assembly, one would then say "the value of PRESSURE is 1836" to refer to the address of the symbol. This must be distinguished from a reference to the numeric value of the operand (say, 1013) stored at the address (1836) designated by the symbol PRESSURE. To avoid this confusion, and to simplify reference to values of attributes of a symbol other than its address, we will not use "value" in the specialized sense of "address".

Symbolic addresses are not limited to single symbols. Arithmetic expressions involving one or more symbols are often permitted, and are extremely useful. Examples of such **address expressions** are FRONT + 5, 4*OFFSET+I, and PRESSURE-RESERVE. Some assemblers permit more complicated address expressions.

Storage Reservation. In most assembler languages it is not necessary to place a label on each storage reservation or constant definition. The use of address expressions in the source language or of indexing in the machine operations provides easy access to unlabeled locations.

An assembler directive to reserve storage may specify directly the amount to be reserved. This is particularly common if the unit of allocation is fixed, as on most word-addressed machines. Thus one might have assembler codes RSF (reserve storage, first address) and RSL (reserve storage, last address) that require a label and one operand. The directive ALPHA RSF 23 would reserve a block of 23 words and associate the symbol ALPHA with the first word of the block. The directive OMEGA RSL 7 would reserve a block of seven words, and associate the symbol OMEGA with the last word of the block.

If different units of allocation are used for different data types, it is customary to provide a choice of directives. In PAL-11 (for the PDP-11), the directives .ASCII, .BYTE, and .WORD reserve space for a character string, byte, and word, respectively. It may be convenient to specify quantities and units and rely on the assembler to compute the amount of storage required. The DS (define storage) operation of the IBM 370 assemblers is of this type. The directive WORK DS 15D,6F causes the reservation of 144 bytes (fifteen 8-byte double words and six 4-byte full words). The address of the label WORK is the address of the first byte of the 144.

Data Generation. Data to be placed in the object code are usually encoded in the assembler-language program in an easily-written form. Although a machine may encode numbers in binary, the programmer is likely to think of their values in decimal. It is necessary to specify, either explicitly or implicitly, both the source and the target encodings.

Near one extreme might be a machine with two data types and a restricted assembler language. The only data are one-word numbers in either fixed-point or floating-point binary encoding. The assembler language permits decimal encodings only; floating-point is to be used if and only if a decimal point is present. In this situation a single assembler directive suffices. For example, RATES CONST 8000,0.22,12000,0.25,16000,0.28 would reserve storage for six words, the first of them labeled RATES, and generate fixed- and floating-point values in them alternately.

If several encodings are possible, it may be more convenient to provide a distinct assembler directive for each type of conversion. Thus DECIMAL and OCTAL might require operands in decimal and octal, respectively, and implicitly specify their conversion to binary. Another approach to encoding constants is syntactic. MACRO-11 (for the PDP-11) assumes that a string of digits is an octal integer unless it contains a decimal point or a digit greater than 7. A quote before a single character (*e.g.*, 'b) indicates a character. A double quote before two characters (*e.g.*, "ta) indicates a character pair. Any other string is assumed to be a label rather than a constant.

If there are many different types of conversions, the language may be more tractable if a single assembler directive is used. That directive is supplemented with type indicators. Thus the IBM 370 assembler directive DC (define constant) permits 15 types of conversions. For example, DC F'5',H'-9',C'EXAMPLE' causes the generation of the integer 5 as a 4-byte full word, followed by the integer −9 as a 2-byte half word, followed by seven bytes of characters. Repetition factors may be permitted, to assist in such specifications as that of a table all of whose values are initially zero.

Location Counters. The programmer is usually free to select a non-zero origin for the location counter. An assembler directive, perhaps called ORIGIN, has an operand to define the value of the location counter. In some assembler languages, this redefinition of the location counter can occur not only at the start of the source program, but also anywhere else. That feature is useful with assemblers that provide two or more location counters. Resetting even a single location counter offers an easy way to reserve a block of storage.

Multiple location counters permit text to be permuted during translation. One example of a useful permutation is the following. Storage reservation and data generation specifications are written next to the associated source-language instructions, but data fields are assembled into a single area at the end of the program. Another example is to interleave, in the source code, instructions to two or more processors (*e.g.*, a machine and its I/O channels), but to segregate them in the object code.

Scope of Symbols. If two or more modules are to be combined after assembly, some symbolic addresses will be defined in one module and used in another. Most symbols, however, will be referenced only within the module in which they are defined. These symbols are said to be **local** to that module. A symbol defined within a module is called **global** if another module is to reference it. During the assembly of one module, the assembler can identify symbols used but not defined within the module. Each such use is either an error or a reference to a global variable whose definition must be supplied by another module during linking. The assembler cannot tell, however, whether a symbol that is defined in the module being translated will be referenced by another module. Yet this information must be transmitted by the assembler to the linker. Hence, the assembler must itself be informed. One way is to mark the definition of each global symbol with a special tag. Thus

```
*RESULT   SPACE   1
```

might identify RESULT as external to the module, although internally defined. An alternative to the marker is an assembler directive, say INTDEF. The sequence

```
RESULT   INTDEF
         SPACE   1
```

would have the same effect. The SPACE directive can be given a label local to the module, as in

```
RESULT   INTDEF
ANSWER   SPACE   1
```

where the local symbol ANSWER can be used only within the module, whereas the global symbol RESULT can be used either within it or without. The advantage of providing a local label is that in some implementations the use of a global label may be more expensive. The alternative syntax

```
INTDEF RESULT
---
RESULT   SPACE   1
```

does not require adjacency of the definition of the label to its designation as global. It does not allow a local label, however, and it suffers from the irregular use of the operand field for symbol definition rather than for symbol reference.

To permit independent assembly of more than one module during a single invocation of the assembler, it is necessary to distinguish the beginning and end of each assembler-language program. Even if only one assembly is to be performed, assembler directives, often START and END, are provided to delimit the source program. We can think of these as constituting vertical parentheses that define the scope of local symbols.

Redefinable Symbols. A symbol whose address depends upon its context is said to be **redefinable**. It cannot be held in the symbol table in the usual manner, because different occurrences may be associated with different addresses. The most frequently used redefinable symbol has as its address the current value of the location counter; often an asterisk (or a period) is chosen. A common use of such a symbol is in relative branching. Thus BR *-6, wherever it appears in the program, is a branch to an address that is 6 less than the current address.

Another extremely useful type of redefinable symbol is also called a **local label**, but with a more restrictive connotation than merely "nonglobal". Distinguished syntactically from other symbols, it is defined anew each time it occurs in the label field of an instruction. Any use of such a symbol in an operand field refers to the most recent definition. A particularly convenient variation is to permit the reference to be marked either as backward to the most recent definition or as forward to the next definition. If, for example, normal labels are restricted to begin with an alphabetic character, the decimal digits might be reserved as ten local labels. Thus 3B would be a reference to the closest previous occurrence of local label 3; and 1F, to the next forthcoming occurrence of local label 1. We can think of a local label (under this stronger definition) as having a scope restricted to only a portion of the module in which it is defined.

Base Registers. The specification of main storage locations by address fields of machine-language instructions is commonly performed in one of three ways. (1) The address field is a single number that refers directly to the storage location. This is **direct** addressing. (2) The address field is a single number that specifies the displacement of the storage location from the origin of the program segment. Before execution, the operating system places the origin in a base register. During interpretation of the instruction at execution time, the computer automatically adds the displacement to the base register content to yield the storage location. Because the instruction does not refer explicitly to a base register, this is **implicit-base** addressing. (3) The address field is a pair of numbers, of which one designates a base register and the other is the displacement. This is **explicit-base** addressing.

If the target machine employs direct addressing, any storage location is addressable. If it employs implicit-base addressing, addressability is a consequence of limiting the length of program segments to the number of locations that can be distinguished by the displacement. If, however, the target machine employs explicit-base addressing, two constraints limit the assembler's ability to ensure that all program locations will be addressable. One constraint is that the displacement field is usually shorter than for implicit-base addressing, because some bits must be used to designate the base register. This means that the portion of storage addressable from one explicitly-named base register is often smaller than that addressable under implicit-base addressing.

The other constraint is the key requirement that any register used as a base contain a suitable value at execution time. Clearly, the assembler cannot control what instruction will be executed to provide this value. The programmer, however, can write an instruction to load a base register. He must inform the assembler of what value will be in the base register at execution time, to permit it to generate addresses relative to the base register content. If there are multi-purpose registers that can serve either as a base or in another capacity, the programmer must specify which registers are to be used as base registers.

For the IBM 370, the assembler directive USING specifies a register as being available for use as a base, and states its execution-time content. The assembler directive DROP withdraws the register from the list of those available for use as bases. Thus USING *,12 states that register 12 can be used as a base register. It also promises that the register's content will be the address of the current line. (That assembler directive would typically be immediately preceded by the machine instruction BALR 12,0. This "branch and link register" instruction is designed for subroutine linkage. At execution time, it loads the appropriate number into register 12, thus fulfilling the promise.)

Suppose that several registers have been made available for use as bases. In addressing a given symbol, the assembler can use any base register for which the address displacement falls within the acceptable bounds. Consequently, the choice of base register is not fixed for the symbol, and is not among its attributes.

Symbol Attributes. One attribute we have seen is the address. This is the address of the start of the field to which the symbol refers. The address of each symbol is stored in the symbol table. Other attributes are normally stored there, too.

A particularly important attribute is whether a symbol is absolute or relative. The loader uses this information in determining whether an adjustment is necessary when the load module is read into storage. The linker uses the attribute to determine the relocatability of addresses that incorporate external references. Even within the assembler, the attribute is used to determine the relocatability of address expressions.

If multiple location counters are provided, the identity of the location counter to use for a symbol is another of its attributes. In generating a relative address for the symbol, the assembler uses the location counter identity to determine from which origin to count.

The length attribute of a symbol is usually the length of the field named by the symbol. Different assembler languages use different conventions for defining the length attribute. Thus the storage reservation directive ALPHA RSF 23 for a word-addressed machine might imply for the symbol ALPHA a length of 1 or a length of 23. The length attribute is used primarily in variable-field-length instructions to specify the length of the operands in the absence of an explicit length specification.

Some assembler languages permit references to attributes of symbols. References to the length of a symbol may be explicit, as in L(ALPHA), or implicit in using ALPHA as an operand in a variable-field-length instruction. An attribute to which reference can often be made explicitly is the address of a symbol. This permits the programmer to place in a register or storage location the execution-time address of another storage location, an **address constant**. This would typically be written A(FRONT) if FRONT is the symbol associated with that location. The indirect addressing that results can be used in passing parameters, in implementing list structures, and in providing for base addressing.

Alternate Names. The provision of symbolic names for other fields of the instruction than storage addresses is often convenient and valuable. Register designations, shift amounts, field lengths, and address displacements are usually encoded numerically in the assembler-language instruction. Representing these numeric constants symbolically can often enhance program readability and writability. Thus a programmer might wish to use FR4 rather than 4 to name a floating-point register, and COMP, INCR, and LIMIT, rather than 8, 9, and 10, to name loop-control registers that hold comparand, increment, and limit. Assemblers that offer this **definitional** facility may use any of a variety of syntactic forms. Perhaps the most straightforward is the following use of the defined symbol as the label and the defining quantity as the operand.

```
FR4      SET    4
COMP     SET    8
INCR     SET    9
LIMIT    SET    10
```

Some assemblers offer a more general form of this facility, in which the operand may be a symbol, or even a symbolic expression. Thus ENTRY = TOP+2 defines ENTRY as a symbol whose attributes are set to equal the attributes that TOP+2 has at the point where the SET directive is encountered. A subsequent change in the attributes of TOP does not affect ENTRY. This is analogous to call by value (see Section 3.5.2). Normally, of course, the attributes of the defining expression will not change unless it incorporates a redefinable symbol. (An exception can occur in macro assemblers, which are discussed in Section 5.4.) It is possible to redefine ENTRY subsequently by use of another SET directive. Our example also illustrates the representation of an assembler directive by a special symbol (here the equal sign) instead of a name. An interesting application is exemplified by * = * + 256, which advances the location counter, thus reserving 256 units of space.

An apparently similar, but actually quite distinct, form of alternate naming caters to the following dubious practice. Two programmers can independently prepare programs that are to be combined before assembly, yet use different names for the same entity. To avoid the tedious replacement of all occurrences of the name used in one of the programs, a **synonym** or name **equivalence** facility is provided in some assemblers. Thus ZIP EQU ZAP specifies that the symbols ZIP and ZAP are to be considered equivalent symbols throughout the program. Their attributes are the same. Whenever ZIP is used, the effect is the same as if ZAP had been named instead.

This is analogous to call by name (see Section 3.5.3). In at least one system, unfortunately, the mnemonic code EQU is used not for name equivalence, but for the definitional facility that we have called SET.

EQU can provide alternate symbolic names for operation codes also, although the use of a distinct directive for this purpose offers some advantages in processing. Suppose that we prefer MULT to the standard MD for double-precision floating-point multiplication on the IBM 370. We can then code MULT OPSYN MD to make MULT synonymous with MD whenever it occurs as the operation code.

Each of the foregoing alternate naming facilities defines a symbol. The definition may or may not be required to precede any use of a symbol so defined. That requirement is imposed whenever lack of the definition will prevent the assembler from properly advancing the location counter during the first pass. The counter is not advanced, of course, when the SET, EQU, or OPSYN itself is encountered. Less restrictive alternate naming facilities can, of course, be provided at the cost of requiring more than two passes.

Literals. Often a programmer may wish to specify not the address of an operand but rather its value. Consider an instruction to increment a counter by 2. The programmer may prefer simply to write the constant "2" without concern for where that operand is located. An operand specified in this manner, with its value stated literally, is called a **literal**. The word "literal" is sometimes used to mean what is more properly called an **immediate operand**. That is an operand value specified literally as part of the machine-language instruction. These are very common in computers, such as the VAX-11, that devote an addressing mode to immediate operands. In MACRO-11, they are identified by prefixing "#" to the value. An immediate operand is addressed implicitly, because it is located at a fixed offset from the beginning of the instruction. We shall reserve "literal" to refer to an operand that is addressed explicitly.

Although several different instructions might include the same literal, usually only one copy of each literally specified value needs to be generated. The distinct literals are placed together in a **pool** to avoid inserting each literal constant between instructions.

The literal pool is typically generated at the end of the object code. In some assembler languages, however, the programmer can control the placement of the pool. A directive, perhaps LITORG, specifies that the pool of literals appearing up to that point in the text is to be placed at the specified address. This address is usually the current value of the location counter. For machines with explicit-base addressing (*e.g.*, IBM 370), this may be needed to ensure the addressability of literals. A subsequently generated literal pool includes only those literals that have been specified since the previous pool generation.

The assembler language must provide a distinction between numeric literals and numeric addresses, and between character literals and symbolic addresses. One way to distinguish is to use a different instruction format; another is to use a special symbol to mark a literal. Some literals, such as those with a decimal point or an exponent designator, are self-marking and would not need the special symbol. Even so, use of an explicit distinction permits a uniform implementation of all literals. For this purpose, the IBM 370 uses "=", and we shall use "@".

The literal @A(FRONT) has as its value the address constant A(FRONT). If FRONT is a forward reference, the value of the address constant is unknown when the literal is first encountered. It may nevertheless be required to generate the literal before the definition of FRONT is encountered. The interaction of LITORG with address constants is explored in Problem 2.13.

Error Checking. An assembler usually checks the source program for several different types of errors. Especially important is the undefined symbol, which appears as an operand but nowhere as a label. Such an occurrence can be either rejected as an error or assumed to be an external symbol. If the assembler language requires the identification of external symbols, then undefined symbols can be caught at assembly time. Otherwise, they are not caught until linkage is attempted.

A symbol that occurs as a label more than once has a different location counter value associated with each occurrence. Even if its other attributes are the same for each occurrence, its address is not. The resulting error is a multiply-defined symbol.

The detection of undefined and of multiply-defined symbols makes use of inter-statement context, as recorded in the symbol table. Many other invalidities can be checked during examination of one instruction alone. Among these are nonexistent operation codes, wrong number of operands, inappropriate operands, and a variety of syntax errors. Some aspects of the checking process may be simpler if the source language is constrained to a fixed, rather than a free, format.

Listing. The object code output is written onto a machine-readable medium, such as magnetic disk. The programmer may require a human-readable listing of both source and object code, preferably side by side. To assist in debugging, the symbol table and a **concordance** or **cross-reference** table are usually printed. The symbol table lists each symbol together with its address, and perhaps other attributes. The cross-reference table indicates where in the source program each symbol is defined (used as a label) and where it is accessed (used in an operand specification). The two tables are usually sorted in alphabetic order for ease of use. Often they are combined in a single table, as in Figure 2.8, which shows a listing of the assembly performed in Section 2.1. Such a listing can be produced, of course, by a separate listing program that accepts the source code, object code, and symbol table as inputs. Alternatively, it can be produced by the assembler itself during its second pass. If space is tight, a third pass can produce the listing.

Error messages are an important component of the listing. Some assemblers group the error messages at the foot of the source-language program. Many programmers, however, prefer to have any message that is associated with a single source line printed next to that line. Even if this is not done, the message must at least identify the erroneous line. Some error messages (e.g., I/O malfunction, lack of storage) may not apply to a specific line. These should not be interleaved with the program text.

A facility for comments is often provided. One method is to use a word or character reserved for the purpose (e.g., an asterisk in column 1 to make the entire line a comment). Another method of identifying comments is to use an assembler directive (say, COMMENT or REMARK) to specify that the ensuing text is to be skipped by the assembler. The amount to be skipped may be fixed (e.g., the rest of the line) or specified as an operand. It can even be determined by the presence of another assembler directive that terminates skipping. Neither of these methods is convenient for placing comments adjacent to program text. Such a capability can be provided in a

Line	Label	Operation	Operand 1	Operand 2	Address	Length	Machine code
1		COPY	ZERO	OLDER	00	3	13 33 35
2		COPY	ONE	OLD	03	3	13 34 36
3		READ	LIMIT		06	2	12 38
4		WRITE	OLD		08	2	08 36
5	CALCNEXT	LOAD	OLDER		10	2	03 35
6		ADD	OLD		12	2	02 36
7		STORE	NEW		14	2	07 37
8		SUB	LIMIT		16	2	06 38
9		BRPOS	FINAL		18	2	01 30
10		WRITE	NEW		20	2	08 37
11		COPY	OLD	OLDER	22	3	13 36 35
12		COPY	NEW	OLD	25	3	13 37 36
13		BR	CALCNEXT		28	2	00 10
14	FINAL	WRITE	LIMIT		30	2	08 38
15		STOP			32	1	11
16	ZERO	CONST	0		33	1	00
17	ONE	CONST	1		34	1	01
18	OLDER	SPACE			35	1	XX
19	OLD	SPACE			36	1	XX
20	NEW	SPACE			37	1	XX
21	LIMIT	SPACE			38	1	XX

Address	Symbol	Definition	References
10	CALCNEXT	5	13
30	FINAL	14	9
38	LIMIT	21	3 8 14
37	NEW	20	7 10 12
36	OLD	19	2 4 6 11 12
35	OLDER	18	1 5 11
34	ONE	17	2
33	ZERO	16	1

Figure 2.8   Assembly Listing

number of ways. One is to reserve a field on each line for comments. Another is to reserve a character to indicate that the remainder of the line is a comment. Yet another is to treat all characters beyond the rightmost required field as commentary.

Assembler directives may also be provided for control of the listing format, especially if the format of the source-language program is fixed. Other options may include the printing of optional items, or even the suppression of part or all of the listing itself.

Assembler Control. Assembler directives other than those that reserve storage or define constants do not cause the generation of object code. As a result, there is not a one-to-one correspondence between lines of source text and of object text. Thus, even an assembler for a machine in which all data and instruction lengths are fixed and equal (*e.g.*, one word) requires two position counters. One counts lines of source text and the other counts addresses in the object program.

Some assembler directives, such as those for alternate names, must be obeyed during the first pass of the assembler. Others, such as those for listing control, must be obeyed during the second pass. Yet others, such as scope delimiters, affect both passes. Some functions specified by an assembler directive can be implemented on either pass. An example is the generation of constants.

Repetitive Assembly. Sometimes a sequence of statements in source language contains nearly identical repetitions. This occurs commonly in the construction of tables. Much of the tedium of writing the full source code can be relieved by the provision of another assembler directive. This causes one or more source lines that follow it to be assembled repeatedly with minor variations. A common name for the directive is REPEAT or ECHO. Thus

```
            REPEAT  2,(1,10)
    ARG$    CONST   $
    FCT$    SPACE
```

might cause the group of two lines to be repeated ten times. On each successive repetition, the next digit in the range (1,10) is substituted for each occurrence of "$" in the group. This repetitive assembly would have the same effect as assembling the 20 following lines.

```
    ARG1    CONST   1
    FCT1    SPACE
    ARG2    CONST   2
    FCT2    SPACE
    ---     ---
    ARG10   CONST   10
    FCT10   SPACE
```

This facility is but a special case of a much more powerful facility, to be discussed in Chapter 4 and in Section 5.4, for generating source code at assembly time.

2.2.2 Implementations

The many functions described in the foregoing sections can be implemented straightforwardly in a two-pass assembler. As in our rudimentary assembler, Pass 1 is still concerned chiefly with symbol table construction and location counter management. Pass 2 still produces the object code and, if one is to be provided, the listing. The complexity of each pass depends, of course, on just which functions are selected. The basic actions for symbol table construction are listed in Figure 2.9.

Where encountered	Already in table?	Attributes in table?	Action taken
label	no		enter symbol and attributes
label	yes	no	enter attributes
label	yes	yes	*ERROR:* duplicate definition
operand	no		enter symbol
operand	yes		none

Figure 2.9   Rules for Constructing Symbol Table

A major exception to the rules of that figure occurs if a symbol encountered as a label has no attributes to be entered into the table. How can this occur? If the associated operation is SET (define) or EQU (synonym). For the SET operation, the defining expression is evaluated and its attributes (e.g., address and relocatability mode) are entered into the table. This evaluation is similar to the evaluation of an address expression, which is described in the discussion of Pass 2. It is customary in a two-pass assembler to restrict the defining expression to contain no symbols that have themselves not yet been defined. Because of this restriction, the SET operation is most often used only to give symbolic names to constants.

If the label with no attributes is encountered in a synonym directive EQU, it is possible to determine its attributes if the defining symbol has itself been previously defined. Because there is no guarantee, however, that referents of synonyms are defined in advance, a different approach is used uniformly for all occurrences of EQU. The label is entered into the symbol table and marked as being of type "EQU". The defining symbol is also placed in the same symbol table entry, perhaps in the address field if there is room. At the conclusion of Pass 1, the symbol table is scanned, and the defining symbol in each EQU type entry is replaced by a pointer to the table entry for the defining symbol. Thus all symbols defined as each other's synonyms are linked into a chain.

Whether or not a synonym function is provided, the symbol table can be scanned after Pass 1 for symbols without attributes. These are flagged either as undefined symbols or as external symbols, accordingly as the explicit identification of external symbols is required or not. An alternative to the table scan after Pass 1 is to wait until Pass 2, when the absence of definition is obvious.

Location counter management is much simpler than symbol table construction. For a START operation, the location counter is set either to the default (usually zero) or to a specified address. For an ORIGIN operation, it is set to the specified address. For SPACE and CONST operations, the appropriate length is computed (if necessary) and added to the location counter value in preparation for the next line. For other assembler directives, the location counter value remains unchanged. For a machine instruction, the instruction length is added to the location counter value. If instructions are of variable length, the operation code table will need to be consulted. For machines with storage alignment restrictions (*e.g.*, IBM 370), an amount may need to be added to the location counter *before* associating its value with the current source line. If multiple location counters are provided, the foregoing description refers to the location counter in use. The assembler directive to change location counters merely selects the counter to be incremented subsequently.

Although location counter management and symbol table construction are the chief responsibilities of Pass 1, certain other functions are mandatory during that pass. Still other functions may optionally be performed during Pass 1 rather than Pass 2. A mandatory function that was not explicitly described in Section 2.2.1 is nevertheless implicit in any translation. This is the scanning of the source-language text to determine what it says. Both lexical and syntactic analysis are involved; they are discussed, not only for assemblers but for other translators as well, in Chapter 6.

Another mandatory function of Pass 1 is to examine operation fields to determine the instruction length, which must be added to the location counter. If an operation code synonym facility (OPSYN) is provided, each OPSYN must be processed during the first pass to make the length of the defining instruction available. Two approaches to implementing OPSYN suggest themselves. One is to enter in the operation table a pointer to the entry for the defining operation code. The other is to duplicate that entry. The remainder of operation code processing is optional during Pass 1. It is often included either (a) if operation table lookup is performed anyway, or (b) to effect the space saving of replacing the mnemonic operation code by the machine operation code. During Pass 1, then, the operation code may or may not be translated; determination of its format (if multiple formats exist) may or may not be performed.

Errors detected during Pass 1 must be recorded for incorporation in the listing. The generation of constants does not require a completed symbol table, and can be performed during either pass. The space required by the constants, however, does need to be determined during Pass 1 because of its effect on the location counter. Constant fields in an instruction often require little or no data conversion and may well be generated during Pass 1 if the instruction format has been determined.

Although it is possible to defer all processing of literals until Pass 2, unless LITORG is provided, it is usually more convenient to build the literal pool during Pass 1. Each time a literal is encountered, it is entered in a literal table, unless it is a duplicate of a literal already entered. Suppose that the character "@" marks a literal and that the following literals occur in the program in the order shown: @-1000, @1, @'TABLE', @12.75, @1, @3. Then the literal table might be organized as in Figure 2.10, where lengths are stated in bytes. Of course, it is not mandatory to eliminate duplicate literals, and some assemblers do generate a value for each occurrence of a given literal. The first literal of the pool can be assigned the address given by the value of the location counter at the conclusion of the first pass. Subsequent literals are assigned addresses determined by the lengths of the preceding literals.

Pass 1 typically transforms the source program into an **intermediate text** for input to Pass 2. Labels can be omitted, because code generation makes no use of them. Other symbols can be replaced, if desired, by pointers to the symbol table. The replacement is performed as each symbol is encountered, and is possible only if the symbol table construction algorithm does not change the position

of a symbol once it has been entered. Although the use of pointers
may result in some space savings, its chief advantage is elimination
of table searching during Pass 2. In a similar manner, literals can
be replaced by pointers to the literal table. Of course, if a source
listing is to be produced, these labels, symbols, and literals must be
retained.

Length	Value
4	-1000
4	1
5	'TABLE'
8	12.75
4	3

Figure 2.10   Example of Literal Table

Although the symbols are no longer needed during Pass 2 for
generating code, they do serve another purpose, production of the
concordance. This lists each symbol, the number of the source line
in which it is defined, and the number of each line in which it is
referenced. The attributes of the symbol are usually included also.
For maximum usefulness, the concordance should be in alphabetic
order. The required sorting of the symbol table can be performed
at any time after the conclusion of Pass 1. A convenient time for
an assembler that uses magnetic tape is during tape rewind. If mul-
titasking facilities are provided, sorting a copy of the symbol table
can be assigned to a separate task for execution concurrent with
Pass 2. If pointers have replaced symbols in the intermediate text,
sorting the symbol table will invalidate the pointers unless special
action is taken. One solution is to keep an unsorted copy of the table for use in Pass 2. Another solution uses the permutation vector
generated by the sort process. An extra symbol table field stores,
at a symbol's original position in the table, a pointer to its new
position.

During Pass 2 the actual object code is generated. As the
source (or intermediate) text is passed for a second time, the location counter is advanced just as it was during Pass 1. This time the
purpose is not to assign addresses to symbols, but rather to incorporate addresses in the generated code. Operation codes are translated
and instruction formats determined, to the extent that these func-

tions were not carried out during Pass 1. Symbolic addresses that consist of a single symbol are easily handled. For a machine with direct or implicit-base addressing, the symbol is merely replaced by its location counter value from the symbol table.

For a machine with explicit-base addressing, a base register table is used. Whenever a USING directive is encountered during Pass 2, the number of the specified register and the promised value of its content are entered in the table. They remain until the content is changed by another USING or the register is deleted in response to a DROP. The symbol's location counter value *locn* is compared with the register content values *regc* listed in the base register table. There should be a register such that $disp = locn - regc$ falls in the appropriate range (0 to 4095 for the IBM 370). The value of the displacement *disp* and the number of the register are assembled into the object code. If there is more than one such register, then any one of them can be selected.

Addresses that correspond to redefinable local labels are easily generated during Pass 2 (or even Pass 1), provided that they are limited to backward references. For processing efficiency it is customary to use a fixed set of reserved symbols for this purpose. A fixed-size local label table holds the location counter value most recently associated with each redefinable symbol. Table lookup, whether for symbol redefinition or for address generation, is performed directly. Because no hashing or scan is required, this gains speed over use of the regular symbol table. Moreover, the existence of the small table of redefinable symbols permits substantial reduction in the size of the regular symbol table. This size reduction increases speed of access to regular symbols also.

Forward references to redefinable symbols cannot be resolved by the normal Pass 2 mechanism, because entries in the local label table are not fixed. The methods of Section 2.3 can be applied, however, as can the technique used in the UNISAP assembler for the UNIVAC I. That assembler, apparently the first to provide redefinable local labels, used magnetic tape for the input, intermediate, and output texts. After the first pass, the intermediate text had to be repositioned for what we have described as Pass 2 processing. Instead of rewinding, the assembler made an extra pass, reading the intermediate tape backward. During this backward pass, what were originally forward references could be processed in the same manner as were backward references on a forward pass.

Address expressions are evaluated after lookup has determined the location counter value associated with each symbol. Thus the expression `LIMIT+3-CALCNEXT` in the context of the sample program of Section 2.1 would be evaluated as 31, and that value used in the instruction address field. A check must also be made that the address expression is not malformed with respect to relocatability; Chapter 8 explores that matter further.

Each reference to a literal is replaced by the address assigned to the corresponding entry in the literal table. The address correspondences can be established either between passes, or as the literals are encountered during Pass 2.

Other instruction fields, such as shift amounts, index register designations, and lengths, are usually stated explicitly as constants or as symbolic names that have been defined to represent constants. These are easily encoded. Sometimes an implicit specification (*e.g.*, length in IBM 370) requires an attribute to be obtained from the symbol table.

The generation of data is another important responsibility of Pass 2. There is almost always a conversion from source-language encoding to machine encoding. The input form is usually a character string, composed perhaps of decimal digits, the period, plus and minus signs, and perhaps the letter "E". The output form may be the machine encoding of a long-precision floating-point number, a short-precision integer, or a string of bits or of characters. For a rich assembler language, the description of data may well be expressed in what really amounts to a sublanguage of considerable size. The volume of assembler program code that performs the conversions may be very substantial indeed.

Whenever a `CONST` (or `DC`) directive is encountered, the specified constant is generated at the attained point in the object code. For a `SPACE` (or `DS`) directive, the assembler need only emit a directive to the loader to advance the location. As an alternative, the assembler can generate the required amount of fill, usually binary zeros. After the `END` directive has been reached, the entries in the literal table are converted to machine encoding and appended. The alternative is to convert each literal as it is encountered, place its machine representation in the literal table, and append the completed literal table to the end of the object code.

In generating the listing, the assembler needs access to the original text. It is possible, of course, to list the source text during Pass 1 and the object code during Pass 2. If this is done, the correspondences between the two representations become difficult to establish. The listing normally includes source text image with line or sequence numbers, object code with location counter values, error messages, and a concordance. Assembler directives that control printing may or may not be omitted from the listing, depending on the assembler. Whether to print them may itself be an option controlled by an assembler directive! Much simpler for the assembler, of course, is to pass the needed files to a separate lister.

The object code produced by the assembler is still often called an object "deck", and may be said to be "punched" even though punched cards have become obsolete. The object code contains basically three kinds of information: machine-language code for the computer, address and relocation information for the loader, and a global symbol table for the linker. This last item may be a single table that includes both the symbols used within the module but not defined therein, and the symbols defined within the module and marked as being global. More usefully, a separate table may be produced for each.

2.3 ONE-PASS ASSEMBLERS

The translation performed by an assembler is essentially a collection of substitutions: machine operation code for mnemonic, machine address for symbolic, machine encoding of a number for its character representation. Except for one factor, these substitutions could all be performed in one sequential pass over the source text. That factor is the forward reference. The separate passes of the two-pass assembler are required to handle forward references without restriction. If certain limitations are imposed, however, it becomes possible to handle forward references without making two passes. Different sets of restrictions lead to the one-pass module assembler and to the load-and-go assembler. These one-pass assemblers became popular initially for computers whose backing storage was slow or required manual intervention. The handling of punched cards or paper tape between passes was eliminated by eliminating a pass. The widespread availability of backing storage has eliminated the original motivation for one-pass assemblers. Both designs, however, illustrate practical translation techniques. Moreover, the simplicity of the load-and-go assembler continues to make it appropriate for short programs.

2.3.1 Load-and-Go Assembler

The **load-and-go** assembler forgoes the production of object code. Instead, it generates absolute machine code and loads it. Immediately upon completion of the assembly, the code will be executed from the physical main storage locations into which it has been loaded. The following restrictions are imposed by this mode of translation. (1) The program must run in a set of locations fixed at translation time; there is no relocation. (2) The program cannot be combined with one that has been translated separately. (3) There must be enough space in main storage to hold both the assembler and the machine-language program. Load-and-go assemblers are still attractive for most student jobs, which are typically small and subject to frequent change.

Because the assembled program is in main storage, the assembler can fill in each forward reference as its definition is encountered. To do this, it is necessary to record the references to each undefined symbol. The number of such references is unpredictable. It is therefore most convenient to organize the information as a collection of chains, one for each undefined symbol. Each element of a chain is associated with one occurrence of a symbol. The element includes a sign, the main storage location of the corresponding address field in the assembled program, and a chain pointer. The sign indicates whether the undefined symbol appears positively or negatively. An instance of each occurs, for example, in the address expression LIMIT+3-CALCNEXT. The last element of each chain includes a null pointer. The symbol table entry for the undefined symbol holds a pointer to the head of the corresponding chain.

The first occurrence of an undefined symbol causes the symbol to be entered in the symbol table, marked as undefined, with a pointer to a one-element chain. Each successive occurrence causes a new element to be inserted between the symbol table entry and the head of the previously created chain. The operand field that contains an undefined symbol is replaced in the assembled program by the value of those parts of the address expression other than undefined symbols. That value is, of course, zero if the operand consists of the undefined symbol alone. Figure 2.11 shows a portion of an assembler language program that makes forward references. Location counter values have been supplied. They are labeled "location" rather than "address" because for a load-and-go assembler they really do refer to physical storage locations.

Location	Label	Operation	Operand 1
12		READ	PV
--		---	
47		LOAD	PV
49		ADD	THERM+1
51		STORE	PV
--		---	
92	PV	SPACE	
93	THERM	CONST	386.2
94		CONST	374.9

Figure 2.11   Input to Load-and-Go Assembler (location added)

The generated code (based on Figure 2.2), symbol table, and undefined symbol chains are shown in Figure 2.12 as they stand after translation of the STORE instruction. In the illustration, chain elements are assumed to require two words each, with space starting at location 120 available for the chain. Other implementations of the chain are also possible.

When the assembler finally encounters the definition of a previously referenced symbol, it follows the chain associated with the symbol. Each storage location specified by the chain holds machine code that has already been generated. The assembler adds the symbol's location to that machine code. If the sign field of the chain element is negative, the symbol's location is subtracted instead of added. When the end of the chain is reached, the mark in the symbol table entry is reset from "undefined" to "defined". The pointer to the first chain element is replaced by the symbol's absolute location,

Location	Machine Code		Symbol	Marker	Address
12	12 00		PV	undefined	126
--	---		THERM	undefined	124
47	03 00				
49	02 01				
51	07 00				

(a) Assembled program   (b) Symbol table

Location	Sign	Address	Pointer
120	+	13	null
122	+	48	120
124	+	50	null
126	+	52	122

(c) Undefined symbol chains

Figure 2.12   Data Structures after Translation of Location 51

which is the now-known location counter value. The space occupied by the undefined symbol chain is returned to the available space list for further use. The generated code and symbol table are shown in Figure 2.13 as they stand after processing of the symbol THERM. The entry "XX" for the machine code generated at location 92 indicates that the content of that location is unspecified.

A particularly economical implementation of the chain of undefined symbols stores the pointers within the partially translated program itself. The operand field that contains an undefined symbol is replaced in the assembled program by a pointer to the previous

Location	Machine Code		Symbol	Marker	Address
12	12 92		PV	defined	92
--	---		THERM	defined	93
47	03 92				
49	02 94				
51	07 92				
--	---				
92	XX				
93	386.2				

(a) Assembled program   (b) Symbol table

Figure 2.13   Data Structures after Translation of Location 93

use of that symbol. Because this precludes any provision for other parts of an address expression, a further restriction is necessary. Undefined symbols may then not appear in address expressions. Thus BR REPLACE+6 is permitted only if REPLACE occurs as a label earlier in the source program.

Although there is, to be sure, no full Pass 2, the load-and-go assembler is not really a pure one-pass assembler. The chain-following actions really do constitute partial second passes. Because the portions of the program that they examine are necessarily still in main storage, the cost often associated with a conventional second pass is nevertheless avoided.

2.3.2 One-Pass Module Assembler

A **module** assembler, unlike a load-and-go assembler, produces not machine code, but rather object code that can later be linked and loaded. The one-pass module assembler purports to accomplish this in a single pass, despite forward references. The strategy is to rely on the pass that the loader will eventually make over the program. That pass is used as the second assembler pass for those functions that just cannot be performed in one pass. Thus more work is imposed on the loader, but the assembler requires only one pass. The restriction typically imposed on source programs is the prohibition of forward references other than branches. Thus data areas precede the instructions that reference them, and literals are not provided for.

Each undefined symbol must occur in a branch address. It is entered in a **branch-ahead table** along with its sign and the address of the instruction address field in which it appears. If several branches are expected to refer to the same undefined symbol, the branch-ahead table could be implemented as a collection of chains similar to the undefined symbol chains described in Section 2.3.1. Because the number of branches to undefined symbols is usually small, however, it is probably simpler to omit the pointers and just use a conventional table. Each time a label is encountered, the symbol and its attributes are entered into the symbol table. The branch-ahead table is then scanned for all occurrences of that symbol. For each occurrence, the assembler first generates a directive to the loader to adjust the corresponding address field when the program is loaded, and then deletes the entry from the branch-ahead table.

FOR FURTHER STUDY

Barron78 is an excellent short book on simple and macro assemblers, loaders, and linkers. Its Chapters 2 and 4 are devoted particularly to assemblers. Two good brief treatments of assemblers are Chapter 4 of Ullman76 and Section 8.3 of Brooks69, which is insightful but specialized to the IBM 360. More extensive presentations are in Chapter 4 of Graham75, Chapter 9 of Gear80, and Chapter 7 of Beck85, whose hypothetical assembler language is considerably richer than that of this book. Chapter 7 of Morris83 describes the implementation of a load-and-go assembler for the PDP-11.

REVIEW QUESTIONS

2.1 What is a forward reference?

2.2 Explain why the four occurrences of "XX" cannot be omitted from the end of the machine code in the last paragraph of Section 2.1.2.

2.3 Distinguish between the synonym directive EQU and the definition directive SET. If B is redefined after execution of A EQU B, is A redefined? If B is redefined after execution of A SET B, is A redefined?

2.4 Suppose that a program contains both the literal @3 and a directive C3 CONST 3. Is it permissible to assign the same location to the literal as to C3?

2.5 Explain why the literals generated by a two-pass assembler for @A(SUBR) amd @300 must be distinct, even if SUBR is a local symbol whose location is 300.

2.6 What is the difference between the assembler directives SPACE and CONST?

2.7 Is "*+6" a forward reference?

2.8 Distinguish a literal from an immediate operand. State where the value of each is placed, and how it is addressed.

2.9 What is the effect of INTDEF on the location counter?

2.10 Why does the linker need to know the relocatibility attribute of an external symbol?

2.11 Give two different meanings of "local" in the phrase "local label".

2.12 Consider the chain of symbols that a synonym facility defines to be equivalent. Why is the chain usually not constructed during Pass 1 as the symbols are read?

2.13 Consider a two-pass assembler with no between-passes processing. The restriction that no operand of a SET or EQU directive contain a symbol not previously defined is sufficient, but unnecessarily strong. State the weakest restriction that is sufficient.

2.14 What are the advantages and disadvantages of holding symbolic operation codes in a separate symbol table?

2.15 Why can the normal Pass 2 processing not resolve forward references to local labels in assembler language? What advantages does the use of local labels nevertheless offer?

2.16 If the intermediate text contains pointers to the symbol table, can the symbols themselves be dropped from the table before Pass 2?

2.17 Can the symbol table be built during Pass 1 from an examination of label fields only?

2.18 Relative addresses in assembler language are usually expressed in machine-language units, such as bytes. We might prefer to express offsets in units of source-language lines. How can this be accomplished in a two-pass assembler?

2.19 Is a line counter needed if a *GETNEXTLINE* mechanism is provided?

2.20 Code generation makes no use of labels. Can they be dropped from the intermediate text after Pass 1?

2.21 Give a reason for not considering an undefined symbol to be an error.

2.22 Suggest some different bit patterns (for "XX") that might be generated in response to the SPACE directive, and explain the advantages of each.

2.23 If LITORG is to be processed completely during Pass 1, what assembler-language construction must be avoided? Why?

2.24 Why is it possible to defer all processing of literals to Pass 2 if the LITORG directive is not provided? Why is it not possible if LITORG is provided?

2.25 What is the earliest time at which the conversion of a literal from source language to machine language can occur? What is the latest time?

2.26 Name a disadvantage in deferring the conversion of literals to Pass 2.

2.27 Suppose that the assembler language symbol CARD has location counter value 200. Explain why the literals @A(CARD) and @200 must nevertheless be entered into the pool as two distinct literals.

2.28 Why might you want a load-and-go assembler?

2.29 Why does a load-and-go assembler require foreknowledge of actual storage locations?

2.30 How does a load-and-go assembler generate references to literals?

2.31 Is it possible to provide literals in a one-pass module assembler?

2.32 How can a one-pass module assembler handle a branch to an *external* symbol?

PROBLEMS

2.1 Rewrite the program of Figure 2.1 in a form that makes no forward references to either instructions or data.

2.2 Assemble the following program manually, showing both the resulting object code and the symbol table. Use starting location 200.

```
        COPY    CST1    I
        COPY    CST1    FACT
        READ    N
TOP     LOAD    N
        SUB     I
        BRPOS   OUT
        LOAD    I
        ADD     CST1
        STORE   I
        MULT    FACT
        STORE   FACT
        BR      TOP
OUT     WRITE   FACT
        STOP
N       SPACE
FACT    SPACE
I       SPACE
CST1    CONST   1
```

2.3 Let "@" mark a literal and "A(*symbol*)" be an address constant. Using Figure 2.2, show the generated object code that corresponds to the following source text. Identify each object-code word as absolute or relative. (The program is not intended to be useful.)

```
        LOAD    @A(FRONT)
        ADD     @3
        STORE   NEXT
FRONT   CONST   99
NEXT    SPACE
```

2.4 Assemble the following program manually, showing both the resulting object code and the symbol table. Use starting location 100.

```
                         READ    N
                         COPY    ONE      FACT
                         COPY    ONE      IDX
              HEAD       LOAD    N
                         SUB     IDX
                         BRZERO  ALL
                         BRNEG   ALL
                         LOAD    IDX
                         ADD     ONE
                         STORE   IDX
                         MULT    FACT
                         STORE   FACT
                         BR      HEAD
              ALL        WRITE   FACT
                         STOP
              N          SPACE
              IDX        SPACE
              FACT       SPACE
              ONE        CONST   1
```

2.5 Disassemble the following object code manually, showing a possible assembler-language representation and the corresponding symbol table. Assume that address expressions are not allowed. Be a careful detective in analyzing the last two lines.

```
              00    3    13 22    23
              03    2    12 24
              05    2    03 24
              07    2    05 21
              09    2    06 23
              11    2    01 15
              13    2    00 03
              15    2    03 24
              17    2    07 23
              19    2    00 03
              21    1    11
              22    1    00
              23    2    22 22
```

2.6 Write an address expression to designate the start of the Jth full word of the six full words in the area reserved by the IBM 370 Assembler instruction WORK DS 15D,6F (see "Storage Reservation" in Section 2.2.1).

2.7 Let "@" mark a literal and "A(*symbol*)" be an address constant. Using Figure 2.2, show the generated object code that corresponds to the following source text. Identify each object-code word as absolute or relative. (The program is not intended to be useful.)

```
          READ   OFFSET
          LOAD   OFFSET
          ADD    @A(FAR)
          STORE  NEAR
          BR     FAR+1
NEAR      SPACE
OFFSET    SPACE
FAR       CONST  A(NEAR)
```

2.8 Let EQU be a synonym directive, SET a definition directive, and * the current value of the location counter. Explain (**a**) the difference between the following directives, and (**b**) how each can be implemented in a two-pass assembler.

```
BACK6     EQU    *-6
BACK6     SET    *-6
```

2.9 How can an assembler permit the use in a literal of a symbol defined by the SET directive to represent a given value, as in the following? Each literal takes its value from the most recent previous SET directive. Describe the required actions carefully.

```
LIMIT     SET    4
          ---
          ADD    @LIMIT
          ---
LIMIT     SET    6
          ---
          DIVIDE @LIMIT
```

2.10 Let OPSYN be the operation code synonym facility mentioned in the third paragraph under "Alternate Names" in Section 2.3.1.
(**a**) How is it distinct from EQU or SET?
(**b**) How can it be implemented?
(**c**) Why is it helpful to require *all* occurrences of OPSYN to precede *any* instructions?

2.11 Design an implementation of literals (without `LITORG`) that does all the processing on Pass 2. State exactly what is generated and when.

2.12 [Donovan] Explain how to process `LITORG` on Pass 1 only, given that address constants are not permitted. State exactly what is generated and when.

2.13 Let `LITORG` be an instruction to assign the current location counter value as the origin of a literal pool. Design an implementation of literals, including `LITORG`, and state precisely and fully what actions each pass performs. Make sure that your implementation is capable of handling the following situation (where "`@`" marks a literal).

```
        ---     @A(PLACE)
        ---     @3
        LITORG
        ---     @3
PLACE   ---
```

2.14 [Donovan] To permit a two-pass assembler to generate code for absolute loading (*i.e.*, without relocation), the assembler directive **ABS** has been defined. Its one operand specifies the execution-time physical location of the origin of the module being assembled.
(**a**) Where may the **ABS** directive appear in the source program?
(**b**) During which pass(es) would the **ABS** be processed and how?

2.15 [Ghezzi] Multiply defined symbols are legal in a certain assembler language. The assembler is to apply the definition closest (in terms of number of source-text lines) to the referencing line. Explain how to implement this feature in a two-pass assembler.

2.16 Consider the translation of the following program by a conventional load-and-go assembler. Assume starting location 100. Show the data structures, as in Figures 2.11–2.13,

(**a**) after the translation of line 6;
(**b**) after the translation of line 12.

1.		COPY	ZERO	SUMPOS
2.	READNEXT	READ	NUMBER	
3.		LOAD	NUMBER	
4.		BRPOS	POSITIVE	
5.		BRNEG	READNEXT	
6.		STOP		
7.	POSITIVE	LOAD	SUMPOS	
8.		ADD	NUMBER	
9.		STORE	SUMPOS	
10.		BR	READNEXT	
11.	ZERO	CONST	0	
12.	NUMBER	SPACE		
13.	SUMPOS	SPACE		

2.17 Consider the translation of the program of Problem 2.16 by a load-and-go assembler that uses the implementation described in the penultimate paragraph of Section 2.3.1. Assuming starting location 200, show the symbol table and the assembled machine-language program
(**a**) after the translation of line 6;
(**b**) after the translation of line 12.

2.18 Change the operand in location 50 of Figure 2.11 to THERM. Illustrate the implementation described in the penultimate paragraph of Section 2.3.1 by showing the assembled program and symbol table
(**a**) after the translation of location 50;
(**b**) after the translation of location 92.

2.19 Show the steps in the translation of the program of Problem 2.16 by a one-pass module assembler. First rewrite the program to avoid forward references to data (*cf.* Problem 2.1).

2.20 Let a one-pass module assembler translate the following program in the assembler language of Figure 2.2. Consider the moment immediately following translation of the STORE instruction. Show, as of that moment, (**a**) the symbol table, (**b**) the branch-ahead table, (**c**) the directives prepared for a relocating loader, and (**d**) the object code generated. Identify the different fields clearly.

```
NEGTWO    CONST   -2
THREE     CONST   3
DATUM     SPACE
          READ    DATUM
LOOPHEAD  LOAD    DATUM
          BRZERO  EXIT
          BRNEG   NEGATIVE
POSITIVE  MULT    THREE
          BR      EITHER
NEGATIVE  MULT    NEGTWO
EITHER    STORE   DATUM
          WRITE   DATUM
          READ    DATUM
          BR      LOOPHEAD
EXIT      STOP
```

2.21 [Ghezzi] Devise an implementation of literals in a one-pass module assembler. Illustrate your method by showing the data structures after the translation of lines 6, 9, and 11 of the following program.

```
 1.            LOAD    @0
 2.            READ    OF
 3.            LOAD    OF
 4.            ADD     @A(FAR)
 5.            STORE   N
 6.            BR      FAR+1
 7.   N        SPACE
 8.   OF       SPACE
 9.   FAR      CONST   A(N)
10.            LOAD    @0
11.            BR      OUT
```

Chapter 3

Program Modules

Since program modules are the basic unit of translation, it is appropriate to explore how various properties of program modules affect the translation process. After all, the programmer has a right to expect that properties of the module as written are preserved in the module as translated. Relevant properties include the degree of reusability of a module, the structural relations among modules, the way a module is invoked, and the type of correspondence of formal to actual parameters. We shall examine each of these in turn.

3.1 DEGREES OF REUSABILITY

The extent to which a program module can be executed more than once with the same effect each time is known as its degree of **reusability**. We distinguish three degrees of reusability. A module may be **nonreusable**, **serially reusable**, or **reenterable**. A *nonreusable* module does not incorporate initialization of values changed by the module. Each execution of the module may therefore yield a different result. A *serially reusable* module does incorporate the required initialization. If one execution of it terminates before another is begun, each execution will have the same result. A *reenterable* module is a serially reusable module that incorporates no modification of itself during execution. Multiple instances of execution will therefore yield the same result, even if one instance has not terminated before the next has begun.

The foregoing three classes of modules stand in a hierarchy of degrees of reusability. A fourth class of module represents not a degree of reusability, but rather a special source of reuse. A **recursive** module is a module having the property that one cause of multiple instances of execution is the module itself. Although some recursive modules are serially reusable only, most are reenterable.

Source-language differences corresponding to the four classes are shown in the procedures of Figure 3.1. Each procedure is intended to return the value of n factorial $(1 \times 2 \times \ldots \times n)$ for a nonnegative integer argument n. Procedure F is nonreusable. It returns the correct value only if the global variables i and r both have value 1 when F is invoked. If they do have these values, then $F(3)$ will indeed return the correct value 6. But a second call $F(3)$ that is executed when i and r have values other than both 1 will return an incorrect result. The resulting lack of reproducibility is a disqualification for most programs, but there is at least one application for which it is not only welcome but mandatory. A pseudorandom number generator must indeed yield reproducible sequences of numbers to permit testing and debugging, but successive calls to the generator must certainly not always return the same value. A more homely example of a nonreusable module is an input routine, which delivers different data upon each invocation.

Procedure FA incorporates the initialization of i and r. It is serially reusable; a second call $FA(3)$ will return the same value 6 as does the first, regardless of any changes that may occur to the values of i and r between executions of FA. Suppose, however, that execution of $FA(3)$ is suspended within the loop but just before entering the loop body with both i and r equal to 2. Let the call $FA(4)$ then be executed in its entirety, while execution of the first call remains suspended. The effect of executing this second call will be to set i to 4 and r to 24, returning the correct value. Execution of the first call, $FA(3)$, would then resume from the loop body, incrementing i to 5 and assigning 120 to r. The condition $i<n$ would not be met, and execution of the first call, $FA(3)$, would terminate with a return of the incorrect value 120. The reusability of the module is thus seen to be serial reusability only.

```
procedure F(n) integer          procedure FA(n) integer
    integer n                       integer n
    begin                           begin
        while i<n do                    i ← 1
            i ← 1 + i                   r ← 1
            r ← i × r                   while i<n do
        return r                            i ← 1 + i
    end                                     r ← i × r
                                        return r
                                    end
```

    Nonreusable   Serially Reusable

```
procedure FAC(n) integer        procedure FACT(n) integer
    integer n                       integer n
    integer i,r                     integer r
    begin                           begin
        i ← 1                           r ← if n<2
        r ← 1                               then 1
        while i<n do                        else n × FACT(n−1)
            i ← 1 + i                   return r
            r ← i × r               end
        return r
    end
```

    Reenterable   Recursive

Figure 3.1 Programs for Computing n Factorial

Procedure FAC is reenterable, because it can be reentered by a second instance of execution before termination of a prior instance, yet without producing incorrect results. This feat is accomplished by making values changed by the module *local* to the module. Most machine-independent languages indicate this by placing declarations of variables within the module, as is done for i and r in the example. A repetition of the previous scenario, in which the execution of $FAC(3)$ is suspended to permit the evaluation of $FAC(4)$, succeeds because *each* instance of execution of FAC has its own copies of the variables named i and r. A reenterable program can thus be shared by many users. Although each user requires separate data areas, a single copy of the procedure code suffices. A reenterable module is therefore sometimes called a "pure" procedure; another common designation is "reentrant". Even if sharing is not

contemplated, reenterable code is usually superior to code that is
only serially reusable, because it is usually easier to read and to
verify.

Procedure $FACT$ is recursive because it calls itself. Execution
of $FACT(3)$ invokes another instance of $FACT$ with 2 as the argument, and this second execution results in the call $FACT(1)$. The
nesting of invocations stops at this point, because $FACT(1)$ is evaluated as 1 without the issuance of a further call of $FACT$. Because
each instance of $FACT$ has its own value for the formal parameter* n, the three instances of execution do not interfere with each
other. Thus the second instance, with $n=2$, receives the value 1
from the call $FACT(1)$, multiplies it by 2, and returns the product 2 as the value of $FACT(2)$ requested by the original instance
of $FACT$ with argument 3. The parameters passed from one instance of execution to another, as well as the return address of
each instance, must not be modified during execution. In practice,
most recursive modules, like $FACT$, are fully reenterable. Anything
that can be computed recursively — with the possible exception
of some functions not classed as "primitive recursive" — can also
be computed iteratively. The programming may nevertheless be
considerably easier if recursion is used. The Towers of Hanoi provide a good example, as do many algorithms for traversing binary
trees.

Some of the information associated with a module in execution
is fixed, such as its instructions, and some information is changeable, such as values of its local variables. Reentrant and recursive
execution require that the changeable information associated with
a partially executed module be stored separately for each instance
of execution, or activation, of the module. The storage area used
is called an **activation record**. All activations of such a module
share a common area of fixed information, but each has a distinct
activation record. There should never be more than one activation
of a nonreusable or serially reusable module, because multiple activations lead to incorrect results. Each of these modules therefore
has at most one activation record. Figure 3.2 depicts the execution
of three activations of a reenterable module.

---

*Formal parameters are discussed in Section 3.4.

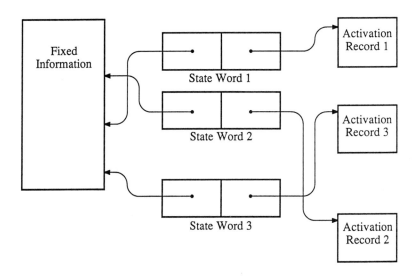

Figure 3.2   Reentrant Execution

The state of each activation can be determined by use of a conceptual **state word**. This holds (1) the address, in the fixed area, of the next instruction to be executed by that activation, and (2) the location of the corresponding activation record. During execution of a module, the pointers that constitute the state word are held in the processing unit's hardware. The instruction counter holds the instruction address; the activation record address is held in a base register or other easily accessible location. When processing is interrupted, the instruction address is stored into the activation record by software. The operating system maintains the list of activation record addresses to assist in making transitions between activations.

The use of a stack of activation records to implement recursion is diagrammed in Figure 3.3. A procedure P has invoked the recursive program of Figure 3.1 with the call $FACT(3)$. An activation record is shown for P; virtually all detail has been suppressed. The call $FACT(3)$ has created the adjacent activation record for $FACT$ with the value 3 assigned to the parameter n, but no values associated yet with either $FACT(n-1)$ or r. The number 7 is

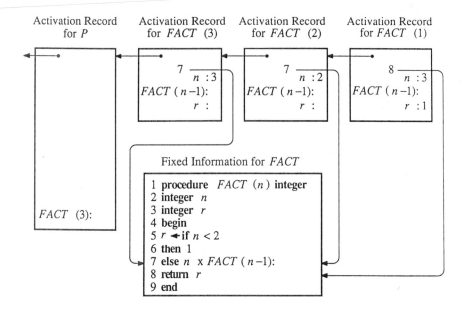

Figure 3.3   Recursion Stack

the address* of the instruction (number of the statement in Figure 3.1) from which execution is to resume in the same first activation of *FACT* after execution of the recursive call *FACT*(2) has terminated.

The activation record for *FACT* is stacked above that for *P*, with a back pointer to permit control to be returned to *P* after execution of *FACT* has terminated. The second call, *FACT*(2), has created the second activation record for *FACT*. This second activation record is identical to the first, except for the pointer used to direct return of control not to *P* but to the first activation of *FACT*. The third activation record for *FACT* was created when the second executed the call *FACT*(1). The status of that third *FACT* module is shown after assignment of the value 1 to *r*, but before the return of control at statement 8. When control is returned, that value 1 will be placed in the cell allocated for *FACT*($n-1$) in the previous activation record,

---

*This is a simplification, of course, because processing resumes from *within* statement 7. If we assume *FACT* to have been translated before execution, then processing resumes not merely from within a statement, but from a particular machine-language instruction. The activation record would hold not the numeral 7, but rather the address of that instruction.

and the second instance of execution will resume at the multiplication in statement 7. The record of the third activation of *FACT* can then be deleted, *i.e.*, popped off the stack. Subsequent assignment of 2 to *r* in the second activation of *FACT* will permit that activation to terminate and the first to resume. Eventually the value 6 will have been computed for *FACT*(3) and delivered to procedure *P*. The stack of activation records for *FACT* will have shrunk back to empty, its state before the call *FACT*(3).

The assembler-language programmer must perform directly the management of activation records for recursive or reenterable modules. The user of a machine-independent language, on the other hand, expects the translator to handle the details automatically. It is particularly important in allocating space for the different activation records of a recursive routine to ensure that they are indeed assigned different locations in storage. This is so, even when all invocations but the first are performed by executing the same calling sequence. The allocation is typically accomplished by issuing, when the recursive call is encountered at execution time, a request to the operating system to provide a distinct storage area. In an assembler-language program, the programmer may either include such requests to the operating system, or directly manage a stack for the parameters and return addresses.

Recursion is not limited to one procedure calling itself directly. If *A* calls *B* and *B* calls *A*, then one call of *A* can engender another call of *A*, and the property of recursion holds for *A* (as it does also for *B*). A formal definition of recursion among a set of modules is possible (*cf.* Problem 3.2). It will be adequate, however, for us to consider the call structure to be recursive if there exists a module whose execution can result in a call of itself.

A call statement existing in a program text may or may not actually be executed when the program is run. It is thus possible to distinguish between a *potential* call (existing in the text at translation time) and an *actual* call (performed at execution time), hence between potentially and actually recursive modules. The detection of potential recursion is possible at translation time, and is performed most readily if all of the modules are compiled at one time. This detection by the compiler becomes unnecessary, however, if the programmer declares each recursive module to be recursive.

3.2 BLOCK STRUCTURE

Many procedural languages are endowed with a feature known as
block structure, which controls the scope of names and also sub-
divides programs into modules. The provision of block structure
restricts the program extent within which an identifier is known, the
so-called **scope** of the identifier. Because different locations in the
program lie within the scopes of different sets of identifiers, they are
said to have different **environments**. The program text is explicitly
divided by the programmer into units generically called blocks, although various names are used for the blocks in different languages.
Examples include procedures in PASCAL, user-defined functions in
APL, and **begin** blocks in PL/I. Some languages have more than one
type of block.

Two blocks in the static text of the program are either disjoint,
having no portion in common, or nested, one block completely enclosing the other. This **static nesting** of blocks in the text is distinct
from the **dynamic nesting** of block activations during execution.
The program of Figure 3.4(a) illustrates both kinds of nesting. There
are three blocks, procedures A, B, and C. In the static text, blocks B
and C are disjoint, and each is enclosed in block A. If block A is activated first and all the calls shown are executed, then A will activate
C, which will in turn activate B. When B has finished executing, it
will return control to C, and C will eventually return control to A.
Thus the dynamic nesting changes dynamically with time, reaching
a maximum depth of three while B is active.

The static nesting structure of text embedding can be represented by a fixed tree of blocks in which the parent of each block
other than a root is the immediately enclosing block. The tree need
not actually be drawn as a directed graph, and the notation of Figure 3.4(b) is often convenient. We can represent the dynamic nesting
structure of activations by a stack of activation records that grows
upon entry to an inner level of dynamic nesting and shrinks on exit
therefrom. A single diagram can capture the dynamic stack at only
one moment; the one chosen in Figure 3.4(c) is that during execution
of block B.

If an identifier is known anywhere within a block, it is known
throughout the block. Thus the block is the unit for determining

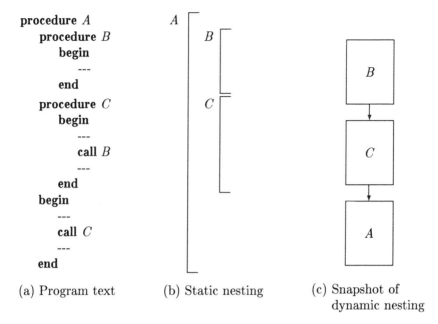

```
procedure A
    procedure B
        begin
            ---
        end
    procedure C
        begin
            ---
            call B
            ---
        end
    begin
        ---
        call C
        ---
    end
```

(a) Program text   (b) Static nesting   (c) Snapshot of dynamic nesting

Figure 3.4   A Block-Structured Program

scope of identifiers and for describing the environment. An identifier that is either declared within a block or named as a formal parameter* of the block is obviously known. It is said to be **local** to that block because knowledge of it derives from within the block. A local identifier is not known outside the block to which it is local. Alternatively, knowledge of an identifier may be imposed on a block from outside the block. Such an identifier is said to be **global** † with respect to that block, although it may be local to some enclosing block. An identifier of which a block has no knowledge may be termed **unknown** to the block.

The rules for determining scope of identifiers vary somewhat among block-structured languages, but it is possible to describe a typical set of rules, based on static nesting. Subject to an exception about to be described, an identifier is local to the block in which it is declared (or named as a formal parameter), global to all blocks

---

*Formal parameters are discussed in Section 3.4.

†Sometimes the term **nonlocal** is used for what we have defined as global, and **global** used for an identifier defined at the outermost level and known to all blocks.

directly or indirectly nested within that block, *i.e.*, *contained* inside
it, and unknown elsewhere. Thus in Figure 3.5(a) the variable x is
local to block A and global to the other four blocks. Variable y, on
the other hand, is local to block B, hence unknown to A and C, and
global to D and E. The scope of either variable is the set of blocks
to which it is not unknown.

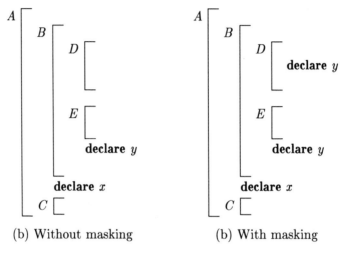

(b) Without masking   (b) With masking

Figure 3.5   Scope of Identifiers

The exception to the foregoing rule occurs when an identifier
local to a given block has the same name as an identifier local to
a contained block. We can think of the identifier that is local to
the inner block as masking knowledge of the other identifier, which
would otherwise be global to the inner block. Thus in Figure 3.5(b)
the variable y declared in block B is no longer global to D, as it is in
(a), because it is masked by the variable y declared in D. There are
two distinct identifiers y in the program. The scope of one is blocks
B and E; the scope of the other is block D. Both identifiers y are
unknown in blocks A and C.

In determining the environment of a block, we must proceed
from that block outward through successive levels of static nesting.
Consider references within block D of Figure 3.5(b) to identifiers x
and y. Because y is local to D, the description of y is immediately
available. Identifier x, on the other hand, is not local to D, and

we must look outside D to find its description. We examine the immediately containing block B, but find no description of x. The description of y that does occur in B is not relevant to the search, because of masking; it describes a variable other than the y that is referenced within D. Our search for x continues with examination of the next outer block A, where we indeed find the description.

Representation of the dynamic nesting of activations is required at execution time to permit control to be returned from a dying block to its activator. Similarly, representation of the static nesting of blocks is necessary at execution time for accessing global identifiers. One possible solution is to consider the activation records as the nodes of the active portion of the static tree structure, and to supply for each a **static link** to point to its enclosing parent. To show the dynamic stack structure a **dynamic link** can be used. These two sets of links are illustrated in Figure 3.6. The static program structure is shown in (a). We assume that blocks A, B, C, D, and E are activated in that sequence; E is a procedure that calls itself recursively. The execution-time representation is depicted in (b) at a time during execution of the third instance of E. The dynamic links are shown on the left, the static links on the right. The set of static links that can be followed from the currently active record constitutes the current **static chain**.

An alternative to the static chain is the **display**, sometimes called the "current-environment vector". The display is a variable-length vector of pointers to the currently accessible blocks, ordered by level in the static tree structure. Access to the display is made by indexing within this vector of pointers, and is therefore much faster than following links in the static chain. The activation-record stack of Figure 3.6(b) is redrawn in Figure 3.6(c) with a display instead of a static chain.

Consider, for example, the current activation of E. The corresponding text is nested statically within D, which is itself nested within B. Suppose that E refers to an identifier declared within B. Suppose also that a static chain is used, as in Figure 3.6(b). Access requires the execution-time traversal of two links in the chain, that from E to D, and that from D to B. Suppose instead that a display is used, as in Figure 3.6(c). Access requires the execution-time use of only one pointer, that to B. The pointer is known at compilation time to lie in the third element of the display. For deeper nesting, the time saving is even greater.

There is a cost, however, for the faster access provided by the display. The program translator must generate code to use the dynamic link in returning control and to use the environment representation (display or static chain) in accessing nonlocal identifiers. It must also generate code to set the appropriate pointer values on entry to each newly activated block, and to reset them on exit. We examine this matter further in Chapter 8.

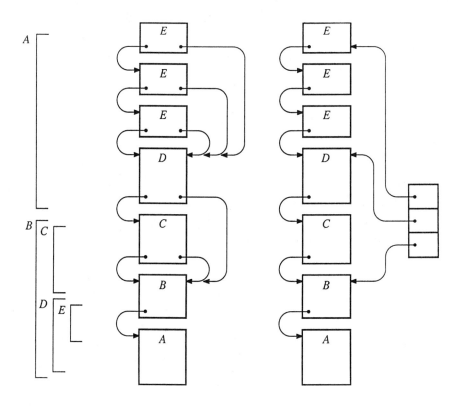

(a) Static structure   (b) Activation-record stack with static links   (c) Activation-record stack with display

Figure 3.6   Run-Time Representation of Nesting

3.3 MODES OF ACTIVATION

A program module can be activated in at least six ways, each of which is primarily associated with a different type of module. Most of the differences among the modes of activation are reflected in the execution-time management of activation records. This is normally a responsibility of the operating system rather than of the language system. Some of the differences, however, are also reflected in the requirements for translation.

3.3.1 Begin Blocks

The simplest module is the **begin** block, introduced in PL/I. Its counterpart in C is the delimitation of scope by the brackets "{" and "}". Execution begins when the instructions in the block are encountered by normal progression from earlier instructions. Execution terminates when normal progression leads to an instruction outside the block. A major purpose of the **begin** block is to provide nesting in the static text of the program, thus delimiting the scope of source-language names.

An equally important purpose in PL/I is the deferral of storage allocation for **automatic** variables, the default. Storage for **automatic** variables is allocated upon block entry, no matter where in the block they are declared. This requires the compiler to process *all* declarations before any other statements. Suppose, however, that an array is to have a bound provided as data. The array cannot be declared until the value of the bound is known. The bound, on the other hand, cannot be read until all declarations, including that of the array, have been processed. The solution has two parts. First is to declare in an outer block the variable that holds the array bound, and to read its value. Second is to enter a **begin** block in which the array may be declared.

For the foregoing purposes, a separate activation record is required. It is created upon entry to the **begin** block, stacked above the activation record of the enclosing block, and deleted upon exit from the **begin** block.

3.3.2 Subroutines

A widely used type of module is the subroutine, with which all but the greenest of computer programmers are familiar. Associated with the subroutine, or called procedure, is a calling block to which it is subordinated in an asymmetric relation of dependence. Execution begins upon specific naming of the called procedure by the calling block and, upon termination, control returns to the caller. Statements such as **call** and **return** are typically used for these actions, although either action may be implicit. In some languages, **return** is implicit in the end of the subroutine text; in some, **call** is implicit in the naming of a procedure. An activation record for the called procedure is created upon invocation, stacked above that for the calling block, and destroyed upon termination. For intermodule communication, parameters can be passed from the calling to the called module. The mechanisms for invoking a subroutine, passing parameters, and returning control are referred to collectively as subroutine linkage. Issues in subroutine linkage are treated in Section 3.4.

What we are referring to as a subroutine is more properly termed a "closed" subroutine. It may or may not be translated as a module separate from the calling block. An "open" subroutine, or "in-line" code, on the other hand, is code embedded in the calling block. It is always translated as a portion of the containing module.

3.3.3 Interrupt Function Modules

The interrupt function module, or exception handler, is also invoked asymmetrically. The invocation may be either explicit or, more commonly, in response to the occurrence of some stated condition during execution of the calling block. Control is normally not returned to the caller.

The archetypal example is the **on** unit of PL/I, activated either by the **signal** statement or, more commonly, by occurrence of the associated condition. There are no parameters. Scope is determined neither statically nor dynamically, but *historically*. The **on** unit (module) to be invoked for the exception is the one most recently encountered during execution. As a result, there may exist no activation record for the module that contains the **on** unit. Even if one does exist, it may lie outside the environment of the invoking module. Consider, for example, the following fragment of program text in PL/I.

> A: **begin**;
>
> ---
>
> **on** *condition-name*
>
> ---
>
> **call** B;
>
> ---
>
> **end** A;
> B: **procedure**;
>
> ---
>
> *condition-name* occurs
>
> ---

The activation record for block B must contain a reference to the exception handler in block A, even though the text within block A is not in B's environment. This permits an activation record for the **on** unit to be constructed if the **on** condition is raised. Moreover, if block A contains two calls of B, each preceded by a different **on** unit, then the reference must be different for each call.

ADA permits not only system-defined but also user-defined exceptions. Its **exception** construct can be invoked either automatically or by execution of the **raise** statement. If the module in which this occurs contains the handler for the exception, that handler is the one invoked. Otherwise, search is made outward into the dynamic environment until an appropriate handler is encountered.

3.3.4 Coroutines

A subroutine **call** creates an activation record for the subroutine, and **return** of control from the subroutine to its caller destroys the activation record. Thus, the subroutine is clearly subordinate to its caller. Unlike the subroutine, the coroutine is a module coordinate with other modules. A coroutine **resume** neither creates nor destroys an activation record. Execution of the coroutine is merely resumed from wherever it last left off, rather than from a fixed entry or reentry point. Its activation record must therefore store the current restart point. Coroutine invocation is thus seen to be symmetric.

Because coroutines are symmetric, and the management of a stack is asymmetric, coroutine activation records cannot share a stack. Instead, each coroutine activation record occupies the bottom of its own stack. This stack grows and shrinks as the coroutine invokes its own subroutines or enters **begin** blocks, and as those modules activate yet others or terminate. Thus the execution-time representation of coroutines requires multiple stacks.

Creation of a coroutine activation record is caused by an initial invocation distinct from the resume. This initial call may be termed an **allocate** because it allocates an activation record. Deletion of the coroutine activation record may occur automatically upon the coroutine executing its last instruction. It may also occur explicitly as the result of a **free** command in another module, typically the one that caused the activation record to be created.

Parameters can be passed to a coroutine, as they can to a subroutine, but at a choice of times. The values of actual parameters can be passed in the **allocate** call, or else in the first **resume** that follows allocation. It may even be possible to pass parameters with later **resume** calls.

The original illustration of coroutines [Conway63] is a program for printing programs read from cards, with a change of notation for the exponentiation operator. Each occurrence of the character pair "**" is replaced by the single character "↑". An "asterisk squasher" coroutine interacts with a coroutine that provides the next input character. A simpler example is the following recipe for conversation. "While the other person talks, listen" and "while the other person listens, talk" constitute an appropriate pair of coroutines.

Coroutines can sometimes substitute for a multipass algorithm. Figure 3.7 depicts in (a) an algorithm that makes three successive passes over a sequential file. In the coroutine implementation (b), coroutine A resumes coroutine B when Pass 1 would have written a record to the first intermediate file; coroutine B resumes A when Pass 2 would have read a record and resumes C when Pass 2 would have written a record to the second intermediate file; coroutine C resumes B when Pass 3 would have read a record. The one-pass coroutine algorithm saves the time needed to pack, write, read, and unpack the intermediate data records. It requires enough space, however, to hold all the programs at once. Some algorithms, of course, are essentially multipass and cannot conveniently be replaced by coroutines.

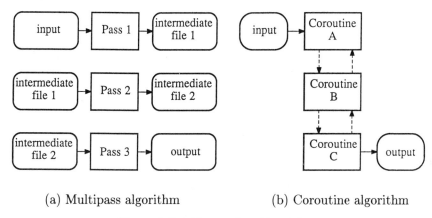

(a) Multipass algorithm   (b) Coroutine algorithm

Figure 3.7   Alternative Algorithms

Coroutines provide synchronization among interleaved cooperating processes. They also provide a means to specify independent concurrent processes, as in MODULA–2. On a uniprocessor system, the apparent concurrency is an illusion, because only one is in execution at a time. In a translator designed for a multiprocessor system, however, this concurrency can become real.

Coroutines also provide, for the efficient simulation of concurrent processes and are so used in the language SIMULA, where the coroutines are known as **classes** or **activities**. MODULA–2 also provides coroutines. Simple examples in which coroutines are clearly more efficient than subroutines are difficult to produce; meaningful examples are often complex. This is one reason why few languages provide coroutines, and why the use of coroutines has long been a neglected art.

3.3.5 Events

A fifth mode of activation can be superimposed on subroutines or coroutines. Each module, instead of issuing a **call**, **return**, or **resume** command, issues instead a **scheduling** command. This is a request to the operating system's process scheduler to issue the **call**, **return**, or **resume**. Use of this control program component to determine execution sequence can result in greater efficiency of resource utilization. In this mode, program modules are often called **events**, and scheduling information for each event whose execution has been requested is an **event notice**. Whenever execution of one event ceases, control is passed to the scheduler, which examines the event notices and selects one event for execution. The search over all event notices can be traded for extra processing time earlier to insert each event notice into an **event queue**. The queue is typically ordered on a criterion such as simulated time or dispatching priority. Event queues provide for global supervision of the scheduling of module activation.

3.3.6 Concurrent Modules

Events are executed consecutively as the result of scheduled invocations. Unscheduled sequencing, a sixth mode, may be used instead when multiple processing units are available to provide true concurrency rather than only interleaving. A module can invoke another module to be executed in parallel with the instruction sequence that follows the invocation, often termed an **attach** or **fork** invocation. In this situation, the sequence of execution of the different modules is unspecified, whereas for coroutines it is specified by the **resume** calls and for events by the scheduler. This absence of sequence specification raises important problems of synchronization, solutions to which are discussed in books on operating systems.

The attachment of a module in parallel is represented by the bifurcation of the activation-record stack. Both the original parent module and the newly attached child module can continue to invoke subroutines, each on its own partial stack. If a child attaches children of its own, further bifurcation results. The partial stacks may or may not have independent lives, depending upon whether a child module is required to expire before its parent. When either a parent or its child terminates, the previously forked stack loses a tine.

Another form of concurrent execution is specified by such constructions as the **cobegin-coend** pair [Dijkstra65]. Because the enclosed parallel instruction streams, such as ADA's **rendezvous**, share the same environment, it might appear that we do not need distinct activation records. But synchronization statements within those streams may require one stream to become temporarily inactive. It is thus appropriate to have for each stream a different activation record, even though all contain the same values of the static link and dynamic link.

3.4 SUBROUTINE LINKAGE

A **formal parameter** of a subroutine or coroutine procedure is an identifier, within that procedure, that is replaced, during execution of the procedure, by another identifier or by an expression. The replacing identifier or expression is the corresponding **actual parameter**. The formal parameters are named in the definition of the procedure. Thus A and B are formal parameters of P in the following.

subroutine $P(A,B)$	FORTRAN
procedure $P(A,B)$	ALGOL,PASCAL
P **procedure** (A,B);	PL/I
$\nabla A\ P\ B$	APL

The actual parameters are named in the invocation of the procedure. Thus the statements

call $P(X,Y*Z)$	FORTRAN
$P(X,Y*Z)$	ALGOL, PASCAL
call $P(X,Y*Z)$;	PL/I
$X\ P\ Y\times Z$	APL

all specify the variable X as the actual parameter corresponding to the formal parameter A of procedure P, and the expression Y times Z as the actual parameter corresponding to the formal parameter B. An actual parameter expression may be a constant, as in **call** $P(X,5)$. Whether a constant is handled as a variety of expression or is treated specially depends on the language. The most important distinction in actual parameters, however, is whether they are variables.

When one module calls or resumes another, it communicates information by means of parameters and preserves enough status information to permit its own resumption. This activity is termed **linkage**, and must not be confused with the "linkage" performed by the linker in binding intermodule symbolic references. The linkage with which we are concerned here is performed at execution time, by executing instructions that have been prepared by the translator. Although linkage applies to coroutines as well as to subroutines, the ensuing description is couched in terms of subroutines. The changes required for coroutines are for the most part straightforward.

There are four common ways to transmit and receive parameters. We shall discuss each in turn and present a sample implementation. In each of the four implementations, the called procedure makes a private copy of the value of each actual parameter. This is only one of several ways to establish parameter correspondence. Others are discussed in Section 3.5.

A **common data** area for parameters can be shared by both calling and called routines. The use of storage that is global to the two routines requires both to use the same names or addresses, which are external references, to access the parameters. The advantage of using such global variables for communication is simplicity. Disadvantages are the need to know external names, the time to translate external references, and, in some systems, particularly those with explicit-base addressing, restrictions on addressability. For the sample correspondence in the first paragraph of this section, we might implement as follows a common data area for transmitting the parameters (not their names).

```
LOAD    X                          LOAD    PARM1
STORE   PARM1                      STORE   A
LOAD    Y                          LOAD    PARM2
MULT    Z                          STORE   B
STORE   PARM2

        Caller                             Called
```

Processing unit **registers**, if available in the machine, provide another locus for parameters. This, too, permits simple communication as long as the registers are not needed for other purposes. Disadvantages are that several registers are likely to be needed for frequently used values such as increments and limits, for the return address, and perhaps for base-register addressing. The consequence may be fewer available registers than parameters to be passed. The following is a sample implementation. LOAD and STORE now specify which of several registers is involved, rather than the sole, implicitly addressed, accumulator of the original instruction set. We follow here the convention of using the predefined synonym Ri for i in referring to a general register.

```
LOAD    R1      X                  STORE   R1      A
LOAD    R2      Y                  STORE   R2      B
MULT    R2      Z

        Caller                             Called
```

All parameters for one call can be grouped into a **parameter area** in storage, and its starting address passed to the called routine. This has the advantages of keeping the registers free and of being easy to implement. The need to pass an address is at worst a minor disadvantage, and the use of a parameter area is often attractive. In the following implementation, register R0 is used to pass the parameter area address. We adopt here the convention of appending "+" to an operation code to indicate the use of one level of indirect addressing.

```
      COPY   X       PARM           STORE  R0        ADDRABCD
      LOAD   R1      Y              COPY+  ADDRA     A
      MULT   R1      Z              COPY+  ADDRA+1   B
      STORE  R1      PARM+1
      LOAD   R0      @A(PARM)
      ---                           ---
PARM  SPACE                    A    SPACE
      SPACE                    B    SPACE
            Caller                        Called
```

A **shared stack** of parameters works as follows. The calling routine transmits the parameters by pushing them onto the stack. The called routine receives the parameters by popping them from the stack. Before returning control, it can push them back on if necessary. Subroutines nested dynamically at multiple levels can share a single stack. Advantages of the shared stack are that it can consume less storage space than separate parameter areas and that it is convenient for recursive calls. One disadvantage is the execution time required. A more serious disadvantage is the need to provide either an implicitly addressed stack mechanism in the hardware or else software stack manipulation with a fixed address. The following implementation assumes that PUSH and POP push an operand from the accumulator to an unnamed stack and pop an operand from the stack to the accumulator.

```
      LOAD   X                     POP
      PUSH                         STORE  B
      LOAD   Y                     POP
      MULT   Z                     STORE  A
      PUSH
            Caller                        Called
```

Whatever method is used to communicate parameters, a further requirement exists. For all but the simplest routines, we must save the calling routine's program status when a subroutine is called and restore it upon return from the subroutine. A program's status information includes: (1) its register contents; (2) its cache contents, if a cache is provided; (3) its instruction counter setting, condition bits, timer request, and interrupt status; (4) its regions of main storage and, if paging or segmentation is used, the associated tables and backing storage; (5) logically associated operating system storage, such as job queue entries; and (6) outstanding I/O requests and the positions of noncyclic I/O devices and volumes.

Fortunately, when subroutine calls are issued, most of this information is not in danger of loss. Usually, only the register contents need be saved and a return address passed. To save the required information, two entities are required: an **owner** of space to hold the information and an **agent** to perform the storing and restoring. The two possibilities for each are the calling and called routines. If the agent is the caller, the save-restore code for *each call* must be included in the caller. Alternatively, a single copy of that code, which is invoked as needed, can be used. Of course, that particular copy then becomes another subroutine, although a very limited one. If the agent is the called routine, the save-restore code must be incorporated there, but often one copy will suffice. The most that will be required is one copy of the save code per entry point and one of the restore code per return point.

If the storage area owner is the routine that is not the agent for storing and restoring, the agent needs to learn the storage area's location. Suppose first that the called routine is the owner and the caller is the agent. The storage space could be provided by convention at a fixed distance from the beginning of the called routine. A more flexible solution would be to put there a pointer to the storage area. Then if multiple entry points are used, multiple storage areas would be obviated by provision of a pointer at the same fixed offset relative to each entry point. Suppose, on the other hand, that the caller is the owner and the called routine is the agent. The caller can pass the storage area location to the called routine in the same manner as the parameters. Because only one call by a given routine can be outstanding at a time, a separate storage area is not needed for each call in the calling routine. If the routine is recursive, one storage area is needed per activation.

Each programming system has a subroutine linkage convention. It is not only adopted for use among components of the operating system, but also imposed on the users, because of the interactions between their programs and the operating system. An attractive solution for multiple-register processing units is for the calling routine to own the space, the called routine to do the work, and one of the registers to point to a parameter area. Whatever solution is chosen, however, the translation programs are involved in two ways. As elements of the programming system, they must use its linkage convention in their own functioning. As translators they must produce user programs that employ those conventions.

3.5 PARAMETER CORRESPONDENCE

When a procedure is invoked, the calling module passes to it an explicit or implicit list of addresses of the actual parameters. The called procedure copies these addresses, if necessary, into its own activation record and uses them to establish the correspondences between actual and formal parameters. The nature of the correspondences depends upon the programming language and, for some languages, upon the programmer's choice. Three principal types of correspondence are described in the following sections.

3.5.1 Call by Reference

Under the call by reference correspondence, the calling module first determines whether the actual parameter is an expression. If so, it evaluates the expression and places the value in a temporary location. The calling module calculates, if necessary, the address of the actual parameter variable, constant, or temporary location. It then passes that address to the called procedure, which uses it to refer to the actual parameter. Call by reference is therefore also termed "call by address". Call by reference is the normal type of correspondence in FORTRAN. It is also the correspondence used for **var** parameters in PASCAL.

Consider the procedure *SUMSQ* of Figure 3.8. Its purpose is to sum (into *tot*) the squares of those elements of vector (*vec*) whose indices lie in the range zero through one less than a limit value (*lim*).

```
procedure SUMSQ(vec, lim, tot)
    real array vec
    integer lim
    real tot
    integer idx
    begin
        tot ← 0
        idx ← lim
        repeat
            idx ← idx−1
            tot ← tot + (vec[idx] *vec[idx])
        until idx=0
    end
```

Figure 3.8 Called Subroutine

Let *SUMSQ* be invoked by execution of the call statement *SUMSQ*(*points, top, sum*). The calling module might pass the *addresses* of the origin of the array *points* and of the variables *top* and *sum* in storage locations with symbolic addresses ADDRVEC, ADDRLIM, and ADDRTOT. The calling module would be unaware of the names given to the formal parameters, but we choose these names for readability of our examples. A straightforward implementation of *SUMSQ* in which all three parameters are called by reference is shown in Figure 3.9. Observe that every access to an actual parameter makes use of indirection, even if the parameter has been accessed previously.

Suppose that our *SUMSQ* is invoked instead by the call statement *SUMSQ*(*points, top, x*+2) Here the formal parameter *tot* to which an assignment is to be made corresponds not to a variable but to an expression. What happens? The calling module evaluates the expression $x+2$, stores its value in a temporary location, and passes the address of that location in ADDR3. The called procedure computes the correct result and stores it in the temporary location allocated to $x+2$. But that temporary location is not accessed again, and the value computed by *SUMSQ* is lost.

```
                LOAD    @0              initialize sum
                STORE+  ADDRTOT
                LOAD+   ADDRLIM         initialize index
                STORE   IDX
        BODY    SUB     @1              decrement index
                STORE   IDX
                LOAD+   ADDRVEC+IDX     square element
                MULT+   ADDRVEC+IDX
                ADD+    ADDRTOT         add square
                STORE+  ADDRTOT
                LOAD    IDX             test index
                BRNZ    BODY
```

Figure 3.9 Implementation of Call by Reference

Suppose next that the actual parameter corresponding to *tot* is a constant. The assignment of value will overwrite the constant, yielding incorrect results if the constant is used later in the program. This insidious error, actually possible in early versions of FORTRAN, is easily prevented. The programmer simply uses a temporary location to hold a constant actual parameter, as should be done for any expression other than a variable.

3.5.2 Call by Copy

The repeated use of indirection observed in call by reference can be avoided by permitting the called procedure to make access to a local copy of an actual parameter. Three closely related forms of parameter correspondence rely on this approach. As is done under call by reference, the calling module passes the address of a variable or of a temporary location that holds the value of a constant or other expression. Under the **call by value** correspondence, the called procedure takes the value stored at that address and copies it into its own location. That location is then used like any other local variable. The called procedure cannot change an actual parameter, not even a variable, because it does not write into the caller's storage. In an alternative implementation, the calling module, rather than the called procedure, makes the copy. In determining where to place the copy, it might use a location at a fixed offset from the entry point, or follow a pointer from such a location. The key distinction, however, is not which module makes the copy, but rather that there is a copy.

Call by value avoids the indirection in each parameter access at the vedit tailprice of extra storage (particularly expensive for arrays) for copies of the actual parameters. It is the normal type of correspondence for "arguments" in APL. Because call by value provides only one-way communication from the calling module to the called procedure, it is not practiced in isolation. To transmit information back to the caller, the procedure may be a function procedure that returns a value. Alternatively, it may use a type of correspondence other than call by value for one or more of the other parameters.

Under the **call by result** correspondence, as for call by value, the called procedure has a location that corresponds to the formal parameter. This location is used like any other local variable, except on termination of the procedure. The actual parameter address, passed at invocation time, is used by the called procedure at termination to deliver the *result*. It does so by copying the result from the local location to the actual parameter location in the calling module's storage. Call by result is the normal type of correspondence for return of "results" in APL, and it is a natural type to use in conjunction with call by value.

Implementation of call by copy is also straightforward. The procedure body includes the use of each location that corresponds to a parameter called by value. It is preceded by a **prologue** to initialize these locations by copying the values from the locations of the actual parameters. The procedure body also includes the initialization of each location that corresponds to a parameter called by result. It is followed by an **epilogue** to deliver their final values by copying them into the locations of the actual parameters. A call by copy implementation of the procedure *SUMSQ* of Figure 3.8 is presented in Figure 3.10. Horizontal rules separate the body from the prologue and from the epilogue. The indirection in COPY+ applies only to the first operand.

Indirection is limited to the initialization, in the prologue, of variables called by value and the delivery, in the epilogue, of variables called by result. Only one indirect reference is required to any element of a variable called under either correspondence. Multiple references during execution of the procedure body make local, hence rapid, accesses to the local copy. A major cost of call by copy, however, is the space required to hold the copies. For large arrays, this can be almost disqualifying.

	LOAD+	ADDRLIM	prologue for *lim*,
	STORE	LIM	called by value
	STORE	I	prologue for *vec*,
PROLOGUE	SUB	@1	called by value
	COPY+	ADDRVEC+I VEC+I	
	BRNZ	PROLOGUE	

	LOAD	@0	initialize sum
	STORE	TOT	
	LOAD	LIM	initialize index
BODY	SUB	@1	decrement index
	STORE	IDX	
	LOAD	VEC+IDX	square element
	MULT	VEC+IDX	
	ADD	TOT	add square
	STORE	TOT	
	LOAD	IDX	test index
	BRNZ	BODY	

	LOAD	TOT	epilogue for *tot*,
	STORE+	ADDRTOT	called by result

LIM	SPACE	
TOT	SPACE	
VEC	SPACES	

Figure 3.10   Implementation of Call by Copy

If the value of the local variable corresponding to the formal parameter is *both* initialized upon entry to the procedure *and* delivered upon exit therefrom, the parameter correspondence is termed **call by value result**. This type of correspondence was introduced as an option in ALGOL W and is also available in ALGOL 68. Call by result is sometimes designated "call by reference result" to distinguish it from call by value result. Implementation of call by value result requires both a prologue and an epilogue for the same variable. It therefore uses more space than does call by reference, and more time on both procedure entry and exit. In compensation, however, it uses less time in making each access to the parameter.

The procedure of Figure 3.8 cannot, as it stands, be called by value result. It has no parameter that both accepts a value from and delivers a value to the calling procedure. We can convert it to such a procedure, however, simply by deleting the statement *tot* ← 0. The effect of the procedure then becomes the incrementation (rather than the replacement) of the value of *tot* by the sum of the squares of the array elements. The required change in the implementation shown in Figure 3.10 includes only the removal of the first two lines of the procedure body and their replacement in the prologue by the following pair.

```
LOAD+   ADDRTOT   prologue for tot,
STORE   TOT       called by value
```

It might seem that the difference between call by reference and call by copy is one of efficiency considerations alone and does not extend to the effects of the two types of correspondence. That such is not the case is illustrated by the program of Figure 3.11. Invocation of *PRINT* will write the value 3 if the parameter x is passed by reference, but the value 2 if x is passed by value result. The difference arises from the nonlocal reference by *INCR* to the variable that is also the actual parameter of the call.

The designers of ADA found a clever way to avoid this insidious distinction. The three forms of parameter correspondence in ADA are called **in**, **in out**, and **out**. In and out parameters are like value and result parameters, respectively, except that actual copying is not required. In-out parameters are like both reference parameters and value result parameters. If the effect of the program depends upon which correspondence is used, the program is erroneous.

```
procedure PRINT
    integer y
    procedure INCR(x)
        integer x
        begin
            y ← 1
            x ← x+2
        end
    begin
        y ← 0
        INCR(y)
        write y
    end
```

Figure 3.11   Program to Illustrate Parameter Correspondence

An interesting terminology is used informally by PL/I program-mers. They refer to a construction such as "**call** $P((A))$" as being a "call by value", although technically it is a call by reference. Because the actual parameter (which includes the inner parentheses) is an expression, the caller makes a copy of the value to pass to the called procedure. Consequently, the latter can write only into the temporary storage associated with the copy, and the variable A cannot be overwritten. The effect is indeed that of call by value.

3.5.3 Call by Name

Under the call by name correspondence, each occurrence of the name of the formal parameter is considered to be replaced textually by the actual parameter. This type of correspondence is therefore sometimes called the "replacement rule". Such a rule, which was introduced as the standard type of correspondence in ALGOL 60, appears very elegant — pure textual substitution is to be performed — but it holds traps for the unwary.

One trap is illustrated by

$$
\begin{aligned}
&\textbf{procedure } P(a,b) \\
&\quad \textbf{begin} \\
&\qquad a \leftarrow 1 \\
&\qquad b \leftarrow b{+}1 \\
&\qquad a \leftarrow 2 \\
&\qquad b \leftarrow b{+}2 \\
&\quad \textbf{end}
\end{aligned}
$$

when invoked by the call $P(i,x[i])$, because the result is not to increment $x[i]$ by 3 while setting i equal to 2. The replacement rule specifies that for this invocation of P the statements to be executed are

$$
\begin{aligned}
i &\leftarrow 1 \\
x[i] &\leftarrow x[i] + 1 \\
i &\leftarrow 2 \\
x[i] &\leftarrow x[i] + 2
\end{aligned}
$$

and it is seen that both $x[1]$ and $x[2]$ will be incremented, whereas $x[i]$ will not (unless i had value 1 or 2 at the moment of invocation).

A second trap is that the actual parameter substituted into the text of the *called* procedure has a meaning specified in the *calling* module. The identifier i that appeared in the foregoing call is not to be confused with an identifier i that is known to the called procedure but unknown to the caller.

Call by name cannot be implemented efficiently by actually performing the text substitution that defines its effect. It would be necessary to execute the procedure body interpretively at execution time, because there is no practical way to generate at compilation time the code that would result from an arbitrary call. Instead, object code compiled for the procedure includes for each formal parameter a separate routine to evaluate the corresponding actual parameter. This routine, called a **thunk** for historical reasons, belongs to the body of the called procedure, not to a prologue. It is invoked for *each* reference made in the body to the corresponding formal parameter, and returns the address of the value of the actual parameter.

The thunk must first save the environment of the called procedure and reestablish the environment of the calling module, then evaluate the actual parameter in the caller's environment, and finally reinstate the called procedure's environment. The evaluation of the actual parameter may entail a further call (by name, of course), which results in further stacking of environments before a return is possible. For the call in the foregoing example, the translator must generate thunks to evaluate the addresses of i and of $x[i]$ and it must ensure that the addresses of the thunks are available to the code for the procedure body.

Call by name is obviously no favorite of compiler writers. The simplicity of its operational definition — textual substitution — has sometimes been mistaken for conceptual elegance. Not only is call by name awkward and costly to implement, but its use greatly increases the difficulty of proving program correctness. Call by name has not survived into any important modern language.

FOR FURTHER STUDY

Rice65 is a thoughtful note on recursion and iteration. Many of the issues covered in this chapter are treated at length in Chapter 4 of Wegner68, particularly the activation-record stack, block structure (4.5, 4.9), and modes of module activation (4.9, 4.10). Modes of module activation are also discussed in Section 5.2 of Ghezzi82. Some attention to block structure is paid in Chapter 11 of Elson73, the article Berthaud73, and Section 3.6 of Ghezzi82. Griffiths74 offers a clear explanation of displays and of static and dynamic links, as does Aho86 (pages 420–422).

The original description of coroutines is in Conway63. Brief explanations are to be found in Wegner68, (Section 4.10.3), and Knuth73 (Section 1.4.2). Some examples are presented in Section 7.8 of Horowitz84a. An elementary, descriptive treatment of operating system issues is offered by Calingaert82.

Subroutines and linkage conventions are mentioned in Section 1.4.1 of Knuth73. Modes of parameter correspondence are discussed briefly in Elson73 (Section 5.5), and more fully in Gries71 (Section 8.7) and Ullman76 (Section 6.10), and at greater length yet in Pratt75 (Sections 6-9, 6-10) and Rohl75, (Sections 12.6–12.12). A particularly readable exposition appears in Barron77 (Chapter 4). Among more recent treatments are Ghezzi82 (Section 5.2.1) and Aho86 (Section 7.5). The implementation of thunks is described in Ingerman61.

REVIEW QUESTIONS

3.1 Will code compiled from a reenterable module be reenterable?

3.2 Name an architectural feature of a computer that substantially aids reenterability.

3.3 Must a recursive module be reenterable?

3.4 What is the difference between compilers and interpreters in their ability to detect actual (as opposed to potential) recursion?

3.5 What is the scope of labels in APL?

3.6 What activation record management is required to handle a **goto** a label in an enclosing block (a so-called "unusual return")?

3.7 Why are programs with interrupt function modules hard to read?

3.8 What happens to the activation record of a coroutine that resumes another coroutine?

3.9 A coroutine **resume** neither creates nor destroys an activation record. (**a**) How does a coroutine activation record come into being? (**b**) How does it disappear?

3.10 The **cobegin-coend** construction is an n-way fork, particularly useful if multiple processors are available. What kind of activation record structure is required?

3.11 Does the use of a shared stack for passing parameters eliminate any of the differences among the various forms of parameter correspondence? Explain.

3.12 Let a particular computer have a stack implemented in hardware. What are the advantages and disadvantages of using it for passing parameters?

3.13 Must all of a module's calls obey the same subroutine linkage convention?

3.14 When is the use of registers for passing copies of parameters particularly unattractive?

3.15 Suppose that you are programming in a language that offers for *each* parameter, independently of the other parameters, the choice between call by copy and call by reference. Describe the costs of each and the circumstances under which you would prefer each choice to the other, and justify your claim.

PROBLEMS

3.1 Consider the program *FAC* of Figure 3.1. Let an execution of *FAC*(3) be suspended, just before entering the loop body for the second time, to permit the evaluation of *FAC*(4). Show the activation records of both instances of *FAC* at the moment at which the execution of *FAC*(4) is about to enter the loop body for the third time.

3.2 Let M be a set of modules of a program. Define on $M \times M$ the relation **R** "calls". Thus $A\mathbf{R}B$ iff $A,B \in M$ and A calls B.

(a) State a property (*e.g.*, reflexivity, weak asymmetry, *etc.*) of the transitive closure of **R** that holds iff the set M is recursive.

(b) Characterize formally the collection of individual modules that are recursive.

3.3 Write in some programming language (which may be a real one or not) a two-parameter recursive function routine for multiplication. One parameter is the multiplicand MC; the other is a (positive integer) multiplier MP. Using only repeated addition of MC and decrementation of MP by unity, the function returns their product. Number the statements. Let the routine be called with $MC=10$ and $MP=4$. Draw the stack of activation records at its maximum size, showing the content of each. State all calls that are generated and all results that are returned.

3.4 Diagram the execution-time static chain when procedure Q, nested within procedure P and called by P, calls itself.

3.5 Show the activation-record stack during the execution of procedure C of this program. Use first (a) a display, then (b) a full set of static links. Do not show any detail within an activation record.

```
procedure A
    call E
    procedure D
        call C
        procedure C
            put skip list ('in C')
        end C
    end D
    procedure E
        call B
        procedure B
            call D
        end B
    end E
end A
```

3.6 Consider the following program.

```
procedure M
    procedure P1
        begin block B
            call P2
        end B
        call P2
    end P1
    call P2
    call P1
    procedure P2
        call P3
        procedure P3
        end P3
    end P2
end M
```

(a) Describe each stage in the life of the activation-record stack as procedure M is executed, once using a static chain and once using a display. Do not show any detail within an activation record. You may save labor by showing both the static links and the display on the same diagram, although both would not normally be present.

(b) Does there ever exist a static chain link that is not accessible from the current activation record? Why or why not?

(c) Explain how to construct, for any program, the static chain corresponding to a given execution-time display and *vice versa*.

3.7 Let the over-all program and the Pass 1 program that correspond to Figure 3.7(a) be the following. The Pass 2 and Pass 3 programs are similar to the Pass 1 program. Write a program that uses coroutines to implement Figure 3.7(b).

```
procedure MASTER
    file infile, inter1, inter2, outfile
    begin
        PASS1 (infile, inter1)
        PASS2 (inter1, inter2)
        PASS3 (inter2, outfile)
    end
```

```
procedure PASS1(source, dest)
    file source, dest
    record inrec, outrec
    begin
        open (source, dest)
        while not eof (source)
            read (source, inrec)
            PROCESS1 (inrec, outrec)
            write (outrec, dest)
        close (source, dest)
    end
```

3.8 Exhibit and explain the subroutine linkage convention for your operating system.

3.9 Design a coroutine linkage convention for your operating system. Exhibit the actual program code.

3.10 Write for your computer an assembler-language subroutine to execute $i \leftarrow i+1$, where i is a formal parameter called by copy. Incorporate a full prologue and epilogue, and do not remove redundant instructions.

3.11 For the definition

```
procedure SWAP(w,x)
    begin
        t ← w
        w ← x
        x ← t
    end
```

the table lists values of the relevant variables before and after execution of $SWAP(i,a[i])$ under two different modes of parameter correspondence. Determine the values after executing the call by copy instead. Show your analysis.

	before call	after call by reference	after call by name
$a[3]$	5	3	5
$a[5]$	7	7	3
i	3	5	5
t	1	3	3

3.12 In the language of Chapter 2, code subroutines for printing x^2, where x is an integer parameter called (**a**) by reference; and (**b**) by copy. Assume that you may not pass x in a register.

3.13 Write, in any real assembler language available to you, a subroutine to increment I by 1, J by 2, and K by 3, where I, J, and K are integer formal parameters called by copy. Use the standard linkage convention. Make any savings possible because your subroutine does not itself call another. Save and restore the contents of all registers; set the return code to zero. Assume that the calling routine has placed the three actual parameters (not just their addresses) in the parameter list.

3.14 [Gries] Manually execute the following program five times, once under each of the following assumptions, indicating the final values in $v[3]$ and $v[4]$. Consider the formal parameter a to be called (**a**) by reference; (**b**) by value; (**c**) by value result; (**d**) by result; (**e**) by name.

$$
\begin{aligned}
&\textbf{begin} \\
&\quad \textbf{integer } k \\
&\quad \textbf{integer array } v \\
&\\
&\quad \textbf{procedure } P(a) \\
&\quad\quad \textbf{integer } a \\
&\quad\quad \textbf{begin} \\
&\quad\quad\quad a \leftarrow a+1 \\
&\quad\quad\quad v[k] \leftarrow 5 \\
&\quad\quad\quad k \leftarrow 3 \\
&\quad\quad\quad a \leftarrow a+1 \\
&\quad\quad \textbf{end} \\
&\\
&\quad\quad v[3] \leftarrow 6 \\
&\quad\quad v[4] \leftarrow 8 \\
&\quad\quad k \leftarrow 4 \\
&\quad\quad \textbf{call } P(v[k]) \\
&\textbf{end}
\end{aligned}
$$

Hint: all five calls are different, and one of them yields an undefined value.

Chapter 4

Macro Processing

4.1 FUNCTION

A subroutine of the standard type discussed in Section 3.3.2 has been known historically as a **closed subroutine**. It is characterized by the incorporation of only a single copy of its text in the complete program. Its execution is triggered by execution of the program statement that calls the subroutine. Parameters passed to the subroutine tailor its function within limits established when the subroutine was constructed. Closed subroutines thus reduce the over-all size of a program, as well as the effort of writing it, by permitting a call statement to serve as an abbreviation for an entire subroutine.

The savings in space and effort cost time, however, for calling the closed subroutine, for passing and accessing parameters, and for returning from the subroutine. The **open subroutine**, also known as "in-line code", offers a faster alternative at the cost of space and effort. A copy of the open subroutine is written in the program in place of a call of a closed subroutine. Modifications of the text of the open subroutine, performed not at execution time but rather at programming time, tailor its function as desired by the programmer. Multiple copies of specialized program text are thus incorporated in the program, rather than a single copy of generalized text.

The tedium of writing many identical or nearly identical copies of the same text is readily transferred from the programmer to the computer. Translation programs have been developed to assist in the repetitive and/or parameterized generation of program text. If the desired text is to be in a machine-independent language, the assisting translator is usually called a **preprocessor**. If the text is to be in an assembler language, the assisting translator is called a **macro processor**. If the translator is not specialized to generating text in a particular language, it may be called a **string processor** (referring to arbitrary text strings) or a **macro generator**.

Whether the application is to machine-independent languages, assembler languages, or arbitrary strings, the required processing is much the same. We shall adopt uniform terminology regardless of the application, using "macro" for a specification of how program text is to be generated and "macro processor" for a translator that accomplishes the task. We shall describe macro processing, both in this chapter and in the next, primarily in terms of the application to assembler-language programming. This permits us to use our hypothetical assembler language for illustration. The techniques described are not limited to assembler-language text, however, but are applicable in general. The use of macro processing with machine-independent languages is explored in Chapter 10.

The assembler-language programmer often repeats groups of instructions. One group might increment a counter in storage, a second might extract characters from variously specified positions of a card image, and a third might perform fixed-point arithmetic with specified scaling and rounding. By using a single instruction, called a **macro instruction**, to represent each such group of assembler-language instructions, the programmer is spared the tedium of repetitive coding. Moreover, we can think of the macro instructions as statements in a machine-independent language that is particularly useful to the programmer, who has defined them personally. Sometimes the designers of the programming system can anticipate that many programmers might wish to have certain instruction sequences available. Examples include calling sequences for the routines that provide system services such as input and output, process synchronization, and storage allocation. Macros provided in the programming system for all users are called **system macros**.

The output of a macro processor is usually a program in the source language of another translator. Its input will then contain both program text that is ready for the subsequent translation and macro definitions that are to be **expanded** into such text. The definition of a macro has two parts. One is a **prototype** statement, which names the macro and its formal parameters. The other is a **skeleton** (often also called "body"), which serves as a model of the output to be generated. Some authors refer to the prototype as a "template". We have avoided that terminology because the skeleton, as well as the prototype, can be viewed as a template.

Because the same source language is used both for statements within macro definitions and for those without, macro definitions must be explicitly distinguished from the surrounding text. This is most readily done by the use of delimiters. Two syntactic forms of delimiter use are common. The opening delimiter may be combined with the prototype statement, as in Figure 4.1(a). There the directive MCDEFN serves as the opening delimiter; the name of the macro instruction (INCR) occupies the label field, and its parameters (L and A) appear in the operand field. The closing delimiter is MCEND. Figure 4.1(b) illustrates a prototype that is not commingled with a delimiter; there MCDEFN is separate from the prototype. The skeleton is the same as that of the previous example. The directive END could be used as the closing delimiter for macros as well as for assembler-language text. Its use would be unambiguous, because of nesting, but then END could not appear in the skeleton, and the macro processor would be unable to generate an END instruction.

We can think of the skeleton as an open subroutine that is inserted into the program text at the point of call. Indeed, the use of a macro is termed a **call**. It is signaled by the appearance of a macro instruction, such as those that are shown opposite the corresponding prototype instructions in the definitions of Figure 4.1. Replacement of a macro instruction by the skeleton, with actual values substituted for the parameters, is known as **macro expansion**. Figure 4.1(c) shows the result of expanding either call.

This straightforward macro expansion is in fact a call by name: pure textual substitution is performed. In view of the bad press given to call by name, why do we tolerate it in macro processing? Because, in most macro processors, there is only one environment. We are

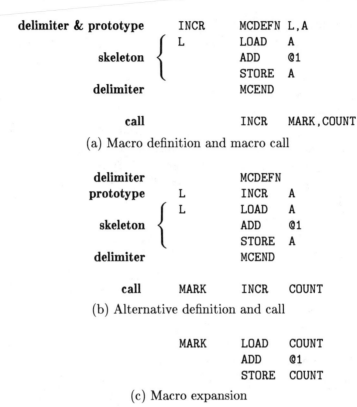

(a) Macro definition and macro call

(b) Alternative definition and call

(c) Macro expansion

Figure 4.1   Macro Processing

spared the need to reestablish previously existing environments to determine what substitution to perform.

4.2 PARAMETER SYNTAX

During expansion, the actual parameters named in the call are substituted for the formal parameters that appear in the skeleton and are named in the prototype. Both actual and formal parameters are, of course, character strings. The correspondence of formal parameter occurrences in the skeleton to their occurrences in the prototype is fixed by the macro definition, and can be established at the time the definition is processed. The substitution of actual values depends on the call, and must be accomplished separately for each call. If the prototype and the call each include several parameters, it is necessary to identify which actual parameter corresponds to which formal parameter.

Two syntactic approaches to parameter identification are in widespread use: positional and keyword. **Positional** parameters are distinguished by the position that they occupy in the list of parameters. Figure 4.1(a) illustrates positional parameters. The two formal parameters, L and A, are named in a list in the operand field. The actual parameters of the call, MARK and COUNT, are also given as a list in which adjacent entries are separated by a syntactic marker (here, the comma). The first actual parameter, MARK, is substituted for the first formal parameter, L; the second actual parameter, COUNT, is substituted for the second formal parameter, A. In general, the ith actual parameter is substituted for the ith formal parameter.

Use of the empty character string (or of blanks) as an actual parameter is often termed **omission** of the parameter. Suppose we wish to call the macro defined in Figure 4.1(a) without specifying a label. If the syntactic markers are left in the parameter list, the omission becomes obvious. Thus the call INCR ,COUNT would cause

```
LOAD    COUNT
ADD     @1
STORE   COUNT
```

to be generated. The omission of two successive parameters from the middle of a longer list would leave three consecutive commas. The omission of a parameter can sometimes be positionally evident even if there is no list. In Figure 4.1(b) the formal parameter L occupies the label field. If a prototype is restricted to having at most one parameter in its label field, then omission of an actual parameter from the call is obvious. The call INCR COUNT would specify, under those conditions, the expansion just given.

It is possible to establish positional correspondence without use of the prototype. Formal parameters in the skeleton can have a syntactic form that refers to a position in the actual parameter list. Thus &SYSLIST(i) in an IBM 370 macro skeleton is replaced by the ith operand of the call.

If the number of parameters is large, it can be difficult to remember the correct sequence, or to provide the right number of commas for omitted parameters. This can be remedied by the use of

keyword parameters. The macro call specifies for each actual parameter not just the value, as under positional syntax, but also the name of the corresponding formal parameter. The customary keyword syntax is *formal=actual*. The formal parameters are identified by their appearance in the prototype, with or without the syntactic mark =. The actual parameters can appear in the call in any order, because each is accompanied by the name of the corresponding formal parameter. A macro definition with four keyword parameters (L, A, B, and C) is presented in Figure 4.2. Note, incidentally, the use of a syntactic marker (here, the period) to separate the literal indicator @ from B, thus permitting the latter to be recognized as a parameter. The call INCR L=MARK,A=COUNT,B=1,C=COUNT would result in the expansion already shown in Figure 4.1(c).

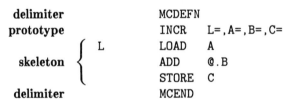

delimiter		MCDEFN	
prototype		INCR	L=,A=,B=,C=
	L	LOAD	A
skeleton		ADD	@.B
		STORE	C
delimiter		MCEND	

Figure 4.2   Macro Definition with Keyword Parameters

Parameter correspondence independent of the prototype can be established for keyword parameters as well as for positional parameters. The mere use of the formal parameter name in the skeleton is enough to establish the correspondence. Identification of a character string as a parameter is accomplished by the syntactic mark ("=" in our examples). Thus the skeleton

```
          L=      LOAD    A=
                  ADD     @.B=
                  STORE   C=
```

could replace that of Figure 4.2.

The processing previously shown for an omitted actual parameter resulted in replacement of the formal parameter by a fixed default value, blanks. Arbitrary default values can be specified instead, whether they calls obey positional or keyword syntax. Thus the definition of Figure 4.3 specifies blanks as the default for L, 1 as the default for B, and ACCUM as the default for both A and C. The definition satisfies the requirements of either parameter syntax. For this definition, a macro processor using positional parameter syntax in calls would expand `INCR MARK,COUNT,,COUNT` into the assembler-language text shown in Figure 4.1(c). A macro processor using keyword parameter syntax in calls would expand `INCR C=COUNT,L=MARK,A=COUNT` into the same text. Unlabeled text to increment the content of `ACCUM` by 2 would be generated from the positional syntax call `INCR ,,2,` or from the keyword syntax call `INCR B=2`.

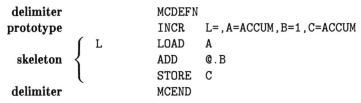

delimiter		MCDEFN	
prototype		INCR	L=,A=ACCUM,B=1,C=ACCUM
	L	LOAD	A
skeleton		ADD	@.B
		STORE	C
delimiter		MCEND	

Figure 4.3   Macro Definition with Default Values

The simplicity of positional correspondence and the flexibility of keyword correspondence can be enjoyed together. It is perfectly feasible to use one syntax for some of the parameters and the other for the remainder. This requires a convention, in the prototype, to enable the macro processor to determine which syntax applies to which parameter.

If a macro skeleton includes a label that is not supplied as a parameter, each call of the macro will generate a distinct occurrence of that label. If the macro is called more than once, the generated assembler-language program will then contain a multiply-defined symbol. To avoid this error, many macro processors maintain a count of the number of times a macro call is expanded, which can be appended (in character string form) to generated labels. The attachment can be performed automatically. Alternatively, the count can be provided as the actual value corresponding to a system-defined formal parameter, say `SER`. Thus the string `MASS.SER` in the skeleton for the macro instruction `REVISE` might be replaced by `MASS0023` in the first expansion of `REVISE` and by `MASS0036` in the second expansion of `REVISE`. This would occur if the two calls of `REVISE` were the 23rd and 36th to be expanded by the macro processor.

A somewhat different problem of generation is represented by comments. Readability of macro processor input is often enhanced by comments that explain the skeleton, but whose presence is not desired in the generated text. We must differentiate such generation-time comments syntactically from execution-time comments that are indeed to be generated. We might agree that any line whose first character is a reverse slash (\) is a comment that is not to be generated. This convention is followed in the macro definition of Figure 4.4.

delimiter		MCDEFN	
comment	\INCREMENT BY LITERAL		
prototype	L	INCR	A
	L	LOAD	A
skeleton		ADD	@1
		STORE	A
delimiter		MCEND	

Figure 4.4   Generation-time Comment in Macro Definition

We have mentioned syntactic devices to distinguish generation-time from execution-time comments, to identify parameters, and to separate a string, such as @.B or MASS.SER, into its component parts. Some assemblers, those for IBM 370 in particular, use a syntactic marker (& as the first character) to distinguish parameters of macros from execution-time symbols. This helps to accentuate for the reader the different binding times* of the two classes of symbols. The distinction is not logically required by the macro processor, however, as long as the parameters are required to be present in the prototype.

4.3 TWO-PASS IMPLEMENTATION

A straightforward implementation of the macro processor is possible if each macro is defined only once. We assume that a macro is restricted to contain neither another macro definition nor a macro call. Two passes over the program text suffice, the first to collect the definitions and the second to expand the calls.

During Pass 1 the macro processor simply copies instructions from input text to intermediate text until it encounters the opening delimiter of a macro definition. At this point it enters **definition mode**. All succeeding instructions of the definition are entered in a

---

*The concept of binding time is discussed in Section 5.1.

macro-definition table. The macro definition is copied only into this table, and not to the intermediate text. Although it is possible to copy these instructions into the table unchanged, the subsequent expansion of each call of the macro is simplified if some editing is performed. We can replace each formal parameter in the skeleton by the number that gives the position of the formal parameter in the prototype's parameter list. Thus the macro definition of Figure 4.5(a) could be stored in the macro-definition table as shown in Figure 4.5(b). There the symbol # serves as a syntactic marker to distinguish a parameter reference from an ordinary symbol. The label parameter was assigned the number 0. The opening delimiter is not needed in the table, because the table is known to contain macro definitions. The closing delimiter is included to mark the end, however, because the length of the definition is not fixed.

	MCDEFN				
SPOT	ABSDIF	A,B,C	SPOT	ABSDIF	A,B,C
SPOT	LOAD	A	#0	LOAD	#1
	SUB	B		SUB	#2
	BRPOS	ST.SER		BRPOS	ST.SER
	LOAD	B		LOAD	#2
	SUB	A		SUB	#1
ST.SER	STORE	C	ST.SER	STORE	#3
	MCEND			MCEND	

(a) In input text (b) In macro-definition table

Figure 4.5 Macro Definition Editing

When the prototype is encountered, its operation field (the macro name) can optionally be stored in a **macro-name table.** This will be used during Pass 2 to distinguish macro calls from other text. If this is done, the prototype may be omitted from the edited definition. After the closing delimiter is entered in the macro-definition table, the macro processor leaves definition mode to resume copying. If system macros are provided, their definitions are incorporated in the macro-definition table and their names in the macro-name table before the macro processor is used.

During Pass 2 the macro processor reads as input the intermediate text prepared by Pass 1. Macro definitions are no longer present, but macro calls are. The operation field of each instruction is compared with entries in the operation table or in the optional macro-name table. If it is not a macro name, the instruction is copied unchanged to the output text. If the operation field is a macro name, then a macro call has been encountered and the macro processor enters **expansion mode**. The corresponding prototype is found, either by searching the macro-definition table, or by following a pointer that was placed in the macro-name table when the definition was collected during Pass 1. By comparing the call with the prototype, the macro processor prepares a list of the actual parameters to be substituted. For the definition in Figure 4.5(b), the call `ABSDIF INPRES,OUTPRES,PRESSURE` would establish the following list (assuming 8-character label and operand fields).

```
#0 '            '
#1 'INPRES   '
#2 'OUTPRES  '
#3 'PRESSURE '
```

Positional parameters are identified by counting; keyword parameters are identified by comparing the parameter names in the call with those in the prototype. For omitted parameters, default values are placed in the list.

The macro processor now copies the instructions of the skeleton into the output text. In so doing, it replaces each occurrence of `#i` by the ith value in the list of actual parameters, and each occurrence of `.SER` by the serial number of the expansion. When the closing delimiter is encountered, the macro processor leaves it uncopied, discards the actual-parameter list, and returns from expansion mode to copy mode.

The advantages of this two-pass division of labor are twofold. (1) Space requirements are modest, only the tables and the program for one pass being needed in storage. (2) Forward references are permitted — a macro call can precede the associated definition in the text. Forward references to macro definitions in the input text are not as important, however, as forward references to symbols in assembler-language text. This is because requiring macros to be defined before use imposes no hardship. Passing the text twice then incurs unnecessary cost. A more fundamental disadvantage of this implementation is that it does not permit macros to be redefined.

4.4 ONE-PASS IMPLEMENTATION

It is not unusual to expect multiple calls of one macro during a single invocation of the macro processor. What is less obvious is the desirability of multiple definitions of a macro. We consider each macro definition with the same name as an existing definition to be a redefinition of the correspondence between a call and its expansion. One of the many uses of redefinition is to override system macros. If we allow redefinition, we must expand each macro call according to the most recent definition of its macro. It is therefore no longer appropriate to defer macro expansion until all macro definitions have been collected.

The required processing can be performed in a single pass over the input text. Forward references can no longer be permitted; *every* call must be of a previously defined macro. As stated earlier, this is not a serious restriction.

We continue to assume that macro definitions contain neither macro calls nor other macro definitions. Hence, the macro processor can never be in both definition mode and expansion mode at the same time. It is either in one of those two modes or in copy mode. The actions during these three modes are precisely those described in Section 4.3. The algorithm is presented in Figure 4.6. In this and succeeding algorithms, an instance of *opcode* will be recognized as a "prototype" if it is read from the first line of a macro definition or from a line that follows the delimiter MCDEFN. It will be recognized as a "macro call" only if it names a macro but is not recognized as a prototype.

The major effect of permitting macros to be redefined is upon the organization of the macro-definition table. There is no guarantee that any definition of a macro will not require more space than its previous definition. This precludes our rewriting a new definition in the place of its predecessor. The space occupied by a superseded definition can be liberated, unless a facility is desired for reverting to a previous definition, as in overriding a system macro only temporarily. One way to organize the macro-definition table is to chain definitions, as shown in Figure 4.7. In definition mode, the macro processor places each new definition at the head of the chain. In expansion mode, it scans the chain for a definition of the called macro;

$d \leftarrow$ **false** {definition-mode switch}
$e \leftarrow$ **false** {expansion-mode switch}
read *line* from *input*
while *line* $\neq$ **empty do**
   if d **then** {in definition mode}
         case *opcode* **of**
           prototype:
           MCEND: $d \leftarrow$ **false** {leave definition mode}
           other: replace ith formal parameter by #i
         write *line* to *macro definition*
    else {in copy mode or expansion mode}
         case *opcode* **of**
           prototype:
           macro call: $e \leftarrow$ **true** {enter expansion mode}
                      PREPARE actual-parameter list
           MCDEFN: $d \leftarrow$ **true** {enter definition mode}
                        ALLOCATE new *macro definition* in table
           MCEND: $e \leftarrow$ **false** {leave expansion mode}
                        DISCARD actual-parameter list
           other: **if** e **then** replace #i by *actual-parameter list*[i]
                    write *line* to *output*
   if e **then** {in expansion mode}
         read *line* from *macro definition*
    else **read** *line* from *input*

Figure 4.6   Macro Processing without Nesting

the first definition it encounters is the most recent. The definitions in
the chain may, but need not, be contiguous. An alternative to linking
all the definitions in a single chain is to use a separate chain for
each macro name, with a macro-name table pointing to the current

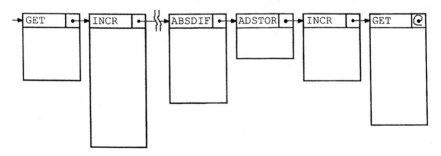

Figure 4.7   Chained Macro-Definition Table

definition. Reversion to the previous definition is accomplished easily with either chaining discipline.

How can a macro processor determine whether the current instruction's operation field is an operation code or a macro call? This is similar to the determination, in an assembler, of whether an opcode field holds a machine instruction or an assembler directive. For the macro processor, the answer depends upon whether operation codes and macro names are stored in separate tables or together in a combined table. If there are two tables, it depends also upon which one is searched first.

One approach is to search a separate operation table first. If the current instruction's operation field is not found, it is assumed to be a macro call, and the macro-definition table chain is then searched for the most recent definition. In the absence of a high density of macro calls, this is the most efficient method.

A second approach is to search a separate macro-definition table first. Only if the operation field is not found is the operation table searched. The advantage of this second approach is that it permits existing operation codes to be redefined by the programmer. It incurs the cost of searching the entire macro-definition table even for a regular operation code for which no macro has been defined.

The searching time under either of these approaches can be reduced by the provision of a macro-name table with separate chains for each macro name. The distinction between the two search strategies dictates whether the macro-name table is searched before or after the operation code table.

The third approach combines operation codes and macro names into a single table. To allow uniform table entries, macro definitions are not entered in the table, but are accessible by chaining. The absence of a second table management routine and of the need to choose between tables simplifies the program. On the other hand, every search now takes longer than in the appropriate single table.

4.5 NESTED DEFINITIONS

If the restrictions imposed in Section 4.3 are removed, then the skeleton of one macro (A) may contain a definition of another macro (B),

as in Figure 4.8. The definition of B is said to be **nested** within that
of A. It is important to realize that the act of defining macro A does
not define macro B. The definition of A merely specifies that the text
into which a call of A is to be expanded includes a definition of macro
B. Thus it is a *call* of macro A that causes macro B to be defined.
Each subsequent call of A also defines B. Because the text of B may
include formal parameters of A, each call of A with different actual
parameters can result in B being redefined. The level of nesting of
macro definitions is not limited to one. Macro B, for example, might
include the definition of a third macro C, which could not be called
until after a call of B had defined C.

```
A        MCDEFN
         - - -
B        MCDEFN
         - - -
         MCEND
         - - -
         MCEND
```

Figure 4.8   Nested Macro Definitions

The inner macros MULTSC and DIVSC of Figure 4.9 are intended
to provide fixed-point multiplication and division, scaled to the arbitrary radix point position RP. The instructions SHIFTL and SHIFTR
are assumed to shift the accumulator content left and right, respectively, by the number of positions given in the operand field. If
operation at radix point 3 is desired for a while, the call SCALE 3 is
written. Its expansion augments the macro-definition table by the
versions of MULTSC and DIVSC shown in Figure 4.10. If radix point 5
is desired later, the call SCALE 5 redefines the two inner macros.

The one-pass macro processor of Section 4.4, as written, cannot
prevent the closing delimiter of an *inner* macro from causing an
exit from definition mode. Nor does it provide for distinguishing
the formal parameters of one macro from those of another macro
nested within it. To implement nested macro definitions, therefore,
we extend that macro processor with two modifications.

The first modification ensures that an exit from definition mode
is caused by the closing delimiter of the *outer* macro only. In defini-

```
MCDEFN
SCALE  RP
MCDEFN
MULTSC A,B,C
LOAD   A
MULT   B
SHIFTR RP
STORE  C
MCEND
MCDEFN
DIVSC  A,B,C
LOAD   A
DIVIDE B
SHIFTL RP
STORE  C
MCEND
MCEND
```

Figure 4.9   Macro to Generate Scaled Arithmetic Macros

tion mode, a **definition-level counter** is incremented by 1 for each opening delimiter encountered and decremented by 1 for each closing delimiter. If the counter is set to 0 before entry to definition mode, then the later reduction of its value to 0 is the signal that definition mode has ended. For example, in defining the macro SCALE (Figure 4.9), the sequence of values of the counter will be 0, 1, 2, 1, 2, 1, 0.

The second modification prevents confusing the formal parameters of one macro with those of another macro nested within it. Inner macro B may have a formal parameter U, which is identical in name to a formal parameter U of outer macro A. When A is called with corresponding actual parameter R, occurrences of U within A are to be replaced by R, *except* those that are also within B. This is because the property that U is a formal parameter of B is not to be upset by the coincidental choice of the same name for a for-

```
MULTSC A,B,C        DIVSC  A,B,C
LOAD   A            LOAD   A
MULT   B            DIVIDE B
SHIFTR 3            SHIFTL 3
STORE  C            STORE  C
MCEND               MCEND
```

Figure 4.10   Macro Definitions Generated by SCALE 3

mal parameter of an enclosing macro. Just as in block-structured
machine-independent languages, the declaration within macro B of U
as a formal parameter masks the parameter U of macro A. Thus an
occurrence of U within the skeleton of B is not bound by assignment
of a value to A's formal parameter U during a call of A. On the other
hand, if macro A has also a formal parameter V, but B does not, then
an occurrence of V within the skeleton of B is indeed bound to the
value assigned to V during a call of A. Consequently, when the definition of A is processed, the editing of formal parameter occurrences
must distinguish among those bound at the different levels of macro
nesting.

A convenient solution is provided by the use of a **formal-
parameter stack*** to assign *pairs* of numbers to parameters entered in the macro-definition table. As definition level d is entered,
the name of its ith formal parameter is placed on the stack, together
with the number pair (d,i). Every symbol in the entire macro definition is compared with the stack entries, starting with the most
recent, until a match is found. If the symbol occurrence in the text
is associated with the pair (d,i), then as it is copied to the macro-
definition table it is replaced by #(d,i). If the symbol is not found
in the formal-parameter stack, it is copied unchanged. When the
closing delimiter is encountered, the stack entries for the current
level are discarded. The stack is thus empty when definition mode
is entered, and is again empty when definition mode is left. The
formal-parameter stack is created and used only during definition
mode processing of the *outermost* macro of a set of nested definitions. Figure 4.11 shows three nested definitions, the maximum
extent of the formal-parameter stack, and the result of editing the
nested definitions. The arrow shows where the stack top was during
editing of the sixth line of input text.

During expansion mode, the actual parameters of the call replace the called macro's formal parameters, which are identified by
having level 1 in the number pairs #$(1,i)$. Each embedded macro
definition is appended to the macro-definition table, with the level
number of all remaining formal parameter references decremented
by 1. Consequently, the newly defined macros have the levels of

---

*This is often called a "macro-definition stack", a term that can lead to
confusion with a stack-organized macro-definition table.

Formal-parameter stack	Input text		Macro-definition table entry	
	MCDEFN			
top	X	A,B,C,D	X	A,B,C,D
		A,B,C,D		#(1,1),#(1,2),#(1,3),#(1,4)
G 3,4	MCDEFN		MCDEFN	
E 3,3	Y	A,B,E,F	Y	A,B,E,F
C 3,2		A,B,C,D		#(2,1),#(2,2),#(1,3),#(1,4)
A 3,1	MCDEFN		MCDEFN	
F 2,4←	Z	A,C,E,G	Z	A,C,E,G
E 2,3		A,B,C,D		#(3,1),#(2,2),#(3,2),#(1,4)
B 2,2		E,F,G,H		#(3,3),#(2,4),#(3,4),H
A 2,1	MCEND		MCEND	
D 1,4		E,F,G,H		#(2,3),#(2,4),G,H
C 1,3	MCEND		MCEND	
B 1,2		E,F,G,H		E,F,G,H
A 1,1	MCEND		MCEND	

Figure 4.11 Formal Parameters in Nested Definitions

their formal parameters now set to 1 and are ready to be called in their turn. Text not within an embedded macro is generated in the normal manner. The algorithm is given in Figure 4.12.

Figure 4.13 illustrates the execution of the algorithm by showing a 10-line input text and the steps in macro processing. The parameter names indicate which are formal and which are actual. Line numbers have been supplied for ease of reading. The values shown for d and e are those that hold before execution of the **case** statement.

Figure 4.14 shows the output text and new macro-definition table entry that result from the call X P,Q,R,S to the macro defined in Figure 4.11.

In one interesting application of nested definitions the name of the inner macro is a formal parameter of the outer macro, as in Figure 4.15. The purpose of CREATE is to define a set of macros, each bearing the name of a subroutine, and each to be expanded into a standard sequence for calling that subroutine. Thus the calls CREATE INSERT, CREATE DELETE, and CREATE REVISE would define three macros, INSERT, DELETE, and REVISE. A subsequent call

$d \leftarrow 0$ {definition-level counter}
$e \leftarrow$ **false** {expansion-mode switch}
read *line* from *input*
while *line* $\neq$ **empty do**
   case *opcode* **of**
      MCDEFN: $d \leftarrow d + 1$
               if $d=1$ **then** *ALLOCATE new macro definition*
                    else **write** *line* to *new macro definition*
      prototype: **if not** e **then** *PUSH* ith formal parameter and
                              (d,i) on *formal-parameter stack*
               if $d>0$ **then write** *line* to *new macro definition*
      macro call: $e \leftarrow$ **true**
               PREPARE actual-parameter list
      MCEND: **if** $d=0$ **then** *DISCARD actual-parameter list*
                    $e \leftarrow$ **false**
                else **if not** e **then** *POP formal-parameter*
                                   stack {level d}
                   $d \leftarrow d - 1$
                   write *line* to *new macro definition*
      other: **if** e **then** replace #(k,i) by
                        if $k=1$ **then** *actual-parameter list*$[i]$
                               else #$(k-1,i)$
                if (**not** e) **and** $d > 0$ **then**
                    replace each formal parameter by topmost
                    corresponding #(k, i) from *formal-parameter stack*
                if $d=0$ **then write** *line* to *output*
                    else **write** *line* to *new macro definition*
   if e **then** {in expansion mode}
          read *line* from *old macro definition*
                named in current *macro call*
   else **read** *line* from *input*

Figure 4.12   Macro Processing with Nested Definitions

DELETE LOCN would result in execution of the standard subroutine
calling sequence with LOCN used as the location of the parameter
list and DELETE as the location of the called subroutine. Note that
the macro of Figure 4.15 is not suitable input for the algorithm of
Figure 4.12. The reason is that the algorithm does not examine the
operation code field of a prototype to determine whether it contains
a formal parameter.

Line	Input	
1.	MCDEFN	
2.	A	FORMAL1
3.	LOAD	FORMAL1
4.	MCDEFN	
5.	B	FORMAL2
6.	STORE	FORMAL2
7.	MCEND	
8.	MCEND	
9.	A	ACTUAL1
10.	B	ACTUAL2

(a) Source text

Line read	d	e	Line written	Macro definitions		Output	
1	0	false					
2	1	false	11	A	FORMAL1		
3	1	false	12	LOAD	#(1,1)		
4	1	false	13	MCDEFN			
5	2	false	14	B	FORMAL2		
6	2	false	15	STORE	#(2,1)		
7	2	false	16	MCEND			
8	1	false	17	MCEND			
9	0	false					
11	0	true					
12	0	true	18			LOAD	ACTUAL1
13	0	true					
14	1	true	19	B	FORMAL2		
15	1	true	20	STORE	#(1,1)		
16	1	true	21	MCEND			
17	0	true					
10	0	false					
19	0	true					
20	0	true	22			STORE	ACTUAL2
21	0	true					

(b) Successive actions

Figure 4.13   Macro Processing Trace

Output text	New macro-definition table entry	
P,Q,R,S	Y	A,B,E,F
E,F,G,H		#(1,1),#(1,2),R,S
	MCDEFN	
	Z	A,C,E,G
		#(2,1),#(1,2),#(2,2),S
		#(2,3),#(1,4),#(2,4),H
	MCEND	
		#(1,3),#(1,4),G,H
	MCEND	

Figure 4.14   Result of Call X P,Q,R,S

```
        MCDEFN
        CREATE SUBR
        MCDEFN
        SUBR   PARMLIST
        - - -
        - - -  PARMLIST
        - - -
        BR     SUBR
        MCEND
        MCEND
```

Figure 4.15   Macro to Generate Subroutine Call Macros

4.6 NESTED CALLS

Just as the text of one macro definition can contain another definition, so can the text of a macro definition contain a macro call, as
in

```
        A         MCDEFN
                  - - -
                  B
                  - - -
                  MCEND
```

where B is a macro instruction. When macro A is called, the call
of macro B will be encountered, requiring the macro processor to
suspend expansion of A and begin expansion of B. Thus the static

nesting of a call within a definition engenders the dynamic nesting of a call within a call.

Nested calls are particularly convenient for defining macros in terms of other macros. The macro DISCR of Figure 4.16(a) computes the discriminant $d = b^2 - 4ac$ of the quadratic polynomial $ax^2 + bx + c$, using arithmetic scaled to radix point 3. It includes three calls of the macro MULTSC defined in Figure 4.10. If each call of MULTSC were expanded before its inclusion in DISCR, the definition of DISCR would appear as in Figure 4.16(b). The skeleton of this second definition includes 14 instructions, versus 5 for the definition with embedded calls. The first definition is easier to write and easier to understand. An occasional drawback is the hiding of inefficiencies that are evident only in the longer form of the definition. Here, the adjacent instructions STORE TEMP1 and LOAD TEMP1 are clearly superfluous, and the instruction STORE TEMP2 can also be seen to be redundant. Nevertheless, the nesting of calls is a valuable facility.

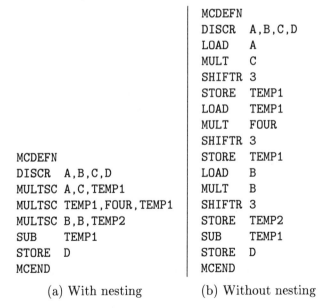

```
                                MCDEFN
                                DISCR   A,B,C,D
                                LOAD    A
                                MULT    C
                                SHIFTR  3
                                STORE   TEMP1
                                LOAD    TEMP1
                                MULT    FOUR
                                SHIFTR  3
        MCDEFN                  STORE   TEMP1
        DISCR   A,B,C,D         LOAD    B
        MULTSC  A,C,TEMP1       MULT    B
        MULTSC  TEMP1,FOUR,TEMP1  SHIFTR  3
        MULTSC  B,B,TEMP2       STORE   TEMP2
        SUB     TEMP1           SUB     TEMP1
        STORE   D               STORE   D
        MCEND                   MCEND
```

          (a) With nesting   (b) Without nesting

Figure 4.16   Use of Nested Calls

Expansion of the call DISCR P,Q,R,S is most readily understood as the two-level process symbolized in Figure 4.17. The first-level expansion replaces DISCR P,Q,R,S by the skeleton of Figure

4.16(a), with the formal parameters A,B,C,D replaced by the actual parameters P,Q,R,S. The second-level expansion replaces each call of MULTSC by the skeleton of Figure 4.10, with formal parameters A,B,C replaced each time by the appropriate actual parameters. If the expansion were actually performed in two stages, it would be necessary to back up after the first-stage generation of STORE S and re-scan from MULTSC P,R,TEMP1. Even if only one level of static nesting of calls within definitions is permitted, there is no limit to the number of levels of the resulting dynamic nesting of calls within calls. Expansion of nested calls by multiple passes would therefore be extremely inefficient.

Outer call	First-level expansion	Second-level expansion	
DISCR P,Q,R,S	MULTSC P,R,TEMP1	LOAD	P
		MULT	R
		SHIFTR	3
		STORE	TEMP1
	MULTSC TEMP1,FOUR,TEMP1	LOAD	TEMP1
		MULT	FOUR
		SHIFTR	3
		STORE	TEMP1
	MULTSC Q,Q,TEMP2	LOAD	Q
		MULT	Q
		SHIFTR	3
		STORE	TEMP2
	SUB TEMP1	SUB	TEMP1
	STORE S	STORE	S

Figure 4.17   Expansion of Nested Macro Calls

A single-pass implementation is used instead to keep track of the dynamic nesting. An expansion that occurs conceptually in n stages is generated practically by stacking to depth n. Suppose that the call DISCR P,Q,R,S is encountered on line 38 of the input text. Comparison of the call with the prototype identifies P,Q,R,S as the actual parameters. These are placed on an **actual-parameter stack** (also called "macro-expansion stack") together with the number, 39, of the input text line from which macro expansion is to resume. The first line of the skeleton is then generated as MULTSC

P,R,TEMP1. Table lookup determines this to be a macro call and the second level of expansion is entered.

The actual parameters P,R,TEMP1 are stacked together with the number, 2, of the next line of the outer-level macro-definition skeleton from which expansion is to resume. The inner macro definition is then expanded, using the actual parameter values from the top of the actual-parameter stack, until the closing delimiter is encountered. At this point the stack is popped. The actual parameters are discarded, and the line number is used to direct the continuation of expansion from line 2 of the skeleton of DISCR. After the last line (5) of the skeleton of DISCR has been expanded, the closing delimiter causes the first stack entry to be popped, leaving an empty stack that signals departure from expansion mode, and normal processing resumes from input text line 39. Figure 4.18 shows the actual-parameter stack during expansion of the third MULTSC instruction.

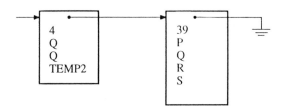

Figure 4.18   Actual-Parameter Stack
During Processing of MULTSC Q,Q,TEMP2

In general, the depth of the actual-parameter stack serves as a **macro-expansion level** counter. As each level is entered, its actual parameters are stacked together with the location from which expansion is to resume in the macro definition at the next outer level. Each element of the actual-parameter stack thus contains the complete actual-parameter list for the call at the corresponding level. The actual parameters are used during expansion at the current level, then are discarded upon final exit from the level. Implementation of the stack entries requires considerable care, because the number of actual parameters can vary from one macro to another, and the length of each actual parameter can vary from one call to another.

If nested macro definitions are not allowed, the stack mechanism for actual parameters can be added directly to the simple one-pass macro processor of Section 4.4. If both nested calls and nested definitions are permitted, the mechanism can be added to the macro processor of Section 4.5.

FOR FURTHER STUDY

Books specialized to macro processors include Campbell73, which devotes substantial space to a variety of applications, and Cole81. Shorter general treatments appear in Part 1 of Brown74 and in Chapter 4 of Beck85. The first three consider the macro processing of arbitrary text as well as of assembler-language programs, and all four describe several specific macro processors.

Revesz85 describes an elegant implementation of nested definitions that does not require number-pair entries in the formal-parameter stack.

Chapter 3 of Wegner68 is devoted to general-purpose macro generators, and Section 2.6 considers the application to assemblers. That section presents concisely the implementation of a macro assembler with nested calls and definitions.

Section 8.5 of Brooks69 embodies a treatment of parameter syntax that is careful, but restricted to the IBM OS Assembler language. A more recent treatment is in Section 4.2.4 of Beck85.

REVIEW QUESTIONS

4.1 What are the similarities and differences between the use of macros at translation time and the use of subroutines at execution time?

4.2 Can one pass a parameter to an open subroutine at execution time?

4.3 Do we really want to be able to generate the END directive?

4.4 How can the value of an assembler-language variable be bound at macro-processing time?

4.5 What actions and data structures are common both to macro processing and to assembly?

4.6 Under what circumstances can the syntactic marker in a list of positional actual parameters be omitted when a parameter is omitted?

4.7 In an edited macro definition, under what circumstances do we need to keep formal parameters in their unedited form?

4.8 If a macro that has a label in its body is called more than once, duplicate labels will be generated. Explain how a macro processor can be made to generate unique labels instead.

4.9 Is it possible to redefine macros when using a two-pass macro processor?

4.10 Which of the three processing modes (copy, definition, expansion) are entered on which pass of a two-pass macro processor?

4.11 What are the principal advantage and principal disadvantage of using a macro-name table?

4.12 During expansion, the macro processor discards the closing delimiter. Why does it not also discard the opening delimiter?

4.13 The two-pass algorithm processes all macro definitions before processing any calls. Is the same true of the one-pass algorithm?

4.14 Does the implementation of Fig. 4.6 permit the redefinition of operation codes?

4.15 In implementing a macro-name table, what is the advantage of maintaining a chain for each name instead of just a pointer to the most recent definition?

4.16 Can a macro processor be simultaneously in copy and definition modes if nested definitions are permitted? Explain.

4.17 Consider the definition of a macro B nested within the definition of macro A.
(**a**) Can a call to macro B also appear within macro A? If not, why not? If so, explain any restrictions.
(**b**) Can a call to macro B appear outside macro A? If not, why not? If so, explain any restrictions.

4.18 Suppose that the definitions of macros B and C are both nested within that of A, but disjoint from each other. Will the use of entries of the form "#(d,i)" in the macro-definition table work correctly?

4.19 We wish to distinguish among identically named formal parameters of nested macro definitions that use keyword syntax. A friend proposes that each macro be edited when it is defined, by replacing each occurrence of each formal parameter P in the body by P=, except within portions of the body that are delimited by MCDEFN and MCEND. Is our friend's proposal satisfactory? If so, what makes it work? If not, what is needed instead?

4.20 In entries of the form "#(d,i)" in the macro-definition table, is the token "#" necessary?

4.21 Can a macro processor be simultaneously in expansion and definition modes if nested definitions are permitted? Explain.

4.22 When an inner macro is being defined during the expansion of an outer macro, why is a formal-parameter stack not used?

4.23 Consider a macro call nested within another *call* (not within another definition). Is that nesting static or dynamic?

4.24 What implementation of nested calls can be used instead of an actual-parameter stack?

4.25 State for each of the following data structures (**i**) the problem it is intended to solve; (**ii**) when it is used, and (**iii**) how it is used.
(**a**) actual-parameter stack;
(**b**) formal-parameter stack;
(**c**) macro-definition table;
(**d**) macro-name table.

PROBLEMS

4.1 Rewrite the macro definition of Figure 4.2, using formal parameters in the body only. Repeat for both (**a**) positional syntax and (**b**) keyword syntax.

4.2 Let some of the parameters of a macro obey positional syntax, whereas others obey keyword syntax.

(**a**) What are the constraints on the order in which parameters appear in the prototype?

(**b**) What are the constraints on the order in which parameters appear in the call?

(**c**) Is it possible to specify default values for parameters of both types? Describe a mechanism or explain why none is possible.

4.3 Given the macro definition

```
          MCDEFN
LABEL     MOD     DIVIDEND,DIVISOR,REMAINDR
LABEL     LOAD    DIVIDEND
HEAD.SER  SUB     DIVISOR
          BRPOS   HEAD.SER
          BRZERO  HEAD.SER
          ADD     DIVISOR
          STORE   REMAINDR
          MCEND
```

show (**a**) the edited macro definition as it might stand in the macro-definition table, and (**b**) the result of expanding the call

```
PUZZLE    MOD     COCONUTS,MONKEYS,LEFTOVER
```

during the seventeenth expansion performed by the macro processor.

4.4 Given the macro definition

```
          MCDEFN
APPLY     OP,A,B,C
          LOAD    A
          OP      B
          STORE   C
          MCEND
```

show **(a)** the preprocessed macro definition as it might stand in the macro-definition table, and **(b)** the result of expanding the call

```
APPLY   DIVIDE,SUM,COUNT,MEAN
```

4.5 Rewrite the program of Figure 4.6 to incorporate a single **case** statement.

4.6 Consider a standard one-pass macro processor that uses DEFINE and END to delimit macro definition, and CALL to signal macro expansion. Each of the following program sequences lists all the statements that reference macros A and B, and omits other statements. For each sequence state which of the following actions is begun, and in what order: definition of A, definition of B, expansion of A, and expansion of B. Describe any error condition that occurs (and assume that it terminates processing).

```
(a)  DEFINE   A       (b)  DEFINE   A       (c)  DEFINE   A
     DEFINE   B            DEFINE   B            CALL     B
     END      B            CALL     B            DEFINE   B
     CALL     B            END      B            END      B
     END      A            END      A            END      A
     CALL     A            CALL     A            CALL     A

(d)  DEFINE   A       (e)  DEFINE   A
     CALL     B            DEFINE   B
     DEFINE   B            CALL     A
     END      B            END      B
     END      A            END      A
                           CALL     A
                           CALL     B
```

4.7 Continue the processing illustrated in Figs. 4.11 and 4.14.

    (a) Show the output text and new macro definition that result from the call Y K,L,M,N.

    (b) Show the output text that results from the subsequent call Z T,U,V,W.

4.8 Show the output text generated by a macro processor from the following input.

```
MCDEFN
OUTER   A=,B=
MCDEFN
INNER   A=,C=
LOAD    A
MULT    C
MULT    @4
STORE   *+4
BR      *+3
SPACE
LOAD    B
MULT    B
SUB     *-5
MCEND
STORE   A
MCEND
OUTER   B=BRAVO,A=DELTA
INNER   A=ALFA,C=CHARLIE
```

4.9 Execute the program of Figure 4.12 manually, using as input the following text, to which line numbers have been affixed. Show the macro-definition table entries, numbering their lines serially from 21 in the order of their creation. Show the sequence in which source-text and macro-definition lines are read, together with the values of d and e during reading. Show the output text generated, numbering the lines.

```
 1.    MCDEFN
 2.    OUTER   PARM1
 3.    MCDEFN
 4.    INNER   PARM2
 5.    MULT    PARM2
 6.    MCEND
 7.    LOAD    PARM1
 8.    MCEND
 9.    OUTER   ARG1
10.    INNER   ARG2
```

4.10 Rewrite the program of Figure 4.12 to permit the name of an inner macro definition to be a formal parameter of an outer definition.

4.11 To the program of Figure 4.6, add an actual-parameter stack mechanism to handle nested calls. Execute your program manually, using as input the definition of Figure 4.16(a) followed by the call DISCR P,Q,R,S. Show the macro-definition table entries and the output text generated, numbering their lines serially from 31 in the order of their creation. Show the sequence in which source-text and macro-definition lines are read, together with the values of *d* and *e* during reading.

4.12 To the program of Figure 4.13, which already handles nested definitions, add an actual-parameter stack mechanism to handle nested calls. Execute your program manually, using as input the following text, to which line numbers have been affixed. Show the macro-definition table entries and the output text generated, numbering their lines serially from 41 in the order of their creation. Show the sequence in which source-text and macro-definition lines are read, together with the values of *d* and *e* during reading.

```
 1.    MCDEFN
 2.    FIRST  A
 3.    LOAD   A
 4.    MCEND
 5.    MCDEFN
 6.    SECOND A
 7.    FIRST  X
 8.    MCDEFN
 9.    THIRD  A
10.    FIRST  A
11.    MCEND
12.    STORE  A
13.    MCEND
14.    SECOND Y
15.    THIRD  Z
```

Chapter 5

Interpretation and Generation

5.1 ATTRIBUTE BINDING

A key concept central to translation is that of **binding**. We say that an attribute is **bound** when its value is specified. The time at which the specification occurs is known as **binding time**. A source-language symbol for a variable, for example, has attributes subject to binding. Its type is usually bound at compilation time by the compiler's action controlled by a declaration statement. The variable's location in main storage is bound at load time by the loader's action controlled by a start address that may be supplied by the operating system. For a load-and-go assembler, however, the location is bound at assembly time. The variable's value is bound at execution time by the machine's action controlled by instructions that correspond perhaps to an assignment statement.

Observe that binding time is not necessarily the time at which the directive to bind is issued. Thus declaration statements and assignment statements are both present at compilation time, but only the former result in compilation-time binding. Observe also that a given attribute is not necessarily bound at a fixed time. The value of an assembler-language variable may be (1) bound at macro processing time; (2) fully bound at assembly time, by a CONST specification; (3) partially bound at assembly time, by synonymy with a second

127

variable, whose value is specified later; (4) partially or fully bound at linking time, if the variable is externally defined; or (5) bound at execution time.

Although the attributes of symbols are those whose binding is of the greatest importance to translators, many entities other than symbols have attributes subject to binding at different times. The number of concurrently executing processes under an operating system may (1) be fixed when the operating system is generated, (2) be subject to change by the machine operator, or (3) vary dynamically during execution. The binding of the I/O medium for a data set may occur at compilation time or be deferred until devices need to be allocated before execution. The priority of different classes of interrupts may be built into the hardware, hence bound when the system is manufactured. Alternatively, it may be bindable by the operating system during execution.

In both operating systems and translators, late binding of an attribute provides flexibility. Consider, for example, the scheduling-time specification of the I/O medium. This permits the programmer to run a program with a test file on disk and then switch to a real data file on tape, without recompiling. Execution-time binding of array sizes enhances the programmer's ability to process variable amounts of data. The price of late binding is complexity, because provision must be made earlier for the eventual appearance of any of several different specifications.

Early binding, on the other hand, offers simplicity at the price of rigidity. Compilation-time binding of array sizes simplifies both the function of the compiler and the management of storage at execution time. But the programmer must abide by the initial choice of array size or else recompile the program. Compilation-time specification of I/O devices precludes deciding for each run what medium to use for a data file. There is no need, however, to defer part of the translation until execution time, when it will be performed for each execution rather than only once per compilation.

Attribute binding and binding time must be borne in mind whenever systems of programs are built. Their role in translators influences not only the organization of different types of translators but also the implementation of translation mechanisms.

5.2 TRANSLATION MECHANISMS

The usual task in using a computer is to produce output results, given input data and a computer program. If the program is in machine language, all that is needed is to let the program control the computer. If a different source language is used instead, translation becomes necessary. Two basic approaches to translation are available, **generation** and **interpretation**.

The generative approach to translation is depicted in Figure 5.1. The source-language program is translated into a program in target language, usually machine language, and that resulting program is subsequently executed with input data to obtain the desired results. The two stages, translation and execution, are not only distinct conceptually but also separated in practice. Translation can precede execution by an arbitrary length of time. Moreover, execution can be repeated for different input data without repeating the translation.

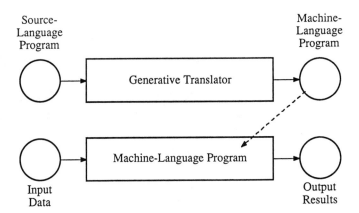

Figure 5.1   Generative Translation

The machine on which the translation is performed, the **host** machine, is often the same as the one that is to run the translated code. Thus a PASCAL compiler for the DEC VAX-11 would normally be written to run on the VAX. There is no requirement, however, that translators other than load-and-go translators and the loader be written to run on the machine for which they produce code. The prefix **cross-** designates a translator whose host and target machines are different. Thus an assembler for the Motorola 68000 that runs on the CDC 7600 is a **cross-assembler**, and a C compiler for the Data General MV10000 that runs on an IBM 370 is a **cross-compiler**. Cross-translators are particularly convenient if the target machine is small relative to the space required by the translator, or if its operating system provides a poor programming environment to the user.

The interpretive approach to translation is symbolized in Figure 5.2. The source-language program is translated into actions that use the input data to yield the output results; no machine-language form of the program is produced. Translation and execution are intimately linked. Translation time is deferred until execution time and the source-language program is translated each time it is executed.

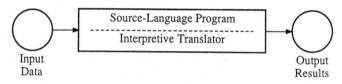

Figure 5.2   Interpretive Translation

A major advantage of generation over interpretation is the greater execution-time efficiency that results from not repeating the translation. Assemblers, linkers, loaders, and most compilers are among the translators that employ generation exclusively or primarily. Macro processors translate chiefly by generation. Some programs called "generators" are also among the translators based on generation.

A translator based on interpretation is an **interpreter**. Some writers use "interpreter" for a translator that performs some generation to obtain a text that is then executed by interpretation. We use the term here in the narrower sense associated with pure interpretation.

Translation by interpretation is deferred until data attributes have been bound. This makes interpreters particularly easy to construct, and they are therefore widely used despite execution-time inefficiencies. Virtually all translators for LISP and for unrestricted APL, and most of those for SNOBOL, are interpreters. The UCSD P-System PASCAL compiler generates first an intermediate language program (in P-code), which is then executed interpretively. The **get** and **put** routines of some operating systems are interpreters, although in others they are generated from information bound when an **open** of the associated file is executed. Nearly all operating systems obey user commands by means of a program, the command language interpreter, which bears the name of the translation technique. Most conditional generators (see Section 5.3) include a measure of interpretive execution. The processing unit of a computer is itself an interpreter for the machine language of the computer. This is particularly evident in computers that implement the interpretation by microprogram.

5.2.1 Interpretation

The basic function of interpretation is to execute successive source-language statements by translating them into actions. The implementation of this function in an interpreter, whether built of hardware or software, is particularly straightforward. For each statement the same sequence of steps is performed:

(1) Obtain statement.
(2) Determine action.
(3) Perform action.

Before examining interpretation by software, consider the familiar hardware interpreter, a computer executing a machine-language program. The execution (interpretation) sequence is the following:

(1) Fetch an instruction (statement) from the location specified by the instruction counter (IC).
(2) Advance the IC in preparation for the next fetch.
(3) Decode the instruction.
(4) Execute the instruction.

After step 4, the computer loops back to step 1 to continue executing the program. The normal sequential execution of instructions is modified by (successful) branch instructions. Their execution (on step 4) replaces the value that was set into the IC on step 2, and by halt instructions, which terminate the looping.

In a software interpreter, the cyclic operation is much the same. The looping action gives its name to the control mechanism of an interpreter, the **interpretive loop** (also "control loop"). Its four steps are similar to those of the computer interpreting machine language:

(1) Fetch a source-language statement from the position specified by the statement counter (pseudo-IC).

(2) Advance the statement counter.

(3) Analyze the statement to determine what operation to perform, and upon what operands.

(4) Execute the statement by calling a subroutine appropriate to the specified operation.

The structure of an interpreter is quite simple. There is a set of operation subroutines for performing the operations in the source language and an interpretive loop for sequencing the subroutines.

There is usually one subroutine for each instruction defined in the source language. Thus an interpreter for a three-address machine-type language (e.g., add A to B and store the result in C) would incorporate a subroutine for "add", one for "subtract", one for "branch", etc. On the other hand, a more complex language may have several instructions that call for related actions. Here, more subroutines than just one per statement type would help. Thus a FORTRAN interpreter might have an exponentiation subroutine that is called by an expression evaluation subroutine, which is itself called by an assignment subroutine when the statement $D := B**2 - 4*A*C$ is executed.

The interpretive loop selects the principal subroutine to be executed for each source-language statement. It also selects the operands. If these are specified symbolically, the interpretive loop needs to maintain a symbol table and assign actual storage locations to correspond to the symbols. To assist in determining the operands and the operations to perform, the interpretive loop may call on other subroutines for lexical and syntactic analysis. Some of this analysis may be performed as a prelude to interpretation. Execution of the interpretive loop, once begun, continues until a source statement causes it to halt, either intentionally or as the result of an error. Otherwise, the interpretive loop accomplishes sequencing of source language statements by updating the statement counter.

As an illustration, consider an interpreter for a three-address source language. Each statement includes an operation code, two operand addresses, and one result address. The program and data areas occupy the first 1000 storage locations in a decimal machine with words of 12 digits, which we number left to right from 0 to 11.

Digits 0–1 are the operation code, digit 2 must be zero, digits 3–5 and 6–8 the first and second operand addresses, and digits 9–11 are the result address. Storage locations 1000–1999 are reserved for the interpretive subroutines, each of which is allocated ten words beginning at the location obtained from the operation code (*e.g.*, 63) by appending a one at the left and a zero at the right (*e.g.*, 1630). The interpretive loop, which can be placed anywhere from location 2000 on, is shown in Figure 5.3. The instruction set of Figure 2.2 is used once again, augmented by the indirect addressing introduced in Chapter 3. The interpreter assumes that the source-language program begins at location 0.

```
          LOAD    @0
          STORE   STMTCNTR
CONTROL   LOAD+   STMTCNTR
          STORE   INSTR
          LOAD    STMTCNTR
          ADD     @1
          STORE   STMTCNTR
          LOAD+   INSTR[3..5]
          STORE   OPD1
          LOAD+   INSTR[6..8]
          STORE   OPD2
          LOAD    INSTR[0..2]
          ADD     @1000
          STORE   SUBRADDR
          BR+     SUBRADDR
STMTCNTR  SPACE   1 {statement counter}
INSTR     SPACE   1 {source-language statement}
OPD1      SPACE   1 {first operand}
OPD2      SPACE   1 {second operand}
SUBRADDR  SPACE   1 {address of subroutine}
```

Figure 5.3   Interpretive Loop

The address of the appropriate subroutine is found by using instruction digit 2 to provide the zero, and addition of 1000 to provide the one. Upon entry to the subroutine, the values of the two operands have been placed in locations OPD1 and OPD2. The subroutine places the result by use of the STORE+ instruction, and closes the loop by branching back to CONTROL. Figure 5.4 shows subroutines for multiplication and for branching on greater or equal.

```
                              BRGREQ    LOAD    OPD1
                                        SUB     OPD2
MULT      LOAD    OPD1                   BRNEG   FAILURE
          MULT    OPD2        SUCCESS    LOAD    INSTR[9..11]
          STORE+  INSTR[9..11]           STORE   STMTCNTR
          BR      CONTROL     FAILURE    BR      CONTROL
```

(a) Multiplication   (b) Conditional branch

Figure 5.4   Operation Subroutines

In implementing this simple structure, we must provide storage for the interpreter program and its data. The program consists of the control loop and the operation subroutines; the data consist of the source-language program and that program's data. Some tables may be required, too. We have already mentioned the use of a symbol table for referencing symbolic operands. Another table is convenient for source languages in which each statement specifies a single operation. This table lists the correspondences of subroutine names or addresses to operation codes.

Because translation is postponed until execution time, such operand attributes as location, type, and value are known at translation time. This information can be used directly by the translator, for example in accessing an element of an array of dynamically specified size. Another example, in APL, is a variable's type, which can change during execution. Generative translation of unrestricted APL is therefore virtually impossible, but interpretation is straightforward. Better error diagnostic messages are another result of postponing translation time until operand attributes are bound.

The immediate availability of results at translation time aids in debugging the source-language program. So does having source-language names available at execution time. Another benefit, particularly if I/O facilities are limited, is the avoidance of the extra I/O that may be required by the two-stage operation of Figure 5.1.

The basic interpreter can be augmented to record facts and statistics of execution. After all, the interpretive loop effects a trace of the source program. Study of the trace information can lead to improvements in the program being interpreted. A special case is the machine **simulator**, an interpreter for the machine language of another computer, which may even be still unbuilt. Execution of the simulator usually includes study of the timing of the simulated machine. If that machine is under development, this study can assist in detailing its design.

Because no machine-language version of the program is produced, substantial space savings are possible. In fact, the source program and interpreter program together may well require less space than does the result of first translating the source program into machine language.

A major difference between interpretive and generative translation is that under interpretation a source-language statement is translated *each time* it is executed. This yields a small saving, to be sure, because the interpreter doesn't even examine source code that is not reached in a particular run. The principal effect, however, is the loss of time in repeatedly translating the statements of a source-language loop. This effect is further compounded by the overhead of performing sequencing operations in source language rather than in machine code. The net result is that interpretation is slow. Interpretive execution of a program typically takes between 20 and 100 times as long as execution of a machine-language version of the program. To be altogether fair, one must count the effort of producing that machine-language program, either by hand or as the result of compilation. Nevertheless, we do not choose interpreters for their execution efficiency. We choose them instead for the space saving, for the ease with which they are constructed, and for the flexibility obtainable by deferring translation until execution time.

5.2.2 Generation

Just as execution of a process specified by the user is the objective of interpretation, so is it also the objective of generation. Whereas interpretation synthesizes *actions* to be performed immediately, generation synthesizes *code* to be executed later. The generation process itself is really just a matter of substitution; target-language code is substituted for source-language code. The complexity of the required substitution depends on the nature of the translation. The generation of a machine-language instruction from an assembler-language instruction is usually rather simple. The generation of machine-language text from a statement in a rich programming language is a much more complex process. Between these two extremes lie such generations as that of expanding a macro call into assembler-language statements.

System-Defined Generation. As the first example of generation, consider the translation of line 11 of the program of Figure 2.5(a), using the symbol table of Figure 2.5(b). Scanning the source text has identified the operation as COPY, operand 1 as OLD, and operand 2 as OLDER. The operation is looked up in the operation table (Figure 2.2), which gives 13 as the value to be substituted for it. The two operands are looked up in the symbol table, which yields 36 and 35 as the corresponding values. The three numbers are combined into 133635, which is the instruction generated by the assembler.

The organization of the generator can be extremely simple. Assume that the lexical scanner assigns to variables *operand1* and *operand2* the symbols, if any, in the respective fields. Assume also that a function procedure *LOCATION* returns the location of its one parameter, as determined from the symbol table. Then a search of the operation table is used to select a subroutine that corresponds to the assembler-language operation code. For COPY, that subroutine would be the following, where the comma represents catenation.

$$word1 \leftarrow 13$$
$$word2 \leftarrow LOCATION(operand1)$$
$$word3 \leftarrow LOCATION(operand2)$$
$$code \leftarrow word1, word2, word3$$

If address expressions are permitted, the call to *LOCATION* is replaced by one to an address evaluation routine that itself calls *LOCATION* as needed. If the assembler language includes extended mnemonics (see Section 2.2.1), the operation table entry specifies not only the text to be placed in the machine-language operation code field. It must also specify other portions of the instruction. For the mythical computer of Chapter 2, the fields of the machine-language instruction coincide with addressable words. For a computer in which they do not coincide, the generator must piece together partial words, using whatever bit-manipulation facilities are available. If a constant is to be generated, complicated conversions may be necessary, but the translation is conceptually still simple.

As a second example of generation, consider the enrichment of the assembler language by an add-to-storage instruction ADST. This

instruction causes the content of the accumulator to be added to that
of the storage location whose symbolic name is HOLDER. Although
the assembler language has been enlarged by a new instruction, the
machine remains unchanged. The addition must still be performed
by executing an ADD instruction, which will destroy the previous
content of the accumulator. We therefore provide a specific storage
location, named BACKUP, to hold a copy of that value. Each time
ADST is encountered in the source program it is translated as if it had
been replaced, before assembly, by the following four statements.

```
STORE   BACKUP
ADD     HOLDER
STORE   HOLDER
LOAD    BACKUP
```

The replacement could be performed either during a pre-pass of the
entire text or upon recognition of ADST during Pass 1 of the assembler. Although the latter choice is often adopted to avoid an extra
pass of the text, use of a pre-pass will be assumed here for ease of
description. The generation program, shown in Figure 5.5, involves
only substitution.

```
read line
while line ≠ empty do
   if opcode = 'ADST'
      then write '          STORE   BACKUP'
           write '          ADD     HOLDER'
           write '          STORE   HOLDER'
           write '          LOAD    BACKUP'
      else  write line
   read line
```

Figure 5.5   Parameter-Free Generation

We can view the new instruction ADST, of course, as a parameterless macro. The macro processing technique of Chapter 4 serves
to translate it whether it is user-defined or system-defined. In the implementation in that chapter, the text to be substituted is first stored
in and later read from a data structure, the macro-definition table,
which is accessed by the translation program. In the implementation of Figure 5.5, the text to be substituted is not merely accessed
by, but actually embodied in, the translation program. This second

technique is therefore restricted to system-defined macros, unless the translator is itself to be generated after the macro is defined.

If the macros have parameters, values of the actual parameters must be inserted in the appropriate positions of the generated text. The macro ABSDIF, defined in Figure 4.5(a), serves as an example. Assume that the format

columns		
	1– 8	label
	10–15	operation
	17–33	operand(s)

is used for both input and output lines. The heart of the generation program might then be written as in Figure 5.6. The comma again represents catenation, and the details of character extraction have been suppressed in favor of an indexing-type notation. The global numeric variable *serial* holds the serial number of the current macro expansion. The procedure *CHAR* converts a numeric variable into a 4-character string. The procedure *LEXANAL* performs a lexical analysis of the character string named as its first parameter. It delivers to the variables *parm0*, *parm1*, etc., the eight-character string values of the label and of the other macro parameters. The total number of such variables is specified as the second parameter of *LEXANAL*.

```
if line [10..15] = 'ABSDIF'
    then serial ← serial + 1
         ser ← CHAR(serial)
         LEXANAL(line,3)
         write parm0,  ' LOAD   ', parm1
              ,         SUB   ', parm2
              ,         BRPOS ST.', ser
              ,         LOAD   ', parm2
              ,         SUB   ', parm1
         'ST.',ser,'  STORE  ', parm3
```

Figure 5.6   System-Defined Parameterized Generation

A somewhat different organization would be for the generator to have the six output lines, with parameters not filled in, available as global data. The following would be used for ABSDIF.

```
,           LOAD                          ,
,           SUB                           ,
,           BRPOS   ST.                   ,
,           LOAD                          ,
,           SUB                           ,
'ST.        STORE                         ,
```

In translating the ABSDIF instruction, the generator would make a copy of the foregoing lines and insert into the appropriate positions the symbols that appear as the parameters in the instruction.

User-Defined Generation. We have considered a system-defined parameterized macro for an assembler language, and seen how code could be generated to correspond to the choice of parameters. Because the correspondence was predefined, the generator code could be prepared ahead of time. Such advance preparation is not possible, however, if the user is permitted to define his or her own macros. Instead, construction of the generator code must be deferred until after the user-supplied definition has been encountered.

Suppose that the ABSDIF instruction, as previously described, is defined not by the system, but rather by the user. The generation program of Figure 5.6 cannot be prepared in advance of encountering the user's definition; it must be constructed from the definition. Such construction can be performed by a *system-defined* program that accepts an arbitrary prototype and a model of the corresponding text, and generates a generator program that will replace the prototype by the text.

An example prototype might be

```
SPOT        ABSDIF A,B,C
```

and the corresponding text model the edited definition of Figure 4.5(b). The generation mechanisms we have already seen are wholly adequate to this task. For example, the fragment

if *line* $[10..15] = $ 'ABSDIF'

would be generated from

if *line* $[10..15] = $ '

by insertion of the operation field of the prototype. Hence the code to perform the user-defined generation can itself be generated by a system-defined generation that occurs when the user's definition is processed. The task of user-defined generation has thus been reduced to the simpler task of system-defined generation.

Although this process involving two stages of generation is perfectly feasible, in practice it is rarely used in preference to the line-by-line technique of Chapter 4. A program to generate an entire user-defined macro expansion cannot be prepared in advance of the definition. On the other hand, a program to generate one line of an arbitrary macro expansion can be prepared and incorporated in the macro processor. The first stage of generation is already accomplished in effect when the macro processor is built and need not be repeated for every macro definition.

Another example of program translation is that of the PL/I preprocessor input

%**declare** X **character**, Y **fixed**;
%X = '$Y+Z$';
%Y = 5;
$A = X$;

to the following single statement.

$$A = 5+Z;$$

The three preprocessor statements (those marked by a % sign) can be used in the generation of a generator that substitutes $5+Z$ for X in the fourth statement. The process is similar in concept to the two-stage generation process for user-defined macros. The greater richness of machine-independent languages and their preprocessor facilities, however, make that type of implementation even more unwieldy. More satisfactory is a partially interpretive approach. Each preprocessor statement inserts, changes, or deletes entries in a preprocessor symbol table, and the regular statements are translated by an interpretation that uses the current symbol table entries. We chose the foregoing example for its simplicity rather than its utility; most use of preprocessors involves conditional generation, as illustrated in Section 5.3.1.

The generation of intermediate code such as the "quadruples" (see Chapter 8)

```
SUB     A       B       T1
BRNEG   T1      -       +4
MULT    B       D       T2
ADD     T2      A       C
BR      -       -       +3
MULT    A       D       T3
ADD     T3      B       C
```

from the PASCAL statement

$$\textbf{if } A{<}B \textbf{ then } C := B{+}A{*}D$$
$$\textbf{else } C := A{+}B{*}D$$

is typical of compilation. The syntactic and semantic complexity of most machine-independent languages, as opposed to assembler languages and most macro processing, make it appropriate to treat compilation as a separate subject. Much of Chapter 6 and all of Chapters 7 and 8 are devoted to compilation.

5.3 CONDITIONAL GENERATION

5.3.1 The Generation-Time Machine

The preprocessor translation of

$$\%\textbf{declare } I \textbf{ fixed};$$
$$\%\textbf{do } I{=}1 \textbf{ to } 10;$$
$$A(I) = B(I) + C(I);$$
$$\%\textbf{end};$$

into the ten PL/I statements

$$A(1) = B(1) + C(1);$$
$$A(2) = B(2) + C(2);$$
$$---$$
$$A(10) = B(10) + C(10);$$

treats the one regular source-text statement (the one with no % sign) in a manner that depends on specific values (here, 1 and 10) presented at generation time. This adaptation of the output text to generation-time conditions is known as **conditional** generation and often considerably increases the usefulness of a translator. Some assemblers, too, perform conditional assembly. The DAS assembler for the Varian 620/i offered conditional assembly as a means of specializing the generated code at assembly time to either the 16-bit or the 18-bit version of the machine. Another example is the `REPEAT` instruction presented in Section 2.2.1.

The most widespread application of conditional generation, however, is to macro processing. In particular, two functions that are dependent upon conditional generation markedly enhance the utility of macros. One is the validation of operands of macro instructions. The other is the generalization of a single macro-definition skeleton, especially over a variety of data types. These functions require that symbol attributes and means of testing them be available at generation time. Conditional macro processing, because of its importance, will serve as our illustration of conditional generation. The techniques presented apply, with little modification, to conditional assembly and conditional preprocessing.

What generation-time capabilities do we require for conditional generation? The macro processor must be able to evaluate conditions and alter the flow of processing accordingly. Although mechanisms for iteration and selection could be provided in the language, typical facilities usually include only an unconditional branch, a conditional skip or branch, and labels to mark branch destinations. Normal sequential flow is maintained by the input-text line counter. Generation-time variables are also needed, both for temporary storage during expansion and for communication between macros. With facilities for manipulating these variables we complete the requirements for a computer system that operates at generation time, executing programs written in a language of macros with conditional generation. The "processing unit" of this system is implemented in software rather than hardware, but the **generation-time machine** is nonetheless real. Its existence serves as a reminder that we are able to perform any operation at any stage of translation, although not necessarily with equal ease at each stage.

5.3.2 Conditional Macro Processor

The implementation of a macro processor for a macro language with conditional facilities embodies an implementation of the generation-time machine. A closer look at the language of this machine will illustrate what further translation is required.

The generation-time variables are usually distinguished from other symbols by being declared explicitly. The declaration specifies both type and scope. The most common scopes are (1) global to all macro definitions and (2) local to the definition in which the declaration is encountered, and perhaps to definitions nested within that one. Because a macro processor is a text manipulator, character variables are a principal type. Numeric variables, especially integers for counting, and boolean variables, for recording conditions, are usually also provided. A simple declaration format might include the variable symbol in the label field, scope declaration (GLOBAL or LOCAL) in the operation field, and type specification (BOOL, CHAR, or INT) in the operand field. An example would be CNTR LOCAL INT.

Expressions involving these variables can be formed using appropriate operations, typically arithmetic operations on integers, logical operations on booleans, substring and catenation on characters, and comparison on all three types. Assignment of the value of such an expression to a variable is accomplished by an assignment instruction, perhaps like CNTR ASSIGN CNTR+1. The value of a relational expression that includes a comparison operation may be assigned to a boolean variable or used directly as a condition in a sequence control operation.

The sequencing operations usually available correspond to the **goto**, **if** *condition* **then goto**, and **return** statements of machine-independent languages. The second one is alone sufficient, and it might be written in a form such as MCGOIF (INDEX<N)%BEGIN, where %BEGIN appears as the label on the line of input text from which processing is to continue if the condition INDEX<N holds. An alternative to the conditional branch is the conditional skip, say SKIPIF or simply SKIP. It skips one line if the condition is satisfied, and therefore need not specify a label. An unconditional branch must be provided for use with the conditional skip.

Generation-time labels must be distinguished from the previously encountered execution-time labels. This is because they are neither to be entered in the symbol table nor generated in the output text; they just mark positions in the input text. In our hypothetical language, both types of labels are defined by being used in the label field. Since neither type is declared and their positional use is the same, the distinction must be syntactic. Here the character %

is used as a syntactic marker on generation-time labels. Sometimes both a generation-time label and an execution-time label are needed on a statement, but most assembler languages provide only a single label field. This impasse is solved by a dummy operation code that does nothing other than provide an extra input-text line on which a generation-time label can be hung. If that operation code is NULL, the lines

```
%FRONT    NULL
ARG.CNTR CONST   CNTR
```

allow both labels to mark the same effective location.

Although the unconditional branch is a special case of the conditional branch, it is convenient to provide it explicitly. An example would be MCGO %FRONT. Macro expansion may terminate conditionally somewhere within the body of the macro definition. A branch to the closing delimiter would, of course, have the desired effect. To make the definition easier to read and write, however, an expansion **terminator** distinct from the definition delimiter is often provided. An operation code such as MCEXIT can serve in this capacity.

We now present three examples of conditional macros to illustrate the foregoing features. The first is a generalization of the repetitive assembly

```
          REPEAT 2,(1,10)
ARG$      CONST  $
FCT$      SPACE
```

discussed in Section 2.2.1. The call TABLE 1,10 of the macro defined in Figure 5.7 would result in the expansion shown in Chapter 2.

```
          MCDEFN
          TABLE  LOWER,UPPER
CNTR      LOCAL  INT
CNTR      ASSIGN LOWER
%FRONT    NULL
ARG.CNTR CONST   CNTR
FCT.CNTR SPACE
CNTR      ASSIGN CNTR+1
          MCGOIF (CNTR≤UPPER)%FRONT
          MCEND
```

Figure 5.7   Table Generation Macro

The second example is a macro whose expansion delivers to the second argument a copy of the content of the first argument. Because the accumulator is used to effect the operation, its content is first saved in a temporary location and afterwards restored. Thus the expansion of MOVE X,Y is

```
STORE   TEMP
LOAD    X
STORE   Y
LOAD    TEMP
```

If, however, the name of either argument is ACC, then it designates the accumulator content instead of a storage location. As a result, the call MOVE ACC,Y yields the one-line expansion STORE Y and the call MOVE X,ACC produces LOAD X. The macro is defined in Figure 5.8, which uses a conditional skip but no branching to arbitrary lines of text. If conditional branches were used instead, two branches would suffice instead of four skips.

```
MCDEFN
MOVE    A,B
SKIPIF  (A='ACC') or (B='ACC')
STORE   TEMP
SKIPIF  A='ACC'
LOAD    A
SKIPIF  B='ACC'
STORE   B
SKIPIF  (A='ACC') or (B='ACC')
LOAD    TEMP
MCEND
```

Figure 5.8 Value Copying Macro

The third example generates code to add two n-element vectors that may be either fixed-point or floating-point. Assume that T(*symbol*) returns the data type of *symbol* as a character string, and that ADDFIX and ADDFLT are machine instructions for adding numbers of the two types. The starting addresses of the operand vectors are A and B; that of the result vector is C; zero-origin indexing is used. We do not specify here the mechanism for generating error messages. Figure 5.9 shows the vector addition macro. Note that if a call of VECADD precedes the definition of the symbol passed to it as an actual parameter corresponding to the formal parameter A, then T(A) is a forward reference to a symbol attribute. Note also the syntactic distinction between A+.INDEX in an operand field to be generated and INDEX+1 in a generation-time assignment. The period segregates INDEX as a generation-time symbol whose value, rather than the symbol itself, is to be generated. All macro processors must provide for this distinction, but they are not restricted to the particular convention illustrated here.

```
 1.                 MCDEFN
 2.                 VECADD A,B,C,N
 3.     INDEX       LOCAL  INT
 4.     TYPEA       LOCAL  CHAR
 5.     TYPEB       LOCAL  CHAR
 6.     TYPEA       ASSIGN T(A)
 7.     TYPEB       ASSIGN T(B)
 8.                 MCGOIF (TYPEA=TYPEB)%OK
 9.                 generate error message
10.                 MCEXIT
11.     %OK         NULL
12.     INDEX       ASSIGN 0
13.     %BEGIN      LOAD   A+.INDEX
14.                 MCGOIF (TYPEA='FLOAT')%FLOAT
15.                 ADDFIX B+.INDEX
16.                 MCGO   %BOTH
17.     %FLOAT      ADDFLT B+.INDEX
18.     %BOTH       STORE  C+.INDEX
19.     INDEX       ASSIGN INDEX+1
20.                 MCGOIF (INDEX<N)%BEGIN
21.                 MCEND
```

Figure 5.9   Vector Addition Macro

For another example of a forward reference to an attribute of an assembler-language symbol consider a set of programs to hash alphanumeric part numbers of various lengths. Each program hashes part numbers of one specific length. It requires a mask twice as long as the part number and consisting of binary ones for the middle half of its length and zeros at the ends. A single macro is provided to generate that mask, whatever the required length. It is called by each of the hashing programs, which passes as an actual parameter the symbol that represents the part number. The macro definition must refer to the field length associated with that symbol, which will be defined only later in the text when the program that contains the macro call is reached.

Conditional assembler language is seen to resemble machine-independent languages in many ways. Variables are declared and their values assigned; subroutines (macros) are defined and invoked; expressions are evaluated and compared; sequence control is exercised. How should this language be translated? Generation of machine-language code to be incorporated in the conditional generator is attractive because of potential space savings. The input text line `INDEX ASSIGN INDEX+1` could easily occupy 80 characters in a fixed-format conditional assembler program. It could be compiled to a load, add, store sequence that might be no more than 15% as long. Nevertheless, a separate generator (or compiler) is not commonly used on macro definitions. Although historical reasons may be a primary cause, there is a good technical reason. An interpreter is easier to write, and it is probably not worth while to compile a macro definition that may be called only once, as many are.

Thus the instructions about how to generate are usually executed interpretively, the conditional macro processor racing around to generation-time labels as it executes the conditional and unconditional branches. To avoid the danger of endless looping during macro expansion, we can impose a limit on the number of successful generation-time branches performed.

5.4 MACRO ASSEMBLER

The combination of a macro processor with an assembler is the widely used translator known as a **macro assembler**. A straightforward implementation couples an assembler, which may or may not be conditional, with a distinct macro processor whose output serves as the assembler's input. An alternative approach is to embed macro processing within an assembler. This makes it possible to avoid duplicating actions and data structures common to both, and to tailor the macro processing more directly to the assembler-language application. Because of the restriction to a particular application, the resulting translator is sometimes called an **applied** macro assembler. The phrase "macro assembler" by itself does not make explicit whether the macro processing is performed independently of the assembly.

Implementation of an applied macro assembler may take either of two forms, macro processing during assembler Pass 1 or after Pass 1. To effect macro processing during Pass 1 of the assembler it suffices to incorporate the regular Pass 1 actions into the one-pass algorithm for the desired complexity of macro processing. Each of the macro processing algorithms of Chapter 4 includes the statement "**write** *line* to *output*", which is executed whenever a line other than a macro call or a delimiter is encountered outside definition mode. That statement is simply replaced by normal Pass 1 processing. If *line* is a machine instruction, the location counter is advanced and symbol table management is performed. If *line* is an assembler directive, the appropriate Pass 1 action is performed.

The chief advantage of embedding macro processing in the first pass of the assembler is to keep the total number of passes down to two. A corresponding disadvantage is that quite a lot must be packed into the first-pass program, which may become unpleasantly large. Another drawback is that forward references to attributes of symbols not yet defined cannot be made during macro processing.

Some of these drawbacks disappear if the macro processing is deferred until after the completion of assembler Pass 1. Because macro definition is not begun until Pass 1 has built the symbol table, both macro definitions and macro calls can make forward references to attributes of symbols. Macro expansion does, however, cause insertions in the assembler-language program text, thus invalidating the location values in the symbol table. Other attributes, however, such as field length, name length, and relocatability mode, remain unchanged by the expansion process.

At least one of the IBM 370 assemblers is an applied macro assembler of this type, and makes four passes. Pass 1 is essentially the first pass of the assembler, although some editing of macro definitions is performed. Pass 2 performs the macro processing, with reference to the symbol table. Pass 3 reconstructs the symbol table, incorporating symbols generated during Pass 2 and providing correct location values that reflect the expansion performed during Pass 2. The second pass of the assembler is Pass 4. The disadvantages of having to make several passes are counterbalanced by two major ad-

vantages. One is the language feature that permits macros to refer
forward to symbol attributes. The other is the reduction in program
size for any given pass. In fact, tight space constraints were a major
design criterion of that macro assembler.

Extra passes are useful not only for processing macros within an
assembler. A third assembler pass would permit forward references
by the SET-type definitional facility. Other potential uses of a third
pass are the optimization of index register assignments and such
simple code optimization as removing the redundant STORE-LOAD pair
from the second-level expansion in Figure 4.17.

FOR FURTHER STUDY

The concept of binding is addressed briefly by Wegner68 (Section
1.1.7), Brooks69 (pages 386–388), Freeman75 (Section 11.7.1), and
Horowitz84a (Section 4.2). One of the best treatments is that of
Elson73, which devotes Chapter 5 to the subject.

The process of generation is treated at least implicitly in all
of the references on assemblers, macro processors, and compilers.
A brief, but sound, explicit presentation is that in Section 8.5 of
Brooks69. The contrast between generation and interpretation is
presented carefully in Lee74 (pages 27–38). Berthaud73 distinguishes
clearly between generative and interpretive translation in the implementation of a compiler. The classic article McIlroy60 first proposed
the thesis that anything doable at execution time is doable at translation time.

Interpreters are described infrequently. Two good expositions,
however, are those of Brooks69 (Section 8.2) and of Glass69.

REVIEW QUESTIONS

5.1 How does an interpreter handle forward references? Why do
they not present the problem that they do to an assembler or compiler?

5.2 The PL/I program fragment

```
MIDTERM: procedure options (main);
declare (I,N) fixed decimal;
get list (N);
declare A(1:N) float decimal;
do I=1 to N;
    A(I) = SQRT(I);
end;
```

is not legal because the second declaration cannot be processed at compilation time. (A **begin** block is normally used instead. Storage for the array can then be allocated in the activation record for the **begin** block.) If the construction were legal, could an interpreter translate it successfully? Explain.

5.3 What approach can we use to reduce user-defined generation to system-defined generation?

5.4 What kind of resource saving is normally offered by generation? By interpretation?

5.5 A macro can serve the same purpose as the REPEAT statement of assembler language. A minor difference is that the macro may allow more variation. State a major difference.

5.6 Suggest an alternative to the lexical differentiation (*e.g.*, "%") between generation-time and execution-time labels.

5.7 What hashing method might require a mask "consisting of binary ones for the middle half of its length and zeros at the ends"?

5.8 In an applied macro assembler, will macro processing after assembler Pass 1 work if a macro expansion redefines symbols defined by EQU or SET?

PROBLEMS

5.1 Write an operation subroutine for COPY, to accompany the interpretive loop of Figure 5.3.

5.2 Define, as is done in Section 5.2.2 for ADST, a new instruction called INCR that increments the content of a storage location. Assume the operations of Figure 2.2. Do not provide for saving the content of the accumulator, hence do not make use of BACKUP. There are two parameters. One parameter is the symbolic name of the storage location; a second parameter is written as the integer to be added. Write a generation program that will replace each occurrence of the INCR instruction by the appropriate lines of assembler-language code. Use whatever assembler features are appropriate.

5.3 It is often illuminating to think of facilities for macro processing and conditional translation as providing a *translation-time* machine. This is distinct from the *execution-time* machine that executes the translated program. Identify the translation-time analogues of variables, declarations, branches, labels, subroutines, assignments, the instruction counter, and other actions and facilities of a computer.

5.4 Rewrite the definition in Figure 5.8, using conditional branching instead of SKIPIF. Follow the syntax conventions of this chapter.

5.5 The macro defined in Figure 5.9 is called by the statement

```
VECADD ADDEND,AUGEND,SUM,4
```

for which each of the first three actual parameters is known to be of type 'FLOAT'. State the sequence in which lines are read from the macro definition during expansion of the call, and show the output text generated.

5.6 The conditional assembler directive IFF tests its one operand, an assembly-time boolean variable. The lines between the IFF and a later ENDIF are assembled if and only if that variable has value **false**. The directive IFT works similarly with value **true**. Assume the provision of multiple location counters. Describe an implementation in which IFF and IFT are processed during Pass 1.

5.7 Using the language defined implicitly in Section 5.3.2 with the substring notation of Figure 5.3, write a definition for the following macro. The prototype is

ROOM NAME,LENGTH

where NAME is a character-string symbol parameter and LENGTH
a positive integer parameter. If the initial letter of the symbol is
in the range I..N, the macro generates the stated integer number
of occurrences of SPACE 1 and labels the first of them with the
symbol. If the initial letter is different and the integer is even,
the macro generates one-half the stated number of occurrences
of SPACE 2 and labels the first of them with the symbol. If the
initial letter is different and the integer is odd, the macro calls
a parameterless macro ERROR.

Repeat the exercise using a real macro assembler, if one is available to you. This will assist you in keeping the binding times
clearly in mind.

Chapter 6

Source-Program Analysis

6.1 OVERVIEW

Before generating code or calling an interpretive subroutine, a translator must determine the content of the source-language text to be translated. Unlike generation and interpretation, which are processes whose goal is synthesis, the determination of source-language content is analytic. Lexical analysis is required to separate the source-language text into the elements that constitute the language. Syntactic analysis is required to ascertain the structural relationships among those elements. These analyses of the source-language text are independent, at least in principle, of later stages of translation. True, it may be convenient to combine syntactic and semantic analysis in a compiler, but this is a practical convenience rather than a theoretical necessity. Lexical and syntactic analysis can be performed independently of whether generation or interpretation is to follow, and independently of the choice of target language or of host language. The extent and nature of the initial processing do depend, however, on the source language of the program text being analyzed. Both the type of language and the extent to which its format is fixed influence the analyses.

Before discussing the different requirements that may be imposed, let us agree on a few definitions. The elementary unit of text is the **character**. Printed or displayed, a character normally occupies one column of output (and is sometimes called a "graphic" or a "grapheme"). Examples of characters are shown in Figure 6.1(a). The input of a character may require a single keystroke on computer or terminal, but sometimes more than one stroke is required. For example, the upper and lower case versions of the same letter are distinguished by the presence or absence of certain shifts. Overstruck characters are sometimes produced by combining two distinct components and an intervening backspace. A character among the "upper 128" on an IBM PC can be produced by holding down the alternate case key ⟨Alt⟩ and pressing three digits on the numeric keypad. We shall use the term **stroke** for the individual elements that can be combined into characters. The last character of Figure 6.1(a) is a composite character produced by four* strokes ⟨Alt⟩ 1 3 0. A character's individual strokes are sometimes converted into the requisite character by hardware, but often the translator must provide the function.

A	'BALANCE'
.	3.14159E+00
c	**procedure**
/	/
=	:=
é	é
(a) Characters	(b) Tokens

Figure 6.1   Example Language Elements

The characters in turn are grouped into **tokens**, the smallest language units that convey meaning. Figure 6.1(b) shows some examples of tokens. The word "symbol" is often used as a synonym for "token", especially in British usage. Unfortunately, it is also used occasionally for "character" or even "stroke". Hence we shall not attempt to define "symbol" precisely.

The task of lexical analysis, then, is to subdivide the source-language text into tokens and to identify the **type** of each token, whether identifier, constant, operator, *etc.* The task of syntactic analysis is to determine how groups of tokens are interrelated.

For an assembler language, the syntactic analysis is usually simple. It must distinguish keyword parameters from positional param-

---

*If one counts separately the depression and release of the alternate case key, *five* strokes are combined.

eters, determine the structure of address expressions, and distinguish generation-time variables from execution-time variables. By and large, however, the syntax of assembler language is constrained to be simple; interline syntax is especially restricted. Many assemblers make lexical analysis easier by using a fixed format that dictates that only certain types of token are permitted in certain locations.

Consider a language with many control structures and an extensive hierarchy of one-character operators, but allowing only one-character operands. An interpreter for this language would need a lexical analyzer hardly more intricate than a table lookup routine. Its syntax analyzer, however, would need to handle both complicated expressions and extensive interstatement syntax.

An APL interpreter, on the other hand, requires more lexical analysis and less syntactic analysis. The paucity of control structures simplifies the interstatement syntax; the positional hierarchy of operators (see Section 6.2.2) displays the syntactic structure in a form that permits almost direct execution. The use of overstruck characters imposes greater demands on the lexical analyzer. Compilers for languages like PASCAL or ADA normally require a moderate amount of lexical analysis followed by substantial syntactic analysis.

Although the requirements of various translators differ in extent, the nature of the lexical and syntactic analysis is much the same for all. We therefore discuss here the initial source language processing for translators in general rather than separately for each type of translator. We treat syntactic analysis first, in Section 6.2, because of its central importance to translation and for two other reasons. (1) Lexical analysis can apply concepts and techniques of syntactic analysis. (2) Some of the requirements on lexical analysis are imposed by syntactic analysis. Then, in Section 6.3, we examine lexical analysis. Because of the simple syntax of most assembler languages, Section 6.2 emphasizes machine-independent languages. Section 6.3, on the other hand, applies to all levels of language.

6.2 SYNTACTIC ANALYSIS

In this section we assume that lexical analysis of the source-language text has already been performed. The task at hand therefore is to determine the syntactic structure of a string of tokens. For this part of the translation process, unlike many others, a substantial body of highly developed theory guides our efforts. This theory is a formal mathematical development. It proceeds from axioms about languages, including computer languages, toward theorems that describe the properties of the languages and of algorithms for analyzing the languages syntactically. In this book, our view is not that of the pure mathematician who values the theorems for their intrinsic interest. It is rather that of the applied mathematician who uses the theorems to guide the engineering effort of implementing translators. Although the methods we describe are based on theorems, our most immediate debt to the theory will be the use of formalisms for the specification of syntax and the determination of syntactic structure.

6.2.1 Grammars and Parse Trees

Systematic generation of code or performance of actions, given arbitrary source-language text, is facilitated by a precise description of how the tokens of the language may be combined into program text. The standard formalism for providing such a description is a **grammar** for the language.

A grammar actually defines a language by specifying which symbols are used in writing the language and which strings of symbols are permitted in the language. Instead of enumerating the acceptable strings, whose number is typically unbounded, the grammar comprises four elements. One is the collection of symbols that are used in writing strings in the language. These symbols are called **terminal** symbols. Another element is a collection of **nonterminal** symbols used not in writing the language but in describing it. Each of these two nonempty collections, called a **vocabulary**, or "alphabet", is finite and includes no symbol in common with the other. Thus a grammar might have the terminal vocabulary {0,1} and the nonterminal vocabulary {a,b,s}. A third element of the grammar is a finite (and nonempty) set of rules.

The nature of the rules depends on the type of grammar. Programming languages are usually described by grammars of the type called **context-free**, and the remainder of this description is correct only for such grammars. Each rule specifies the replacement of a single nonterminal symbol by a finite (and nonempty) string of symbols, each of which may be either terminal or nonterminal. The replacement specified by a rule is optional rather than mandatory.

Thus one possible rule might specify that if the nonterminal symbol a appears in a string, it may be replaced by the string "11a". The fourth element of a grammar is the designation of one of the nonterminal symbols as the initial string from which other strings are generated by successive application of rules. Because this distinguished symbol is called the **start** symbol or **sentence** symbol, the letter s is often used, as in the following grammar:

1. $s \leftrightarrow a\, b$
2. $a \leftrightarrow 1\, 1$
3. $a \leftrightarrow 1\, 1\, a$
4. $b \leftrightarrow 0$
5. $b \leftrightarrow 0\, b$.

In representing a grammar, it is customary to use the notation called **Backus-Naur form** (BNF). Unfortunately, there are many variants of BNF in common use and the differences among them often tend to confuse readers. Our version is a variant of the one cogently recommended in Williams82. We shall refer to it as **SN**, for our Syntax Notation. Each rule of the grammar is written as a nonterminal symbol followed by "$\leftrightarrow$", then by the string of symbols (nonterminal and/or terminal) that replace the nonterminal, and optionally by a final period.

We shall enlist the aid of the typesetter in helping us to distinguish among nonterminal symbols, terminal symbols, and SN symbols. All nonterminal symbols are alphabetic and printed in slanted lightface font. Examples include a and *expression*. Any symbol printed in boldface font or in the monospace font introduced in Chapter 2 for assembler language is a terminal symbol. So are most other symbols. Examples include **procedure**, :=, and `STORE`.

SN symbols are few, and never include letters. We shall introduce them explicitly as the need arises. Whatever we choose to use as SN symbols could, of course, be used as terminal symbols in some language. When a possibility for confusion might exist, we enclose a terminal symbol, but never a SN symbol, in either single or double (but matching) quotation marks. An example is the plus sign, which is both a terminal symbol in many programming languages and a SN symbol. In the former role it appears as '+' or as "+" even when the context makes it clear that it cannot be the SN symbol.

The distinguished nonterminal symbol is the only symbol that does not appear in any string to the right of a double-ended arrow; therefore, it need not be designated explicitly. For convenience, however, we always begin the first rule with the distinguished nonterminal. The numbers written at the left are not part of the grammar; they are affixed for ease of reference.

The language defined by a grammar includes all strings and only those strings that comprise terminal symbols exclusively and are produced from the start symbol by a finite sequence of applications of rules of the grammar. The strings in the language defined by the foregoing grammar all consist of a positive even number of ones followed by a positive number of zeros. The string "110" is therefore in the language (and is in fact the shortest such string), whereas the string "0011" is not in the language. Although each string in this language is of finite length, the maximum possible length is unbounded, and the number of distinct strings in the language is unbounded.

The string "1111000" can be produced from s by application of rule 1, yielding "ab", then rule 3, yielding "11ab", then rule 5, yielding "11a0b", and finally rules 5 (a second time), 4, and 2. The sequence of rules 1,5,5,4,3,2 also serves, as do several others. Each such sequence is called a **derivation** of the string "1111000". For the string and grammar of this example, all derivations reflect the same structure, represented in Figure 6.2 as a tree. Each node corresponds to a symbol. The root node is the start symbol. Each nonterminal symbol node has as its descendants the symbols that replace it under application of a rule of the grammar. Each leaf node is a terminal symbol. The terminals from left to right constitute the string whose syntactic structure is represented by the tree.

Before looking at further examples of grammars, we present the remaining conventions of SN. The vertical stroke indicates alternation, as in the use of

$$letordig \;\leftrightarrow\; letter \mid digit$$

instead of the pair

$$letordig \;\leftrightarrow\; letter$$
$$letordig \;\leftrightarrow\; digit \,.$$

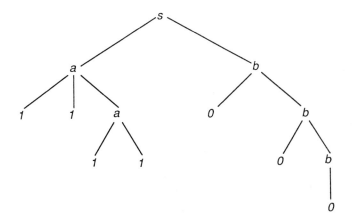

Figure 6.2   Derivation Tree for 1111000

The alternation symbol avoids repeated writing of the left-hand non-terminal and the ↔ symbol; it increases economy of expression, but does not increase the power of SN. Another such facility is provided by the pair of symbols for optional inclusion. A symbol string enclosed in square brackets may be included one time or zero times. An example is

  ifstmt ↔ **if** *condition* **then** *stmt* [**else** *stmt*]

instead of

  ifstmt ↔ **if** *condition* **then** *stmt* |
            if *condition* **then** *stmt* **else** *stmt* .

Parentheses indicate grouping, as in

  iostmt ↔ (**read** | **write**) '(' *identifier* ')' .

Observe the distinction between the two pairs of parentheses. The parentheses of the first pair are not enclosed in quotation marks. They are therefore the grouping symbols of SN, and indicate that either **read** or **write** may serve as the first symbol of the replacement string. The parentheses of the second pair do have enclosing quotation marks. Each of them is therefore a terminal symbol that appears in the replacement string.

Indefinite repetition is indicated by postfixing * or + to whatever symbol or group is repeated. The asterisk indicates zero or more occurrences and the plus sign indicates one or more occurrences. Thus an identifier might be defined by

> *identifier* ↔ *letter letordig*∗

instead of

> *identifier* ↔ *letter* | *identifier letordig* .

Although the second form makes the recursiveness of the definition explicit, the first is often more easily grasped. Similarly, a purely alphabetic identifier could be defined by

> *identifier* ↔ *letter*⁺ .

A final convention of SN provides that if a terminal symbol enclosed in quotation marks (of the same type) is itself a quotation mark, it is written twice.

We look now at three examples of the formal specification of the syntax of programming languages or portions of languages. The first example, presented in Figure 6.3, is limited to arithmetic expressions built from the identifiers X, Y, and Z by addition, multiplication, and grouping operators. The first rule defines an expression either as a term, or else as an expression followed by a plus sign and then by a term. The second alternative would by itself constitute a circular definition. Because of the first alternative, however, the second is in fact not circular. Substituting *term* for *expression* in the second alternative shows that an expression can denote the sum of two terms. Substituting the resulting "*term + term*" for *expression* in the second alternative yields "*term + term + term*" as a further possibility. We are thus led to the alternative specification of the first rule as *expression* ↔ *term* ('+' *term*)∗.

> *expression* ↔ *term* | *expression* '+' *term*
> *term* ↔ *factor* | *term* '∗' *factor*
> *factor* ↔ X | Y | Z | '(' *expression* ')'

Figure 6.3 A Syntax for Expressions

The second rule defines a term similarly as a product of factors. The third rule defines a factor either as one of the three identifiers or as an expression enclosed in parentheses. This last choice completes the circularity of the three rules as a group, and it may appear difficult to see where to begin. Nevertheless, by starting with the distinguished nonterminal *expression*, it is in fact possible to derive an expression. Proof is offered by the parse tree, shown in Figure 6.4, for the language string "(X+Y)*Z+X".

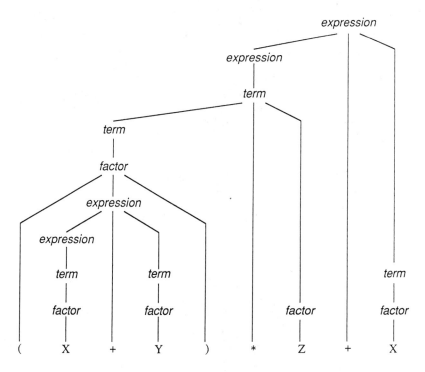

Figure 6.4 Parse Tree for (X+Y)*Z+X

The second example is the specification of a minilanguage. The grammar is presented in Figure 6.5, and Figure 6.6 shows a minilanguage program defined by the grammar. There are eight rules, of which the last uses ellipsis (technically not part of SN) to obviate writing 23 of the terminal symbols. The first rule defines a program as a sequence of statements joined by semicolons, much as the first rule of Figure 6.3 defines an expression as a sequence of terms joined by plus signs. There is, however, an important difference in the formulations of the two recursive alternatives

$$expression \quad \leftrightarrow \quad expression \ '+' \ term$$
$$program \quad \leftrightarrow \quad statement \ ; \ program \ .$$

In the first example, the repeated nonterminal *expression* appears as the leftmost symbol of the replacement string. In the second example, the repeated nonterminal *program* appears as the rightmost symbol of the replacement string. As we shall see, the distinction bears on the choice of parsing method. Moreover, the meaning of language strings is affected by the order of the nonterminal symbols if the joining terminal represents a nonassociative operator, such as subtraction.

$$
\begin{array}{rcl}
program & \leftrightarrow & statement \mid statement \ ; program \\
statement & \leftrightarrow & assignment \mid input/output \mid conditional \mid iterative \\
assignment & \leftrightarrow & identifier \leftarrow identifier \\
input/output & \leftrightarrow & (\ \textbf{read} \mid \textbf{write})\ \text{'('}\ identifier\ \text{')'} \\
conditional & \leftrightarrow & \textbf{if}\ condition\ \textbf{then}\ statement\ \textbf{else}\ statement \\
iterative & \leftrightarrow & \textbf{while}\ condition\ \textbf{do}\ statement \\
condition & \leftrightarrow & identifier\ (\ <\ \mid\ \le\ \mid\ \ge\ \mid\ >\ )\ identifier \\
identifier & \leftrightarrow & A \mid B \mid \ldots \mid Z
\end{array}
$$

Figure 6.5   Grammar for a Minilanguage

```
read (N);
read (X);
while X≥N do read (X);
read(Y);
while Y≥N do read (Y);
if X<Y then A←Y else A←X;
write (A)
```

Figure 6.6   A Minilanguage Program

The third example is a more complete language, the small subset of PASCAL defined in Figure 6.7. The two sets of rules in the figure together constitute a grammar that fully defines the language subset. The partition into two sets reflects a typical division of labor between syntactic and lexical analysis. Figure 6.7(a) is a grammar whose terminal symbols are either specific tokens, such as ':=' and **while,** or classes of tokens that represent identifiers or relations. The rules of Figure 6.7(b) define those two classes, and are easily embodied in a lexical analyzer. The lexical rules do not constitute a grammar, because there is no unique distinguished nonterminal.

program	↔	**var** *decllist* ; *cmpdstmt* '.'
decllist	↔	*declaration* | *declaration* ; *decllist*
declaration	↔	IDENTIFIER : *type*
type	↔	**boolean** | **char** | **integer** | **real**
cmpdstmt	↔	**begin** *stmtlist* **end**
stmtlist	↔	*stmt* | *stmt* ; *stmtlist*
stmt	↔	*simplstmt* | *structstmt*
simplstmt	↔	*assignstmt* | *iostmt*
assignstmt	↔	IDENTIFIER := *expression*
expression	↔	*expression* '+' *term* | *term*
term	↔	*term* '*' *factor* | *factor*
factor	↔	'(' *expression* ')' | IDENTIFIER
iostmt	↔	(**read** | **write**) '(' IDENTIFIER ')'
structstmt	↔	*cmpdstmt* | *ifstmt* | *whilestmt*
ifstmt	↔	**if** *condition* **then** *stmt* [**else** *stmt*]
whilestmt	↔	**while** *condition* **do** *stmt*
condition	↔	*expression* RELATION *expression*

(a) Syntactic rules

IDENTIFIER	↔	*letter* (*letter* | *digit*)*
letter	↔	A | B | ... | Z
digit	↔	0 | 1 | ... | 9
RELATION	↔	< | ≤ | = | ≠ | ≥ | >

(b) Lexical rules

Figure 6.7 Two-Part Grammar for PASCAL Subset

We have distinguished IDENTIFIER and RELATION typographically from the other terminal and nonterminal symbols. In the full grammar, IDENTIFIER and RELATION are nonterminals; in the subset grammar of Figure 6.7(a) they are terminals. To indicate their dual role we call them **semiterminals**.

A grammar may serve either of two purposes. One is to produce strings in the language by the process of **generation**. In generation, we think of the single nonterminal symbol as producing the string of symbols that replaces it. Because of this productive role, rules of the grammar are commonly termed **productions**. The other purpose for a grammar is to determine whether a given string is in the language and, if so, what its structure is. The acceptance or rejection of the string as a member of the language is called **recognition**. The determination of its structure, if it is in the language, is called **parsing**. Even if a source-language program contains syntactic errors, merely signaling that fact is not very helpful to the programmer. More helpful is parsing to determine how much of the program is correct and where the errors lie. For that reason, recognition alone is not attempted during program translation. Parsing is always undertaken instead.

We can think of the process as a reconstruction of the derivation tree given only the leaf nodes and the grammar. In this process, the rules of the grammar may be applied in the direction from replacement string to single nonterminal symbol. Because a rule so used reduces the string to a single symbol, we shall (following Wegner68) term it in this context a **reduction** rather than a production. Our choice of the symmetric symbol $\leftrightarrow$ is intended to reinforce the concept of symmetry between production and reduction.

A programming-language parser can usually rely on a lexical analyzer to reduce character strings to identifiers, constants, reserved words, and operator symbols. The task of parsing is to apply a grammar pretty much like that of Figure 6.7(a) to a source-language program and determine the tree that represents its syntactic structure. Even though not every parser describes the tree directly, the output of any parser must at least reflect it indirectly.

A vast body of knowledge has been developed about parsing programs; the literature is replete with parsing methods. They can be divided into two major classes, whose names indicate the direction followed in constructing the parse tree. **Top-down** parsing starts from the distinguished symbol at the root, which is customarily found (in computer science if not in nature) at the top. It proceeds downward to the string of terminals at the leaves, applying productions of the grammar by substituting strings for single nonterminals. Application of these productions yields intermediate strings composed of both nonterminals and terminals. At each stage, these strings are compared with the known goal (the string of terminals to be parsed), to select the production to apply next. **Bottom-up** parsing, on the other hand, starts from the terminals at the leaves and proceeds upward to the root. It applies reductions of the grammar, substituting single nonterminals for strings. The intermediate strings are compared at each stage with the terminals of the original string, to select the reduction to apply next.

Our primary purpose in this book is not to provide detailed treatment of the major top-down and bottom-up parsing methods. We are concerned rather with exploring the role that parsing plays in the translation process, with understanding, for example, how to harness a parser for service in a compiler. This endeavor does, however, demand familiarity with at least one parsing method. We have chosen to examine two: recursive descent, a top-down method; and operator precedence, a bottom-up method. A grammar for any reasonable machine-independent language is either suitable for recursive descent, or can be rather easily modified to become suitable. Although the algorithm may be slow, it is particularly easy to program, and the translator writer in a hurry can always fall back on recursive descent. Operator precedence is not applicable to all grammars, but it is especially appropriate for evaluating expressions even if the rest of the language is not suitable. It illustrates, perhaps better than does recursive descent, the role of theory in parser design.

Our choice of operator precedence and recursive descent to illustrate parsing methods is not intended to suggest that they are necessarily superior to other methods. A great variety of parsing techniques exist; the two presented here do permit the casual writer of translators to program an effective parser. Further study of parsing methods is highly desirable for anyone planning to undertake a production compiler.

In examining the two parsing methods, we shall concentrate here upon the determination of syntactic structure rather than upon its representation. The choice of representation is important, however, to the subsequent stages of translation, and will be considered more fully in Chapter 7.

6.2.2 Expressions and Precedence

Before defining operator precedence formally, we review informally some intuitive notions about precedence. The simplest context in which to do this is the evaluation of arithmetic expressions, and we begin with a few definitions.

An **operator** in a programming language can be characterized informally as a token that specifies an operation of function evaluation. An **operand** is a token that specifies a value, either literally (as a constant) or indirectly (as an identifier). An **expression** is a sequence of operands, operators, and perhaps grouping indicators (often parentheses), formed according to certain syntactic rules. Each expression is associated with a value that is determined by the values of its operands, the functions specified by its operators, and the sequence in which the latter are applied to values of their arguments. Note that a function can have as an argument either an operand or an expression, and that an operand may be either a constant or an identifier.

The number of arguments required by a function is called its **degree**. Addition is a function of degree 2, hence termed **binary** or **dyadic**. The absolute value function is of degree 1, hence termed **unary** or **monadic**. It is common to apply these terms, by extension, to the operators that represent the functions. We thus speak of the addition operator as being binary.

Because programming-language text is almost invariably one-dimensional, there are three ways to place a binary operator relative to its arguments. Each leads to a notational convention whose name reflects the placement of the operator. In **prefix** notation the operator precedes both arguments, in **postfix** notation it follows both arguments, and in **infix** notation it stands between its arguments. Using one-character source-language tokens for clarity, we can represent the subtraction of B from A as follows.

$$\begin{array}{ll} \text{prefix} & -AB \\ \text{infix} & A-B \\ \text{postfix} & AB- \end{array}$$

If the operator is unary, it precedes its argument in prefix notation and follows its argument in postfix notation. In infix notation, a symmetric choice is available; convention decrees that a unary infix operator precede its argument. Prefix and postfix notations are often called **Polish** notations, after the logician Jan Lukasiewicz, who introduced the former. Postfix is often called **reverse** Polish. Prefix, infix, and postfix notations are generated by the preorder, inorder, and postorder traversals, respectively, of a binary tree whose nodes represent the operators in an expression and whose subtrees represent its operands.

Prefix notation has the advantage of corresponding most closely to traditional mathematics. There the result of applying function f to arguments a and b is typically written $f(a,b)$, and functional composition is written as in $f(h(x))$. The Polish notations accommodate more than two arguments, which infix does not. Infix has nevertheless been adopted for virtually all procedural languages, because it is so very familiar. If more than two arguments are needed, the language can either (as in APL) disguise several arguments as one, or else (as in many other languages) permit excursions into prefix notation. We limit the present discussion to unary and binary operators, because the principal arithmetic and logical operators have degree two or less.

It is necessary, of course, to distinguish whether an operator is unary or binary. Sometimes the distinction is purely lexical. The FORTRAN token * (when it serves as an operator) is always binary. For other tokens, such as | in APL or − in PASCAL, the distinction is syntactic. The infix notation of source language makes it easy to distinguish unary from binary. If the operator has a left argument, it is binary; if not, it is unary. Although this determination requires syntactic analysis, the degree of analysis is so slight that it can be easily performed as an adjunct to lexical analysis. If an operator is preceded by a left parenthesis or by another operator, it is unary; otherwise it is binary.

Expressions such as those defined by the grammar of Figure 6.3 can be evaluated in a single left-to-right scan, with the use of two stacks. An operator stack holds the arithmetic and grouping operators; an operand stack holds identifier values and intermediate results. During the scan, each time an identifier is encountered, its value is pushed onto the operand stack. Each time a left parenthesis is encountered, it is pushed onto the operator stack. Each time an addition operator is encountered, it is pushed onto the operator stack. Before the operator is pushed, however, the topmost token on the operator stack is examined. If that token is a + or *, then the operation that it represents is performed before the stacking occurs. This operation is performed upon the topmost two values on the operand stack. They are popped, and are replaced by the value that results from performing the operation. The operator token that indicated the operation is then popped before the incoming addition operator token is stacked.

Similar processing is performed for each multiplication operator encountered, except that only a * already on top of the operator stack has its operation performed and symbol popped before the incoming operator is stacked. Whenever a right parenthesis is encountered, the topmost token on the operator stack has its operation performed and is popped in turn. This action is repeated until a left parenthesis is found. The two matching parentheses are then discarded. This evaluation process, which might be performed in an interpreter, is very efficient. Figure 6.8(a) shows twelve successive stages in the evaluation of (X+Y)*Z+X. The values of X, Y, and Z are taken to be 1.5, 2.5, and 2, respectively.

What governs the order in which the operators are applied? It is really the priority or **precedence** of the different occurrences of operators. This precedence has two aspects, **inherent** and **positional**. In the language we are now parsing, multiplication has inherent precedence over addition because in either X+Y*Z or X*Y+Z the multiplication is to be performed first. Two occurrences of the same operator, on the other hand, are to be applied in the positional left-to-right order. Both the inherent and the positional precedence are reflected in the grammar of Figure 6.3. In fact, the precedence rules were selected first, and the grammar built to suit.

The precedence rules embodied in the grammar can be represented conveniently by a **precedence function** F, which assigns to each operator a numerical precedence. The precedence of the left parenthesis is lower than that of any operator. A precedence lower yet than that of the left parenthesis is assigned to a dummy operator token '$'. We can think of that token as affixed to the left of the string to be parsed. Another dummy token '#' is affixed to the right of the string. For the grammar of Figure 6.3, suitable values of F would be 3 for multiplication, 2 for addition, 1 for the left parenthesis, and 0 for the $ token.

The precedence function is readily embodied in the straightforward algorithm for expression evaluation presented in Figure 6.9. To save space in this and subsequent programs, we omit the enclosing **begin** and **end**. Two stacks are used, one for operators and one for operands. The dummy token $ is stacked automatically at the outset; it is not physically present in the input string, unlike the # end marker. Left parentheses and operands are always stacked. A right parenthesis is never stacked; it causes the matching left parenthesis to be discarded, after first directing the intervening operator(s) to

Stage	Stack of operators	Current token	Stack of values	Stack of tokens	Code generated for operator
1.	*empty*	(	*empty*	*empty*	
2.	(	X	*empty*	*empty*	
3.	(	+	1.5	X	
4.	+ (	Y	1.5	X	
5.	+ (	)	2.5 1.5	Y X	
6.	*empty*	*	4	TEMP1	LOAD X ADD Y STORE TEMP1
7.	*	Z	4	TEMP1	
8.	*	+	2 4	Z TEMP1	
9.	*empty*	+	8	TEMP2	LOAD TEMP1 MULT Z STORE TEMP2
10.	+	X	8	TEMP2	
11.	+	*none*	1.5 8	X TEMP2	
12.	*empty*	*none*	9.5	TEMP3	LOAD TEMP2 ADD X STORE TEMP3

(a) Evaluation   (b) Code generation

Figure 6.8   Syntactic Analysis of Expression (X+Y)*Z+X

be applied. An operator is stacked only after operators of higher precedence at the top of the stack have been applied. Upon termination, the value of the expression remains the sole element on the operand stack.

A slight modification results not in evaluating the expression, but in generating code to perform the evaluation. Such would be the function of a compiler. Instead of stacking values of operands, the compiler stacks their tokens. On encountering an operator of degree

```
procedure EVAL real
    boolean more {more operators are to be applied}
    opstack ← empty {operator stack}
    valstack ← empty {value stack}
    PUSH '$' onto opstack
    read token from input
    do forever
        case token of
            value:      PUSH value of token onto valstack
                        read token from input
            '(':        PUSH token onto opstack
                        read token from input
            operator:   more ← true
                        while more do
                            if F(opstack[top]) < F(token)
                                then PUSH token onto opstack
                                     more ← false
                                     read token from input
                                else APPLY
            ')':        more ← true
                        while more do
                            if opstack[top] = '('
                                then POP opstack
                                     more ← false
                                     read token from input
                                else APPLY
            '#':        while opstack[top] ≠ '$' do APPLY od
                        return valstack[top]


procedure APPLY
    POP opstack to operator
    k ← degree of operator
    POP k values from valstack to value[1..k]
    apply operator to value[1..k] yielding result
    PUSH result onto valstack
```

Figure 6.9   Evaluation of Infix Expression

k, it generates code that embodies the topmost k operand tokens. New tokens are created to represent temporary results. Figure 6.8(b) shows instructions, in the assembler language of Section 2.1, that could be generated in this fashion.

Operators having equal inherent precedence are assigned a positional precedence by the algorithm. For associative operators, it might appear immaterial whether the precedence decreases from left to right or from right to left. The two resulting directions of evaluation are shown in Figure 6.10 for integer addition, and yield the same result. Note, however, that the two parse trees differ. The addition of floating-point numbers is not associative; the parser and the programmer should agree on the desired sequence. In deriving a parse tree, rather than only evaluating an expression, it is important to conform to the grammar, even for associative operators.

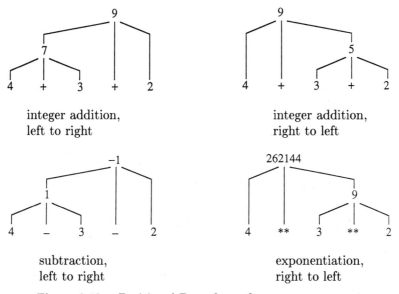

integer addition,
left to right

integer addition,
right to left

subtraction,
left to right

exponentiation,
right to left

Figure 6.10   Positional Precedence for
Associative and Nonassociative Operators

For nonassociative operators, the algorithm of Figure 6.9 assigns positional precedence that decreases from left to right. This is correct for operators such as subtraction in PASCAL or C, but not for others such as exponentiation (see Figure 6.10). The use of *two* precedence functions provides a simple cure. One function (F) is applied to operators already on the stack; the other (G) is applied to those not yet stacked. The use of such **double precedence** functions entails a small change in the program of Figure 6.9. The condition

$$F(opstack[top]) < F(token)$$

is replaced instead by

$$F(opstack[top]) < G(token).$$

The following double precedence functions are adequate for addition, subtraction, multiplication, division, and exponentiation in PL/I (*cf.* Problem 6.7).

	\$	(	+	−	*	/	**
F	0	1	2	2	3	3	4
G			2	2	3	3	5

We might observe here that APL does away very neatly with all of these problems. There is no inherent precedence among operators, except for parentheses, and positional precedence increases from left to right for all operators.

6.2.3 Operator Precedence Parsing

Let us now return to the algorithm for parsing expressions. Examine the parse tree of Figure 6.4. No fewer than 14 reductions are represented, yet the structural information important to translation is entirely contained in the order of performance of only three of them. The reduction of "*expression + term*" to *expression* at the left side of the tree occurs before "*term * factor*" can be reduced to *term*. This second reduction must occur before the remaining reduction of "*expression + term*" to *expression*. It is not important even to what nonterminal symbol those reductions are made, nor to what nonterminals the identifiers are reduced. It is important only to know that "X+Y" is reduced to some nonterminal, which we can designate *temp1*; that "*temp1*Z*" is later reduced to a nonterminal, say *temp2*; and that "*temp2*+X" is finally reduced to a nonterminal. A wholly adequate parse tree, therefore, is that of Figure 6.11, which depicts only eight reductions. The different nonterminals, no longer differentiated, are all represented as *n*.

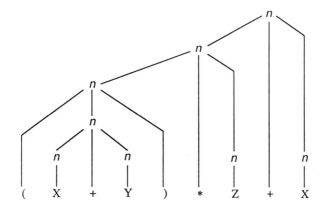

Figure 6.11   Simplified Parse Tree for (X+Y)*Z+X

Let us see how such a simplified parse might be produced. Assume that we can tell, by inspection only of terminal symbols (which we continue to differentiate from each other) when it is time to apply a reduction. We shall shortly describe conditions that justify this assumption. A single left-to-right scan of the source text suffices, together with the use of a single stack that holds both terminal and nonterminal symbols. Each symbol of source text is examined and compared with the stack contents, and one of two actions taken. One action is to **shift** by pushing the incoming symbol onto the stack. The other action is to **reduce** one or more topmost stack symbols, replacing them on the stack by the nonterminal symbol. After reducing, parsing continues by comparing the new stack content with the same source symbol. After shifting, parsing continues by examining the next source symbol. A parser that uses these actions is called a **shift/reduce** parser. The desired sequence of decisions for parsing (X+Y)*Z+X is presented in Figure 6.12, where "reduce k" signifies the reduction of the k topmost stack symbols. The stack is shown at each stage with its top at the right.

The decision whether to shift or reduce is governed by comparison of the topmost terminal on the stack with the source-text terminal currently being examined. For example, if the current symbol is ')' the choice is always to reduce unless the topmost terminal is '('. If the current symbol is +, then an identifier or ')' as topmost terminal calls for reduction, whereas '(' calls for shifting. We have already encountered a very similar algorithm in Figure 6.9. If the decision is to reduce, it must be determined further *how many* symbols are to be reduced. We shall now investigate the conditions that permit this determination, as well as the prior shift/reduce decision, by returning to the underlying grammar.

Stage	Stack content	Current symbol	Remaining string	Shift/reduce decision
1.	*empty*	(	X+Y)*Z+X	shift
2.	(	X	+Y)*Z+X	shift
3.	(X	+	Y)*Z+X	reduce 1
4.	(*n*	+	Y)*Z+X	shift
5.	(*n*+	Y	)*Z+X	shift
6.	(*n*+Y	)	*Z+X	reduce 1
7.	(*n*+*n*	)	*Z+X	reduce 3
8.	(*n*	)	*Z+X	shift
9.	(*n*)	*	Z+X	reduce 3
10.	*n*	*	Z+X	shift
11.	*n**	Z	+X	shift
12.	*n**Z	+	X	reduce 1
13.	*n**n	+	X	reduce 3
14.	*n*	+	X	shift
15.	*n*+	X		shift
16.	*n*+X	*none*		reduce 1
17.	*n*+*n*	*none*		reduce 3
18.	*n*	*none*		

Figure 6.12   Parsing Sequence for (X+Y)*Z+X

An **operator grammar** is one in which no rule has the form $a \leftrightarrow ..bc..$, where b and c are both nonterminals. It can be shown that this restriction guarantees that no string in the language contains two adjacent nonterminals, nor does any intermediate stage in the generation or parsing of a string. The terminology is presumably due to equating "operator" with "terminal". Although this is an oversimplification, the standard designation "operator grammar" cannot well be avoided. The grammars of Figures 6.3, 6.5, and 6.7(a) are all operator grammars.

Between any two terminals of an operator grammar, one or more of three important **precedence relations** may hold. Let **L** and **R** be any two terminals of an operator grammar. It is convenient to think of them as the left and right members of a pair of successive terminals, either in the source text or in the text produced from the source text by applying reductions. The relations $<$, $\doteq$, and $>$ can be defined informally as follows, where a, b, and c are arbitrary nonterminals, which may or may not be distinct.

(1) The relation $\mathbf{L} < \mathbf{R}$ holds if there exist a rule $a \leftrightarrow .. \, \mathbf{L}c \, .. $ and a derivation from c of a string whose leftmost terminal is $\mathbf{R}$. The relation is diagrammed in Figure 6.13(a). We wish to reduce $\mathbf{R}^*$ and succeeding symbols to c before reducing $\mathbf{L}c$.

(2) The relation $\mathbf{L} \doteq \mathbf{R}$ holds if there exists a rule $a \leftrightarrow .. \, \mathbf{LR} \, ..$ or $a \leftrightarrow .. \, \mathbf{L}b\mathbf{R} \, .. \, $. The relation is diagrammed in Figure 6.13(b). We wish to reduce $\mathbf{LR}$ (or $\mathbf{L}b\mathbf{R}$) and surrounding symbols.

(3) The relation $\mathbf{L} \cdot\!> \mathbf{R}$ holds if there exist a rule $a \leftrightarrow .. \, b\mathbf{R}..$ and a derivation from b of a string whose rightmost terminal is $\mathbf{L}$. The relation is diagrammed in Figure 6.13(c). We wish to reduce $\mathbf{L}^*$ and preceding symbols to b before reducing $b\mathbf{R}$.

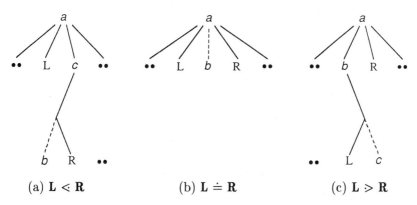

(a) $\mathbf{L} < \mathbf{R}$ (b) $\mathbf{L} \doteq \mathbf{R}$ (c) $\mathbf{L} > \mathbf{R}$

Figure 6.13   Relations in an Operator Grammar

Let us apply the foregoing definitions to the grammar of Figure 6.3, which is readily seen to be an operator grammar. From the rule

---

*Under case (1), if the string derived from c begins with the nonterminal b, we wish to reduce $b\mathbf{R}$ and succeeding symbols. Similarly, under case (3), if the string derived from b ends with the nonterminal c, we wish to reduce $\mathbf{L}c$ and preceding symbols.

expression ↔ *expression* + *term* and the derivation (by a single rule) of *term* * *factor* from *term*, it follows that + <· *. The rule *factor* ↔ '(' *expression* ')' ensures by itself that '(' ≐ ')'. Because it is the only rule with two terminals on its right-hand side, no other pair of terminals can stand in the precedence relation ≐. From that same rule and the further derivation of *expression* + *term* from *expression*, it follows that + ·> ')'.

The use of the arithmetic relation symbols in + <· * reflects the fact that + has lower precedence than * in this grammar. Do not be misled by the choice of symbols, however, into believing that **L** ·> **R** implies **R** <· **L**, or conversely. In particular, it does *not* hold in this grammar for + and ')'.

It may be the case for an operator grammar that an arbitrary ordered pair of terminals stands in at most one of the three precedence relations. If so, that grammar is an **operator precedence grammar**. The grammar of Figure 6.3 is such a grammar; the precedence relation (if any) in which each pair of terminals stands is shown in the **precedence matrix** of Figure 6.14. Blank entries in the table indicate that the sequence **L R** (or **L***b***R**) cannot occur in a legal string or during the reduction of a legal string.

		+	*	(	)	X	Y	Z
	+	·>	<·	<·	·>	<·	<·	<·
	*	·>	·>	<·	·>	<·	<·	<·
	(	<·	<·	<·	≐	<·	<·	<·
L	)	·>	·>		·>			
	X	·>	·>		·>			
	Y	·>	·>		·>			
	Z	·>	·>		·>			

R (column group header)

Figure 6.14 Precedence Matrix for Grammar of Figure 6.3

We can now illustrate the application of the relations tabulated in Figure 6.14 to the parse given in Figure 6.12. If the topmost terminal stands in the relation <· or the relation ≐ to the current symbol, then the current symbol is shifted onto the stack. If the topmost terminal stands in the relation ·> to the current symbol, then one or more stack symbols are reduced. The relations that hold between successive pairs of terminals on the stack determine how many symbols are to be reduced. Suppose, for example, that there are five terminals on the stack, **t5** at the top, preceded by **t4** through **t1**, and that the current token is **t6**. Let the following relations hold between successive terminals.

$$t5 > t6$$
$$t4 \doteq t5$$
$$t3 \doteq t4$$
$$t2 < t3$$
$$t1 < t2$$

The notation

$$t1 < t2 < t3 \doteq t4 \doteq t5 > t6$$

summarizes the relations in a particularly convenient form. The symbols to be reduced include all terminals starting from the top of the stack and continuing until the first < is encountered. These are precisely the terminals enclosed by the < > pair, which we can think of as bracketing the string to be reduced. In the example, terminals **t3**, **t4**, and **t5** are in that string. Moreover, any nonterminals adjacent to any of those terminals are also included. Thus the string to be reduced includes all nonterminal and terminal symbols between **t2** and **t6**. Figure 6.15 shows how the relations are used at stages 5–9 in the parse, both to make the shift/reduce decision and to determine how many symbols need to be reduced. Each relation is written beneath the position between its left and right arguments. The last step in Figure 6.15 illustrates the need for adjoining the dummy terminal $ that stands in the relation < to all other terminals.

The syntactic structure information that the operator precedence parser develops must be used as it is produced. This is because by the end of the parse nothing is left except a single nonterminal. Although it is possible to build the parse tree explicitly, it is usually more convenient to perform instead some of the actions that depend on the syntactic structure. In a compiler, for example, the ensuing semantic processing, although conceptually distinct from syntactic analysis, is often performed in conjunction with parsing. To accomplish this, the parser may invoke a so-called **semantic routine** whenever it performs a reduction.

5. stack & current symbol $ (n +   Y
    terminal symbols $ (+   Y
    relations   <   <   <
    decision   shift   Y

6. stack & current symbol $ (n + Y   )
    terminal symbols $ (+   Y   )
    relations   <   <   <   >
    decision   reduce   Y

7. stack & current symbol $ (n + n   )
    terminal symbols $ (+   )
    relations   <   <   >
    decision   reduce   n + n

8. stack & current symbol $ (n   )
    terminal symbols $ (   )
    relations   <   ≐
    decision   shift   )

9. stack & current symbol $ (n)   *
    terminal symbols $ ( )   *
    relations   <   ≐   >
    decision   reduce   (n)

Figure 6.15   Details of Operator Precedence Parsing

What action would these routines take for the simple grammar of Figure 6.3? When an identifier is reduced to n, the identifier (in a generator) or its value (in an interpreter) is pushed onto an operand stack. When $n+n$ is reduced to n, an interpreter pops the topmost two operand values, adds them, and pushes the sum on the stack. Such interpretation might well be performed by an assembler evaluating an address expression. A generator uses the topmost two operand stack entries in producing code to perform the addition. It replaces them with a reference to the temporary variable that represents their sum. This code is often not yet ready to be executed, but rather is in one of the intermediate forms described in Section 7.2. Similar actions are performed when $n*n$ is reduced to n. The easiest reduction of all is that of (n) to n; no action is required.

So far we have considered operator precedence parsing only for expressions. The technique can be applied to richer languages as well. The minilanguage grammar of Figure 6.5 is also an operator precedence grammar; its precedence matrix is shown in Figure 6.16. Verifying the operator precedence property by hand is exceptionally tedious, even for such a small grammar. Fortunately, the process is readily mechanized.

	;	←	read	write	(	)	if	then	else	while	do	<	≤	≥	>	A..Z
;	<	<	<	<	<		<			<						<
←	>						>	>								<
read					≐											
write					≐											
(						≐										<
)	>						>	>								
if		<	<	<	<			≐		<		<	<	<	<	<
then		<	<	<	<				≐	<						<
else	>	<	<	<	<		>	>		<						<
while											≐	<	<	<	<	<
do	>	<	<	<	<		>	>		<						<
<															>	<
≤															>	<
≥															>	<
>															>	<
A..Z	>	>					>	>	>			>	>	>	>	>

Figure 6.16   Precedence Matrix for the Minilanguage Grammar

For a big grammar, the precedence matrix can be inconveniently large. A more compact representation of the relations between terminals can be given by a pair of precedence functions F and G so constructed that $F(\mathbf{L}) < G(\mathbf{R})$ if $\mathbf{L} < \mathbf{R}$ and similarly for the other two precedence relations. Unfortunately, there are precedence matrices for which suitable double precedence functions do not exist. For most procedural languages representable by operator precedence grammars, however, the construction of double precedence functions is possible.

The operator grammar for the subset of PASCAL defined in Figure 6.7 does not have the operator precedence property. In particular, the relations ; < ; and ; > ; both hold. This does not mean, however, that operator precedence parsing is totally inapplicable if the grammar as a whole is not an operator precedence grammar. One approach is to use operator precedence to parse a subset that does have the operator precedence property (e.g., expressions in the

PASCAL grammar), and to use a different method for the rest of the grammar. Another approach is to supplement an operator precedence parser with special routines to resolve the cases in which more than one precedence relation holds. A third approach is to subdivide the grammar into multiple smaller grammars each of which is an operator precedence grammar. Yet a fourth approach is to rewrite the given grammar as an operator precedence grammar that generates the same language. Although there is no guarantee that any of these approaches is applicable in a particular situation, often one of them can indeed be used to enable parsing by this simple and efficient method.

6.2.4 Recursive Descent Parsing

A straightforward top-down parsing method is that of **recursive descent**. The analysis descends from the start symbol at the root of the parse tree to the program text whose tokens lie at the leaves. Each terminal symbol is recognized by the lexical scanner. Each nonterminal symbol is recognized by a procedure that attempts to recognize the symbols in the right-hand side of a production associated with that nonterminal. Because nonterminals can appear in the right-hand sides of each other's productions, the procedures for recognizing nonterminals are recursive.

A stack of symbols is not maintained explicitly; the information is implicit in the stack of activation records for the procedure calls. The procedures need no local variables and can communicate without parameters by sharing a single global variable. Local variables may well prove convenient, however, for holding attributes of symbols.

In designing the procedures for a recursive descent analyzer, it is often helpful to express the rules of the grammar by **syntax diagrams**. Consider the grammar of Pascal in Figure 6.7(a). The distinguished symbol is *program* and the first procedure to be invoked has as its object the recognition of *program*. The procedure looks in turn for the terminal **var**, a nonterminal *decllist*, the terminal ';', a nonterminal *cmpdstmt*, and finally the terminal '.'. This is symbolized by the following syntax diagram, which can be written directly from the right-hand side of the production for *program*. Rectangular boxes enclose nonterminals and rounded boxes enclose terminals.

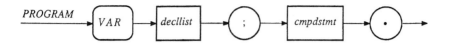

The syntax diagram for *decllist* can also be written directly from its production.

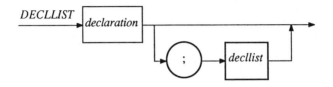

The alternation (symbolized by | in SN) is represented as a choice of paths in the syntax diagram.

The recursive recognition of *decllist* can be portrayed more graphically by directing the flow back to the start of the diagram. This modification yields the following syntax diagram.

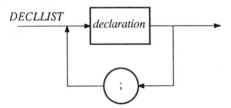

We can make the recursive nature of the production more obvious in SN, too. We can rewrite the rule to match the second syntax diagram directly.

$$decllist \leftrightarrow declaration \ (\ ; \ declaration \ )*$$

A problem should be evident at this point. Does the semicolon that follows an instance of *declaration* presage another instance of *declaration* or an instance of *cmpdstmt*? Substitution of the syntax diagram for *decllist* in place of the box enclosing *decllist* in the syntax diagram for *program* illustrates the problem.

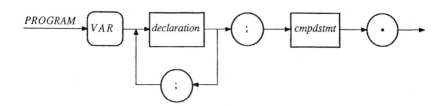

The direction of flow is nondeterministic. Two approaches to the problem suggest themselves. One is to guess at a direction and record the point in the analysis at which the guess is made. If the analysis fails at a later stage, we assume that the guess was incorrect, and employ backtracking to restart from the decision point in a different direction. This approach can always be taken, but may result in often repeating parts of the analysis. The time required to parse a program in this manner can grow as rapidly as exponentially with the length of the program. The designation "recursive descent" is normally withheld from backtrack parsers.

A more satisfactory approach, which is usually possible with procedural languages, is to rewrite the grammar to avoid choices among nonterminals. Because *cmpdstmt* always has **begin** as its first token whereas *declaration* never does, the following revision offers a deterministic choice that eliminates the need to backtrack.

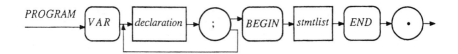

After a semicolon is recognized, the next terminal is scanned to determine whether it is **begin**. If not, it is presumably the first terminal of a declaration. This means that in attempting to recognize a declaration that follows a semicolon we must assume that its first terminal has already been found. Suppose that a single procedure is to recognize a declaration, whether preceded by **var** or by a semicolon. Then the assumption that the first terminal has been found must be made independently of whether the call to the procedure follows the recognition of **var** or of a semicolon. For uniformity, then, *all* of the recognition procedures expect upon entry that the one global variable *token* holds the first terminal symbol of the un-recognized portion of the source program. Similarly, they also ensure that, before exit, the next terminal symbol is placed in *token* for use in subsequent processing.

Any production of the grammar can be recast as a procedure to recognize the single nonterminal on its left-hand side. The recognition procedure for *declaration* is shown in Figure 6.17. We do not need to know here what the procedure *ERROR* does. It may perform any action from merely printing an error message to terminating the parse. The procedure *SCANNER* finds the next terminal symbol of the string being parsed and assigns it as the value of the identifier named as the parameter.

> **procedure** *DECLARATION*
> **if** *token* $\neq$ IDENTIFIER **then** *ERROR*
> *SCANNER* (*token*)
> **if** *token* $\neq$ ':' **then** *ERROR*
> *SCANNER* (*token*)
> *TYPE*

Figure 6.17   Procedure to Recognize *declaration*

Even simpler than the translation of a production into a recognition procedure is the translation of a syntax diagram into a recognition procedure. Each rectangular box becomes a call to another procedure to recognize the enclosed nonterminal; each rounded box becomes a test for the enclosed terminal. The recognition procedure based on the most recent syntax diagram for *program* is shown in Figure 6.18. Because that procedure is the first recognition procedure to be invoked in the recursive descent, we must make provision for reading the first token into *token*. Either *PROGRAM* must begin exceptionally with a call of *SCANNER*, or the invocation of *PROGRAM* must be preceded by such a call. We adopt the latter convention.

The productions for *stmt*, *simplstmt*, and *structstmt* appear to present a choice among several nonterminals. The grammar can be written, however, to recast the choice among the terminals IDEN-TIFIER, **read**, **write**, **begin**, **if**, and **while**. Even if IDENTIFIER were not a terminal of the grammar, the choice would be deterministic. To avoid nondeterminism it is necessary only that $n-1$ of n choices

procedure *PROGRAM*
   if *token* ≠ 'var' **then** *ERROR*
   SCANNER (*token*)
   repeat
      DECLARATION
      if *token* ≠ ';' **then** *ERROR*
      SCANNER (*token*)
   until *token* = 'begin'
   SCANNER (*token*)
   STMTLIST
   if *token* ≠ 'end' **then** *ERROR*
   SCANNER (*token*)
   if *token* ≠ '.' **then** *ERROR*
   SCANNER (*token*)
   if *token* ≠ **empty then** *ERROR*

Figure 6.18 Procedure to Recognize *program*

be introduced by a terminal. If none of those terminals is recognized, the nth direction is chosen. It is required, of course, that none of the $n-1$ terminals can be derived, as the first token, from the nonterminal that introduces the nth choice.

One of the attractions of recursive descent is that the grammar need not be highly constrained, as for operator precedence. There is, however, one important restriction, illustrated by the production for *expression* in Figure 6.7(a). An attempt to create a syntax diagram leads to the following impasse.

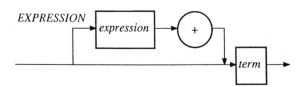

Substitution of the entire diagram for the box enclosing *expression* leads to an infinite regression of diagrams. Replacement of the box by an arrow to the beginning leads nowhere. The problem is caused by the leftmost symbol on the right-hand side of the production being the same as the nonterminal on the left-hand side. This occurrence is known as **direct left recursion**, and renders recursive descent unworkable. Even more insidious is **general left recursion**, in which the application of a sequence of productions may eventually, not just immediately, yield a string whose leftmost symbol is the same as the original nonterminal. It is possible to test a grammar for general left recursion, but difficult to eliminate it. Direct left recursion, on the other hand, is tractable. One attack is to write productions using right recursion rather than left recursion. An example is our choice of

$$decllist \quad \leftrightarrow \quad declaration \mid declaration \; ; decllist$$

rather than the equivalent

$$decllist \quad \leftrightarrow \quad declaration \mid decllist \; ; declaration$$

in writing the grammar of Figure 6.7(a). The substitution of right recursion for left is not always possible, however, because it changes the meaning of nonassociative operators. An alternative attack is to express the repetition directly, as in

$$expression \quad \leftrightarrow \quad term \; (\; '+' \; term \;)^*$$
$$term \quad \leftrightarrow \quad factor \; (\; '*' \; factor \;)^*$$

which lead easily to recognition procedures.

Let us not lose sight of the purpose of the syntactic analysis. How can we combine semantic routines with recognition by recursive descent? As in discussing operator precedence we postpone the details of semantic processing to Chapter 8; here we examine the parsing of expressions only. The procedure for recognizing *term* might be written as *TERM* in Figure 6.19. A call to a semantic routine would be inserted within the loop after the call to *FACTOR*. That semantic routine would pop the topmost two operand stack entries and replace them by a single entry, as described in Section 6.2.3 with respect to operator precedence parsing in either an interpreter or a generator.

procedure *TERM*
  FACTOR
  while *token* = '*' **do**
    SCANNER (*token*)
    FACTOR

Figure 6.19   Procedure to Recognize *term*

6.3 LEXICAL ANALYSIS

6.3.1 Classification of Tokens

The primary task of lexical analysis is to assemble characters into
tokens and to determine which category of terminal symbol of the
grammar each token belongs to. The terminals are often classified
for this purpose into **lexical types**. The major types are words,
constants, and operators, each of which can be further divided into
subtypes.

A word that has a predefined meaning is known as a **keyword**.
Examples include **var** in PASCAL and **sum** in PL/I. The two examples differ in that the meaning of **var** is fully as fixed as that of an
operator, whereas a declaration can override the default meaning of
sum. The former is said to be a **reserved** keyword; the latter is
nonreserved. If a word is not a keyword, it is understood to be an
identifier. A constant may be numeric or nonnumeric and there are
often finer distinctions within each of those subtypes. Operators include, among others, arithmetic operators, grouping symbols such as
parentheses, and the punctuation marks used to separate operands
in lists.

The lexical analyzer usually determines at least to which major
lexical type each token belongs and, except sometimes for words, to
which subtype. It usually reports not only type information but
also the identity of the token, by passing to the syntax analyzer
either the token itself or a pointer into a table. Perhaps there is one
table for words, another for numeric constants, a third for character-
string constants, and yet a fourth for operators. Perhaps a single
table is used instead, with entries of uniform length independent of
the variable lengths of the source-language tokens that the entries
represent. Details of token storage are discussed in Section 7.3.

The determination that **var** is a reserved name in PASCAL can
be performed by either the scanner or the parser. One of them, to be
sure, must check each word against a table of reserved words. The
over-all requirements of initial source-language analysis are pretty
much fixed for a given language. Because the boundary between
lexical and syntactic analysis is not firm, however, the division of
labor between parser and scanner is to some extent arbitrary.

In identifying and classifying tokens, the scanner needs to isolate each token from its neighbors. The beginning and end of each token must be recognizable. The degree to which the format of the source-language text is fixed affects substantially how easy it is to isolate tokens. If the positions of tokens are fixed (*e.g.*, the label in IBM 370 assembler language), the beginning of each token can be found without testing characters. Similarly, if their length is fixed (*e.g.*, identifiers in unextended BASIC), the end of each token can be identified without such testing.

Sometimes one or more tokens (usually, but not necessarily, one character long) are defined to be **delimiters**, which mark the extent of variable-length tokens. Many assembler languages use the comma to delimit multiple operands in an operand field that has a fixed beginning. The Atari assembler makes the following distinction in scanning beyond the mandatory line number. If text follows after a single space, it is a label. If text follows after more than one space or after a tab, it is an opcode. With a format that is wholly fixed it is possible to decide in advance of lexical analysis where to find each token. If there is some format freedom, with enough delimiters, relatively little preprocessing is required to isolate the tokens.

In a free-format language, however, it is usually necessary to perform the isolation of tokens concurrently with their identification. Thus in analyzing the fragment 3.14*$DIAM$ the rules for construction of constants would both delimit 3.14 before the asterisk and identify it as a constant. Here a token serves as a delimiter, although its primary purpose is to represent an operation. In many languages the space serves as a delimiter; in fact, where one space is permitted, multiple spaces usually have the same effect. Spaces, tabs, and newline characters must normally be discarded before syntactic analysis.

Many languages have provision for comments. These, too, must be discarded before syntactic analysis. The ease with which comments can be recognized varies inversely with the freedom allowed the programmer in inserting them. In line-oriented source languages a specified character in a specified position (*e.g.*, C in column 1 for Fortran) flags the entire line as a comment. This is so easily tested that the reading routine used by the scanner can spare the latter the trouble of examining the line at all. Sometimes a reserved character in an arbitrary position flags the remainder of the line as a comment. One example is "%" in the T$_{E}$X formatting language used in composing this book. Another is "!" in some dialects of BASIC. We can consider the reserved character and the end-of-line to be a pair of comment delimiters that are to be discarded, together with the enclosed comment. This is a special case of the specified pair of tokens (*e.g.*, '{' and '}' in PASCAL) that delimit the comment. The use of a reserved character (*e.g.*, the "lamp" symbol in APL) makes comment recognition simpler than if multipurpose characters are used in the comment delimiter. Usually, tokens within a comment are ignored; they may even be permitted to include characters not admitted in the programming language. Specified characters are sometimes used at the start of a token to identify its lexical type. An example is the @ used in Chapter 2 to mark literals.

6.3.2 Scanning Methods

Because there is no firm division between lexical and syntactic analysis, one way to scan source text is to include scanning as part of the parsing. This is accomplished by using a grammar whose terminal symbols are the characters themselves. Recursive descent provides a natural vehicle for this technique. In the grammar of Figure 6.7, for example, we can treat the semiterminal symbols of part (a) as nonterminals, and convert the rules of part (b) into nonterminal recognition procedures. The recognition of reserved words and other multicharacter terminals (*e.g.*, ':=') would be performed not by calling a separate *SCANNER* to obtain a token for testing, but by successive calls to a character-fetching procedure to obtain a character for testing.

Substantial effort may be needed to transform the entire grammar into a form suitable for recursive descent without backtracking. The cost of backtracking in the token identification portion only is not too severe, however, because it is confined to regions of the tree near the leaves and cannot result in undoing as much analysis as can backtracking to points nearer the root. Consequently, the use of recursive descent to perform the complete analysis from character string to parse tree is quite practical.

If the grammar that describes the lexical analysis is simple enough, we can design a particularly efficient scanner. (The reader familiar with formal languages and their acceptors will observe that the grammar must be **regular**; the recognizer is a finite-state automaton.) We begin by describing the scanning process by **state** diagrams. Unlike the syntax diagrams, in which the recognition of symbols is associated with nodes, state diagrams employ arcs to represent the recognition of characters, and reserve the nodes to represent states of the analysis. For example, the recognition of an unsigned integer is represented by the following state diagram.

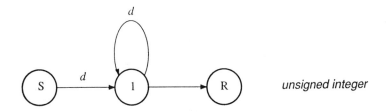

unsigned integer

The scanner begins operation in start state S. Upon recognizing a digit (denoted 'd' to avoid writing "$0|1|\dots|9$") the scanner makes a transition to state 1. Each further digit recognized leaves the scanner in state 1; the first nondigit encountered causes a transition to the recognition state R. In that state the scanner has recognized an unsigned integer and already has read the next character, which may begin another token. Alternatively, that character may be a nontoken delimiter. The label on an arc names the characters whose encounter causes the transition corresponding to the arc. The absence of a label is a synonym for "any other character".

The state diagram

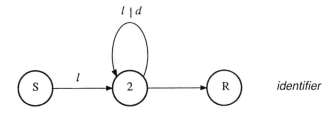

identifier

depicts the recognition of an identifier, with 'l' representing an alphabetic letter and '$|$' used, as in SN, for alternation. We now merge the two state diagrams, which share the same start state and recognition state.

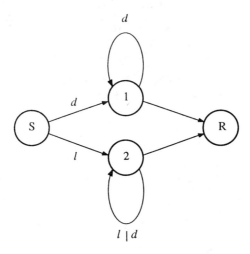

Attainment of state R indicates, as before, that a token was recognized and the next character read. It no longer identifies the token. This information is recoverable from knowledge of whether the state preceding state R was state 1 or state 2. We can easily write a simple program to perform the transitions and keep track of the previous state. It uses a **state-transition table** to represent the state diagram. The table that corresponds to the four-state diagram just presented appears as Figure 6.20. Each row designates a state; each column designates a lexical **class** of characters. (In the table, "other" means neither digit nor letter.) The table entry in position (i,k) is the state to which a character of class k causes a transition from state i.

		Lexical class		
		d	l	other
	S	1	2	
State	1	1	R	R
	2	2	2	R
	R			

Figure 6.20   State-Transition Table

The scanning program is given in Figure 6.21. Each invocation of *GETCHAR* delivers the next character to the first parameter and that character's lexical class to the second. The variables *char* and *class*, which are used as actual parameters, are made global. This preserves their contents from one execution of *SCAN* to the next, and permits them to be initialized by invoking *GETCHAR* before the first execution of *SCAN*. The loop is always executed at least once because we so draw the state diagrams as to prohibit transitions from state S directly to state R. The token is assembled one character at a time. Its type is the simple function *TYPE* of *prevstate*. This scanner, which recognizes one token, is an example of a table-driven program, in which the flow is controlled by an explicit table (here *statetable*, which represents the lexical rules).

procedure *SCAN*(*token,type*)
  {*char* and *class* are global}
  token ← **empty**
  prevstate ← *start*
  currstate ← *statetable*[*prevstate,class*]
  while *currstate* ≠ 'R' **do**
    token ← *token,char* {catenation}
    GETCHAR(*char,class*)
    prevstate ← *currstate*
    currstate ← *statetable*[*prevstate,class*]
  type ← *TYPE*(*prevstate*)

Figure 6.21   Table-Driven Scanner

Observe that two different purposes are being accomplished at the same time by execution of the scanner of Figure 6.21. The program serves both to accept a token and to decide to what type the token belongs. If the characters being analyzed cannot possibly form a token, *type* should at termination be assigned a value that indicates an error.

The transition table of Figure 6.20 is missing some entries. Because the scanner terminates in state R, that state is never succeeded by another. Row R of the table is therefore superfluous and is customarily omitted. When a character of class "other" is encountered in state S, the succeeding state is not specified by the state diagram, hence is omitted from the table. Two interpretations are possible. One is that such a character is not permitted as the initial character

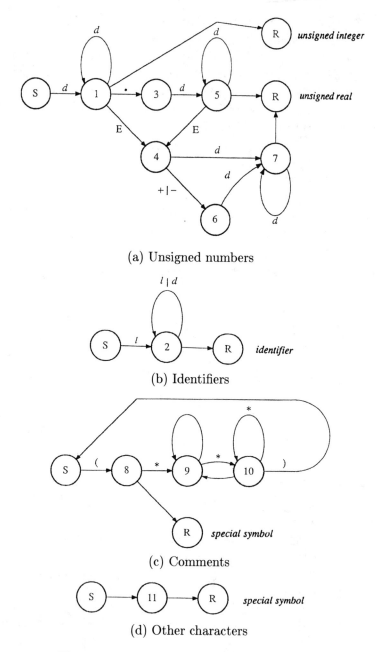

(a) Unsigned numbers

(b) Identifiers

(c) Comments

(d) Other characters

Figure 6.22   State Diagrams of Lexical Rules

of a token in the language and that the corresponding table position should be marked as an error. The other is that the state diagram is only a partial specification of the lexical rules and that another diagram defines the tokens begun by a different initial character. Analysis of that diagram will provide the missing entry, and may well require expansion of the table.

Adopting the second interpretation, we complete our specification in Figure 6.22. Part (a) displays the state diagram corresponding to the following rules for recognizing unsigned numbers.

$$unsignedreal \quad \leftrightarrow \quad unsignedinteger \ fraction$$
$$| \ unsignedinteger \ scalefactor$$
$$| \ unsignedinteger \ fraction \ scalefactor$$

$$unsignedinteger \quad \leftrightarrow \quad digit{+}$$

$$fraction \quad \leftrightarrow \quad \text{`.'} \ unsignedinteger$$

$$scalefactor \quad \leftrightarrow \quad \text{`E'} \ [\ sign \ ] \ unsignedinteger$$

$$sign \quad \leftrightarrow \quad \text{`+'} \ | \ \text{`−'}$$

The diagram previously shown for unsigned integers is incorporated. Error transitions, such as from state 3 for any character other than a decimal digit, are not shown. The state diagram for recognition of identifiers is redrawn as part (b). Part (c) shows how comments introduced by '(*' and terminated by '*)', as in PASCAL without '{' and '}', are ignored. Part (d) completes the specification by defining all initial characters other than '(', letters, or digits to be one-character tokens of special symbols.

6.3.3 Character Recognition

The identification of each character is in principle trivial. A simple table lookup determines the lexical class of each character, and both the character and its class are passed to the scanner. The character is used in assembling the token; the lexical class, in directing the analysis. The state diagrams must be studied carefully to ensure that the lexical classes are properly defined. For the rules described in Figure 6.22, for example, the 26 letters do not all fall in the same class because of the special role that 'E' plays in representing real numbers. Similarly, six of the operator characters (period, plus sign, minus sign, asterisk, and both parentheses) fall into four classes distinct from that of the other nondigit, nonletter characters.

Efficiency of operation is sometimes enhanced by incorporating in the character recognizer some simple functions whose removal from the scanner would greatly decrease the frequency with which the scanner calls the character recognizer. One such function is the discarding of comments. Another is the discarding of nonsignificant blanks. The latter is easily programmed if the scanner informs the character recognizer with each call whether blanks are significant in the current context.

The real challenge in character recognition occurs when the input stream is highly encoded, as is common when unbuffered terminals are used. The identity of many characters depends not on a single stroke, but on multiple strokes that are often not adjacent and may well be far separated from one another. Examples of such strokes are the backspace and shifts into and out of upper case. The strokes used to indicate erasure of a character, of a partial line, or of an entire line, must be interpreted correctly. If shifts are used, the character recognizer can store the value of the most recent shift and consult the appropriate table to interpret each incoming character accordingly. Some of the work may be accomplished in the control program charged with the responsibility of communicating with terminals. If not, it devolves on the translator.

6.3.4 Lexical Ambiguity

Lexical ambiguity occurs when the application of only lexical rules fails to identify a token uniquely. The English words "putting" and "does" are examples of this familiar occurrence in natural language. In procedural languages, one example is a character that can represent either a unary or a binary operator. The minus sign has that property in many languages; in APL many characters have the property. Another sort of example arises in FORTRAN, where all blanks except those within Hollerith constants (*i.e.*, character strings), are nonsignificant and therefore ignored. Thus the text fragment DO33I represents one token in the assignment statement "*DO33I*=7" but three tokens in the loop control statement "**do** 33 *I* = 7, 11". Similarly the fragment 25.E must be split when encountered in the context "25.**eq**" but not in the context "25.E4".

There are three principal approaches to the problem of lexical ambiguity. One is for the scanner to report multiple interpretations to the parser, which then selects whichever one can be correctly parsed. This permits the scanner to be written as a separate pass, with attendant storage economies. Then the intermediate text of tokens and their syntactic types must be encoded to indicate alternate choices. If a separate pass is not made, the calling sequence used by the parser to call the scanner becomes considerably more complicated for all calls, although the ambiguities are relatively infrequent.

A second approach is for the scanner to examine the context of the ambiguous fragment. Although this endows the scanner, technically speaking, with syntactic powers, a very limited examination of lexical classes often suffices. The unary/binary ambiguity is resolved by retaining information about the previous token. If it was a left parenthesis or an operator, then the ambiguous operator is unary; otherwise it is binary. An alternative interpretation, of course, is that the unary and binary operators are represented by the same unambiguous token. There is then no lexical ambiguity, and the parser determines which operator is represented. The 25.E ambiguity can be resolved by indulging in three characters of lookahead after the 5, rather than the usual one character. If Q is found the decimal point belongs to .eq, whereas a digit is part of a real-number constant.

The third approach is for the scanner to make only one lexical analysis at a time, but to cooperate closely with the parser. The parser can reject a lexical analysis that is inconsistent with the parse and call upon the scanner to try again. An extension of this idea is to permit the scanner to call the parser to aid it in disambiguating a fragment. This form of cooperation is particularly suited to implementation by coroutines.

FOR FURTHER STUDY

Several good introductions to grammars and parsing for programming languages are available. A good, brief presentation is Chapter 13 of Rohl75. Intermediate in length are Chapter 8 of Ullman76 and Chapter 3 of Davie81. A more thorough presentation is Chapter 4 of Aho86. Three interesting short communications on the representation of syntax are Knuth64, Wirth77, and Williams82.

Operator precedence parsing is due to Floyd63, who gives a method for constructing double precedence functions, if they exist, from an operator precedence grammar. One of the fullest and most readable expositions of operator precedence parsing is given in Section 4.6 of Aho86. Another good treatment is that in Section 6.1 of Gries71. Those two sources give algorithms for computing the precedence relations for an operator grammar. There is a brief treatment in Hopgood69 (Sections 7.3–7.4), and longer ones in Beck85 (Section 5.1.3) and Tremblay85 (Section 7–2).

Recursive descent parsing was apparently first described in Lucas61. The method is clearly explained in Gries71 (Section 4.3), Beck85 (Section 5.1.3), Hunter85 (Section 4.2), Aho86 (Section 2.4), and in Tremblay85 (Section 6–1.2), which treats error recovery. The book Davie81 treats recursive descent compiling, particularly for a variant of ALGOL W. The more general topic of syntax-directed top-down parsing is considered in Section 5.5 of Aho86 and described fully in Chapter 7 of Barrett79.

One of the most attractive methods of syntactic analysis, not covered in this book, is LR parsing, due to Knuth65. It is described well in Waite84 (Chapter 7), Aho86 (Sections 4.7–4.8), and fully in Barrett86 (Chapter 6).

Lexical scanning is explored by Gries71 (Chapter 3), Rohl75 (Chapter 3), Hunter85 (Chapter 3), Aho86 (Chapter 3), and Waite84 (Chapter 6). The treatments in Chapter 6 of Hopgood69 and in Section 3.7 of Barrett86 include character recognition and line reconstruction.

REVIEW QUESTIONS

6.1 Can one recognize without parsing? Can one parse without recognizing?

6.2 Programming language text was described in Section 6.2.2 as one-dimensional, yet it surely looks two-dimensional. Explain.

6.3 How many stacks are needed for the left-to-right evaluation of a postfix expression?

6.4 On what set are the three relations defined that appear in the definition of operator precedence grammars?

6.5 Correct the following half-truth. "In operator precedence parsing, reduction is applied to the terminals on the stack between $\lessdot$ and $\gtrdot$."

6.6 If it is not possible to derive double precedence functions for a given operator precedence grammar, what can be used instead?

6.7 State advantages and disadvantages of using double precedence functions instead of relations for operator precedence parsing.

6.8 How does nondeterminism arise in recursive descent parsing?

6.9 What approaches exist to handling the nondeterminism?

6.10 For efficiency in parsing, what general programming technique do we wish to avoid?

6.11 Each nonterminal recognition procedure in this book assumes that the first terminal has already been found upon entry to the procedure. Why?

6.12 The PASCAL fragment **if** A **then if** B **then** $C=1$ **else** $C=2$ is unambiguous; the second **then** matches the **else**. Yet a grammar such as that of Figure 6.7 is ambiguous with respect to a nested conditional statement. How could a recursive descent parser based on that ambiguous grammar nevertheless be made to parse such constructions correctly? Give a brief answer.

6.13 How does the use of a separate table for reserved words complicate scanning and simplify parsing?

6.14 Is it possible to recognize some programming-language tokens without scanning beyond their last character?

6.15 How does the degree of input format rigidity affect lexical and syntactic analysis?

6.16 How can a scanner for APL determine whether a token represents a unary or a binary operator?

6.17 Is "$A(8)$", which in PL/I may represent an array element or a function call, lexically ambiguous?

PROBLEMS

6.1 Consider the string

<div align="center">if X<Y then if X>Z then A:=B else A:=C</div>

and the Pascal subset grammar of Figure 6.7.
(**a**) Display all possible parse trees of the string as *stmt*.
(**b**) State for each parse the value, if any, assigned to A under each of the four possible pairs of values of the two conditions. Assume that B has value 0 and C has value 1.
(**c**) Now let the new terminal **fi** be appended to the right end of the replacement substring for *ifstmt*. For each parse, rewrite the string (using **fi** to reflect unambiguously the corresponding structure).

6.2 Construct an example of the ambiguity that can arise in postfix notation if a given token can represent either a unary or a binary operator.

6.3 Trace the execution of the program of Figure 6.9, as modified in the text for double precision, in evaluating
$5+6*(7-2**(12/4)**2)+1$.

6.4 Modify the program of Figure 6.9 to generate code for expression evaluation rather than to evaluate an expression.

6.5 Extend the grammar of Figure 6.3 to include subtraction $(-)$ and exponentiation $(**)$. Give to subtraction the same precedence as to addition, and to exponentiation a higher precedence than to multiplication. For these nonassociative operators, ensure that subtractions are performed left to right and exponentiations right to left.

6.6 Devise algorithms to evaluate a prefix expression,

(**a**) with a single right-to-left pass; and
(**b**) with a single left-to-right pass.

6.7 The priority of operators in PL/I is given by the table

$$** \quad prefix+ \quad prefix- \quad \neg$$
$$* \quad /$$
$$infix+ \quad infix-$$
$$||$$
$$< \quad \neg < \quad <= \quad = \quad \neg = \quad >= \quad \neg >$$
$$\&$$
$$|$$

where operators on a higher line have higher priority than those on a lower line. If two or more operators from the *top* line appear in an expression, the one that stands rightmost in the expression has the highest priority and each succeeding one from right to left has next highest priority. Among operators from any other line of the table, the order of priority is from left to right.

Rewrite the double precedence table near the end of Section 6.2.2 to include *all* unary and binary operators of PL/I. Assume that tokens for unary operators have already been distinguished from binary.

6.8 Execute manually an operator precedence parse of each of the following strings, using the grammar of Figure 6.3. Show for each parse at least the degree of detail given in Figure 6.12. Show also a parse tree in which each nonterminal is marked with the number of the corresponding decision to reduce (*not* the number of the reduction). If a string is not in the language, show as much of the parse as can be completed.

(**a**) X*(Y+Z)
(**b**) X+Y)*Z
(**c**) Y*((X+Y*Z)+X)
(**d**) (X*(Y+Z)+Z

6.9 Construct a grammar that imposes the required positional hierarchy in evaluating APL expressions composed of one-letter identifiers, the eight unary and binary operators +, −, ×, and

÷, and parentheses. Assume that tokens for unary operators have already been distinguished from binary.

6.10 Extend the precedence matrix of Figure 6.14 to incorporate explicitly the dummy tokens that mark the beginning and end of the string.

6.11 Write a set of recursive descent parsing routines for the following grammar. Write them in a manner that associates exponentiation from the right. For example, X↑Y↑Z is to yield the same parse tree as X↑(Y↑Z).

$$
\begin{aligned}
expression &\leftrightarrow term \mid expression \text{ `+' } term \mid expression \text{ `−' } term \\
term &\leftrightarrow factor \mid term \text{ `*' } factor \\
factor &\leftrightarrow element \mid element \text{ `↑' } factor \\
element &\leftrightarrow X \mid Y \mid Z \mid \text{`(' } expression \text{ `)'}
\end{aligned}
$$

6.12 [Ghezzi] The following rules describe a fragment of a language. Write recursive descent parsing routines for rules 1–6. Each routine is to correspond closely to one rule.

```
 1.      prog     ↔  statlist '.'
 2.    statlist   ↔  stat ( ; stat )*
 3.      stat     ↔  asstat | loop | condstat
 4.    asstat     ↔  id := expr
 5.      loop     ↔  while cond do statlist od
 6.  condstat     ↔  if cond then statlist [ else statlist ] fi
 7.      cond     ↔  expr (< | ≤ | = | ≥ | > | ≠) expr
 8.      expr     ↔  ( '+' | '−' term )+
 9.      term     ↔  factor ( ( '*' | '/' ) factor )*
10.    factor     ↔  id | number | '(' expr ')'
```

6.13 Draw a state diagram for the lexical analysis of quoted strings in your favorite programming language.

6.14 The character string DO33I in a FORTRAN program may be either one token or three, depending upon the context. Discuss the relative advantages and disadvantages of the following ways of performing lexical analysis in a FORTRAN compiler.
(**a**) As a separate pass over the entire text
(**b**) As a subroutine called by the syntax analyzer
(**c**) As a coroutine in parallel with the syntax analyzer

6.15 The following state diagram describes the lexical form of a PAS-
CAL comment for a computer that does not provide the single-
character delimiters '{' and '}'. Using SN, write a grammar
that generates the language consisting of all PASCAL comments.
Consider the terminals to be single characters.

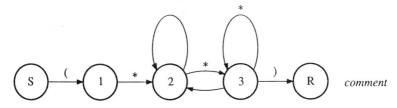

6.16 Construct the state transition table that corresponds to the
state diagrams of Figure 6.22. Choose a minimal set of lexical classes, and work carefully. There are many opportunities
to go astray.

6.17 To the state diagram of Figure 6.22(a), add an error state, plus
arcs and other states as necessary, to represent the detection
of errors in recognizing an unsigned real number. Modify the
program of Figure 6.21 to handle the possibility of errors.

Chapter 7

Data Structures

The symbol table, which we have already encountered in our study of assemblers and macro processors, is a data structure designed to hold names. The literal table is a data structure designed to hold various kinds of literally-specified tokens. Names and other tokens are processed not only by assemblers and macro processors, but by all translators, including compilers. Another important data structure is particular to compilers. To understand its role, we preface our examination of the data structures themselves by a discussion of the functions and characteristics of compilers.

7.1 INTRODUCTION TO COMPILERS

Generative translation from a language that is not machine-oriented into a more easily executed form (*e.g.*, object code for a specific computer) is called **compilation**, and the programs that perform this translation are called **compilers**. From one point of view, compilation is just an extension of macro processing, with the source language generalized beyond the machine orientation of most macro-processor input. Yet the differences between typical macro-assembler languages and most machine-independent languages are not merely quantitative. The qualitative differences are such that compilers are usually not constructed in the same manner as macro assemblers.

We illustrate by examining some of the language features that impose functional requirements on the compiler. We then continue by dissecting a typical compilation.

7.1.1 Source-Language Features

Many features of machine-independent languages contribute to the greater complexity of compilation as compared with assembly. A partial catalog of these features follows.

The declaration of an identifier may be implicit in its use rather than provided explicitly. Examples include labels, undeclared variables, and names of built-in files and functions. Deciding what an implicitly declared identifier represents may be relatively easy, as for labels, or relatively difficult, as in determining whether **sum** in PL/I is the built-in function or a variable. In some languages, an explicit declaration may even be deferred to a point beyond the first use of the identifier.

Elementary variables with different attributes can be organized into a tree-structured aggregate, such as a COBOL group item, a PASCAL **record**, or a C **struct**. The compiler may be required to compute addresses of leaves, or of groups of leaves, which correspond to fully- or partly-qualified names in the source language. The compiler must also be able to decompose into its constituent parts an operation performed **by name** (in PL/I) or **corresponding** (in COBOL).

Address computation for array elements or cross-sections is also required. This is straightforward if the array dimensions are bound at compilation time, but not if the language permits dynamic arrays. In that event the compiler must generate code that will compute the required addresses by use of values that are not available until execution time.

Interrupt function modules require code to test for the conditions that cause the interrupts, as well as for immediate invocation of and eventual return from the modules.

During execution, each invocation of a recursive procedure is represented by copy of its activation record. The compiler must provide at translation time for the production at execution time of an indeterminate number of those copies. It is particularly important not merely that the data areas be distinct, but also that the appropriate different values of link fields be generated for each copy, to permit proper stack management.

The existence of multiple data types, even in the absence of user-defined types as in PASCAL, requires type checking, type conversion, or some of each. If types are specified at compilation time, the compiler can perform checking; otherwise it must generate code to perform execution-time checking. Type conversion, except of constants, must be deferred to execution time.

Facilities for formatting input and output are often very extensive. To generate code from such specifications as those of FORTRAN's **format** or BASIC's **map**, the compiler must translate from a large, nonalgorithmic sublanguage.

The use of pointer variables to qualify references to identifiers imposes two requirements on the compiler. It must establish pointers that will hold the correct execution-time addresses, and it must provide for indirect addressing at execution time. The availability of explicit-base addressing in the target machine greatly simplifies this task.

The variety of storage classes mandates a variety of schemes for accessing storage. A particularly intriguing class is that of the **own** variable (ALGOL) or local **static** variable (C). The variable must remain addressable, with its value intact, even when the only block that can access it is inactive and therefore not represented by an activation record.

The existence of block structure imposes further burdens. Multiple uses of an identifier may refer to the same entity or to different ones, depending on the static nesting of the blocks in which the identifiers are declared. Storage for identifiers local to a block, unless they are **own** or **static**, must be allocated upon each entry to the block and freed upon each exit.

Call by name is another feature that, if provided, greatly complicates the task of the compiler, for the reasons discussed in Section 3.5.3. That section describes briefly the use of thunks to implement call by name.

The last language feature in this catalog occurs in PL/I. Because labels may be passed as parameters, a **goto** may transfer from within a procedure to a label in another block that does not enclose it statically and to which the static chain therefore does not lead.

These and other complicating features of machine-independent languages help explain why compilers for rich languages are complex programs. Nevertheless, the basic process of compilation is readily understandable. Although this chapter can hardly hope to convey all of the material in whole books on compiler design, it does explain methods for handling some of the foregoing language features.

7.1.2 Overview of Compilation

The process of compilation can be performed as a sequence of five major steps. Although two or more of these steps can be implemented together in a particular compiler, they are conceptually distinct and subject to a sequential order imposed by logic. In that order, they are the following:

(1) Lexical analysis;
(2) Syntactic analysis;
(3) Semantic processing;
(4) Storage allocation;
(5) Target code generation.

Lexical analysis in general has been treated in Section 6.3. A concomitant of lexical analysis in a compiler is the construction of a symbol table for user-determined identifiers and of a storage facility for constants. Numeric constants can be handled much as in an assembler's literal table or as in processing immediate operands; string constants, whose lengths can vary widely, need different care.

Syntactic analysis has been discussed briefly in Section 6.2. As mentioned there, lexical analysis may be either performed as a subroutine of the syntactic analysis or combined with it in some manner. Because of the length of programs that may be compiled, it is usually not practical to develop the complete parse tree before continuing the compilation. For this reason, semantic processing is normally undertaken whenever the parser has recognized a language construct. Thus it is common for both lexical analysis and semantic processing routines to be called by the parser. Operator precedence and recursive descent parsers are among those most easily used in compilers. Among other important parsing methods are those called "simple precedence", "bounded context", "LL(1)", and "LR(1)". Rather than discussing them here, however, we refer the reader to more specialized works.

Semantic processing, also called "semantic analysis" or "semantic interpretation", has two facets. One is "interpretation" (not as opposed to "generation", but rather in the conventional sense of the word). This is the determination of the meaning of the language constructs recognized by the syntactic analysis. The other is the representation of that meaning in a form intermediate between the source language and the target language, and called **intermediate code**. Like source language, intermediate code is independent of the details of the target machine. Like the target language, however, it reflects the types of operations available in a target machine. It is often fruitful to think of intermediate code as being composed of calls of macros that can be defined for the target machine language.

Storage allocation includes both the determination of storage requirements and the specification of algorithms to perform addressing calculations at execution time. Storage must be provided, of course, for the variables defined in the source program and for the constants (literals) that appear in it. Storage must also be provided for several kinds of parameters and for temporary results in expression evaluation and type conversion. Addressing calculations range from trivial, as in accessing a local scalar variable, to moderately complex, as in accessing an element of an array declared in an enclosing block and having dynamically specified bounds.

Target code generation is the translation from intermediate code to a machine-dependent representation, sometimes similar to assembler language, but more often object code. Target code generation can be likened to macro expansion for which the prototypes match calls in intermediate code and the skeletons are defined for the target machine. With certain forms of intermediate code, this generation step is in fact just pure macro processing without nesting.

The first two steps, lexical analysis and syntactic analysis, are machine-independent as well as analytic. The last two steps, storage allocation and target code generation, are machine-dependent and synthetic. Semantic processing is both analytic and synthetic, but still machine-independent. The intermediate code stands at the interface between the machine-independent and the machine-dependent steps. Some compilers do not produce an explicit intermediate code. Even for those compilers, however, the concept of intermediate code is fruitful.

An important process in many compilers is the investment of effort to increase the efficiency of the compiled code. This **code improvement**, commonly called "optimization", is performed once per compilation and enjoyed once per execution. The anticipated number of executions per compilation is the major determinant of how much optimization should be undertaken. Some optimization (e.g., elimination of common subexpressions) is machine-independent, and other optimization (e.g., elimination of redundant store instructions) is machine-dependent. If optimization is performed, the five principal steps are augmented by one or two more. Machine-independent optimization is often performed in a separate step, usually after semantic processing. Machine-dependent optimization can be undertaken as a separate final step, but is more often combined with target code generation.

Structural Issues. In a compiler, the algorithms and the data representations are interdependent, just as they are for any other program. In developing a particular compiler, the choice of control and data structures must proceed hand in hand with refinement of the algorithms. In compiler description, however, we are not bound by this interdependence and choose to defer our study of the processing algorithms until after examination of three structural issues. These are (1) how to represent the intermediate code, (2) how to store programmer-specified entities, and (3) how to manage the symbol table. Intermediate code representation is an important issues in compilers, and storage mechanisms are important in both compilers and interpreters. Symbol tables are ubiquitous, appearing in every kind of translator.

7.2 INTERMEDIATE CODE

7.2.1 Postfix

Polish postfix notation is particularly attractive for the computer representation of arithmetic expressions. A minor advantage is the space saving due to the property that parentheses are never required. For example, the 7-token infix expression $(X+Y)*Z$ is represented by the 5-token postfix expression $XY+Z*$. The principal advantage of postfix representation over infix is that single-pass left-to-right evaluation requires only one stack. We do not need an operator stack, because operators are applied as soon as they are encountered.

The one required stack holds only values, and is initially empty. Each time an operand is encountered, its value is pushed onto the stack. Each time an operator of degree i is encountered, the top i values are popped, the operator is applied to them, and the resulting value is stacked. At the conclusion of the scan, the stack will contain precisely one value, that of the expression scanned. This evaluation process, which might be performed in an interpreter, is very efficient. A slight modification results not in evaluating the expression, but in performing the target code generation required in a compiler.

Other programming-language constructs, too, can be readily represented in postfix notation. The assignment statement $A \leftarrow B$ becomes $A\ B \leftarrow$ and the branch **goto** $L1$ becomes $L1$ GOTO. In generating target code for either of these constructs, the entries are popped from the stack, but nothing is pushed onto the stack afterwards, as is done for expressions. The details of target code generation, for other representations as well as for postfix, are considered in Section 8.3.

In evaluating a sum, the left operand is popped from the stack and its *value* used. In performing an assignment, the left operand is popped from the stack and its *address* used. If the left operand is written in the same manner for either operation, lookahead to the operation symbol is needed to determine whether the value or the address is needed. To avoid lookahead, the difference is often represented syntactically in the postfix string. We shall henceforth use "!" to indicate address as opposed to value, the default. We write the assignment as $!A\ B \leftarrow$ instead.

Compound, alternative, and iterative control structures are also easily represented in postfix. Compound statements (*e.g.*, those grouped within a **begin-end** pair) require no special handling. Postfix representations of the individual statements are just catenated in sequence. Alternation and iteration, however, implicitly specify jumping to points in the source text that are not necessarily labeled. We therefore require means of representing jumps that are specified by the compiler rather than directly by the programmer. If the symbols of the postfix text are numbered serially from the beginning, then these numbers can serve as jump destinations. An unconditional jump might have the syntax

⟨destination⟩ JUMP

where ⟨destination⟩ is the serial number of the text symbol, a label, to which the branch is made. The source-language operator **goto** is distinct from JUMP because the operand of **goto** is a pointer to a symbol table entry, not the serial number of a text symbol. Conditional jumps might have operators JPOS, JNEG, JZERO, and the like, with syntax

expression ⟨destination⟩ JPOS.

If the jump condition is satisfied, then the next text symbol to scan after the jump is the one specified; otherwise, normal processing continues. In either event, *expression* and ⟨destination⟩ are popped from the stack and nothing is pushed back on.

To see how alternation can be expressed in postfix notation without requiring any backup in the left-to-right scan of the postfix text, consider the following statement.

if *condition* **then** *stmt1* **else** *stmt2*

The postfix form of the statement is

cond ⟨dest2⟩ JFALSE *stmt1* ⟨destout⟩ JUMP *stmt2*

where ⟨dest2⟩ is the serial number of the first symbol of *stmt2*, and ⟨destout⟩ is the number of the first symbol that follows the text shown. For example, the PASCAL statement

if A<B **then** *C* := *B*+*D*∗4
else *C* := *A*+*D*∗4

might be translated into

```
37 38 39 40  41  42 43 44 45 46 47 48 49   50   51 52 53 54 55 56 57
A  B  −  51 JPZ !C  B  D  4  ∗  +  ←  58 JUMP !C  A  D  4  ∗  +  ←
```

where the serial number of each symbol appears directly above the symbol and JPZ is a jump on accumulator positive or zero.

7.2.2 Quadruples

A convenient way to represent the execution of a binary operator is to list four items: the operator, its two operands, and the destination of the result. Intermediate code is often represented by such

quadruples. If we list the four items in the order described, then the assignment $D := B*B-4*A*C$ could be translated into the following sequence of quadruples.

*	B	B	T1
*	4	A	T2
*	T2	C	T3
−	T1	T3	D

The temporary variables T1, T2, and T3 hold the results of applying each operator. On a single-accumulator machine, T2 could reside in the accumulator, but T1 and T3 would correspond to temporary storage locations.

Unary operators can be represented by leaving one operand position empty. For example, the assignment $P := Q$ might be represented as

:=	Q		P

Jumps can be represented by using the first operand position for the expression to be tested, if any, and the destination position for the target. The latter is given as the serial number of a quadruple. Except as otherwise directed by jumps, quadruples are executed in serial order.

If 10 quadruples using four temporary variables have already been generated when the PASCAL statement

> **if** A<B **then** $C := B+D*4$
> **else** $C := A+D*4$

is encountered, the generated quadruples might be the following.

11.	−	A	B	T5
12.	JPZ	T5		16
13.	*	D	4	T6
14.	+	B	T6	C
15.	JUMP			18
16.	*	D	4	T7
17.	+	A	T7	C

Quadruples have the advantage of corresponding more closely to machine language than does postfix (except for stack machines). Their chief disadvantage is the number of temporary variables that must be described. The next representation to be discussed attacks this problem.

7.2.3 Triples

If the result field is omitted from a quadruple, a **triple** results. When reference must be made to a result, the number of the triple that produced it is used instead. Not only do many temporary variable names vanish from the symbol table, but nearly one-fourth of the space for the intermediate code is saved. The intermediate code for the same PASCAL statement as before can now be written as follows.

11.	−	A	B
12.	JPZ	(11)	(17)
13.	*	D	4
14.	+	B	(13)
15.	←	(14)	C
16.	JUMP		(20)
17.	*	D	4
18.	+	A	(17)
19.	←	(18)	C

Note the requirement to distinguish syntactically between a triple number, e.g., "(13)", and a constant, e.g., "4". Thus triple 13 specifies the multiplication of D by the literal constant 4, whereas triple 14 specifies the addition of B and the result produced by the execution of triple 13. In the conditional jump triple 12, the second field refers to a result, that of executing triple 11, but the third refers to a destination.

7.2.4 Indirect Triples

A given triple, such as (13) or (17) in the foregoing example, can occur many times in one program. This is particularly true if subscripts are used, because identical subscripting calculations are frequently written more than once, as in $X[I] := X[I] + Z[I]$. Multiple occurrences of a given triple can be replaced by multiple references to a single occurrence. The result is an **indirect triple**, referred to by its serial number in a list of all distinct triples. A separate sequence vector specifies the order of execution of the triples. We can rewrite our example in indirect triples as follows.

	distinct triples				sequence
11.	–	A	B	37.	11
12.	JPZ	(11)	43	38.	12
13.	*	D	4	39.	13
14.	+	B	(13)	40.	14
15.	←	(14)	C	41.	15
16.	JUMP		46	42.	16
17.	+	A	(13)	43.	13
18.	←	(17)	C	44.	17
				45.	18

Note that jump targets are no longer given as triple numbers, but
rather as indices to the sequence vector.

For this short example, the use of indirect triples costs space,
rather than saves it. For a longer program, the opposite is more often
true. Indirect triples offer another advantage if code optimization is
to follow. The resulting deletion of redundant triples or re-ordering
of remaining triples can be performed in the sequence vector, obvi-
ating the rearrangement of the much larger list of triples.

7.3 TOKEN STORAGE

The lexical analyzer and symbol table manager together determine
which source-language identifiers name the same entity. In subsequent processing, it is important for the compiler to know that two
occurrences of an identifier do name the same variable or the same
label. It is immaterial, however, what the source-language name is.
The replacement of each identifier token by a pointer to the identifier's entry in the symbol table imposes therefore no limitation on
the compiler's ability to translate. Except in languages with severe
restrictions on identifier length, a substantial space saving may result. There is also some time saving because it is quicker to operate
on a short pointer than on a long identifier.

Another benefit is that uniform-length tokens have replaced
the variable-length identifier tokens. Great simplification can result
from providing tokens of uniform length not just for identifiers but
for all token types. The resulting elements are called **uniform tokens** or **uniform symbols**. Each consists of two fields, a type code

and an index. The index specifies a location in whichever table is
appropriate to the type. There may be, for example, a table of identifiers, a table of constants, a table of reserved words, and a table
of operators. The type code may be just a code, or it may be the
address of the associated table. Some tokens, such as one-character
operators, may indeed be replaced by uniform symbols longer than
the original tokens. Nevertheless, the replacement of identifiers and
constants, especially long character strings, usually does reduce the
size of the program to be compiled. Far more important is the ability to test, copy, and stack tokens of uniform length. Because many
computers compare numbers more easily and rapidly than they do
characters, a further advantage is the replacement of characters and
character strings by numbers. Moreover, numbers are surely much
more convenient to use as indices to tables of tokens or of addresses
of processing routines.

What kinds of tables are required for the uniform symbols to
point to? Identifiers and their attributes are kept in a symbol table,
as already discussed. If the source language has block structure,
a block-structured symbol table, as described in Section 7.4.4, is
required. Reserved words may be placed in the symbol table before
compilation, or they may be kept in a separate table. The latter
choice usually simplifies the parsing at the cost of complicating the
scanning. Because the meaning of reserved words is predefined, it is
possible to omit their attributes from the table. In fact, the table
itself can be discarded if all reserved words are identified in initial
processing before later stages of translation are undertaken. The
same is true of special symbols, such as operators. Syntactic analysis
and semantic processing can proceed quite comfortably given only
the information that a token is the ith reserved word or the kth
special symbol.

The handling of constants is more involved. Character-string
constants are characterized by length that can be highly variable.
To avoid the waste inherent in allocating table entries big enough to
hold the longest possible string, a different approach is customary.
All character-string constants are stored consecutively in a **string
space**. Because their lengths are different, each string constant requires a length specification. One method is to include a length
field in the uniform symbol, but this field lengthens unnecessarily

the uniform symbols for other token types and may complicate their processing. Another method is to insert partition codes between successive entries in the string space, but this requires continual testing during string retrieval. Probably most satisfactory is to place the length of a string in a fixed-length field just before the start of the string. The index in the uniform symbol then points to this field rather than to the first character of the adjacent string.

Numeric constants, like literals in assembler language, must ultimately be converted to machine representation. If this is done upon initial encounter, then a table of fixed-length entries can be used for each type of numeric constant. If constant generation is to be deferred until other target code is generated, the variable length of the source-language representations suggests the use of the string space. In that event, however, it may be necessary at least to determine in advance the type of each constant. This ensures the ability to generate target code for the execution-time type conversions required by the language definition.

7.4 SYMBOL TABLES

The degree to which the meaning of a token is known to the translator depends upon the type of token. The meaning of a constant is simply its value, which is evident from inspection of the constant. Hence, constants are sometimes said to be "self-defining". The meaning of an operator is defined by the language, and is normally implicit in the design of the translator. A word that is a reserved keyword similarly has a predefined meaning. Other words, which are permitted as identifiers in a machine-independent language — or as labels in an assembler language — have meanings defined by the programmer. Upon encountering such a symbol, the translator must be able to refer to its meaning. A **symbol table** is used to hold the meanings associated with user-defined symbols. Normal lexical analysis does not distinguish reserved words from others. To make this distinction, we can keep reserved words in a separate table that is interrogated before the regular symbol table. Alternatively, a single table can be used, in which reserved words are entered automatically, and flagged as such, before translation begins.

The meaning of a symbol is expressed by its attributes. These may be as few in number as one, such as the address of an assembler-language label, or there may be very many. Among possible attributes are source-text line number, type, number of dimensions, length of each dimension, internal tree structure, and storage class. The first reference to a symbol serves as an explicit or implicit declaration and inserts the symbol into the table. Either that access inserts the attributes, or a small number (often only one) of subsequent accesses do. Most accesses retrieve attributes. Usually the symbol is not deleted. Retrievals require a search for the designated symbol; in practice, insertions also require such a search.

Because of these frequent searches, effective symbol table management is crucial to efficient translation, whether in an assembler, macro processor, linker, interpreter, or compiler. The chief differences among the translators are the number of attributes and the potential for block structure. In the following sections we review briefly the appropriateness of several elementary data structures for use in representing symbol tables, particularly emphasizing the use of hashing functions. We conclude by explaining how to handle block structure.

7.4.1 Basic Structures

The simplest structure that one might consider for representing a symbol table is an unsorted linear array. Search is serial and requires $O(n)$ time if there are n symbols in the array. A symbol to be inserted if not found is simply appended to the end of the array at an insignificant extra cost. Although the unsorted array with serial scan is very easy to implement, it uses much time if n is large.

A marked improvement results from replacing the serial scan by a binary search, which takes only $O(\log n)$ time. Binary search requires that the elements of the array be sorted. If an element is to be inserted, it cannot be simply appended. Half of the elements, on the average, must be displaced one position to make room for the insertion, which therefore still takes $O(n)$ time.

In binary search, each element has two possible successors in the search, one if the element compares higher than the search argument, and one if lower. There is thus a tree structure implicit in the table. It is possible to make this tree structure explicit, and to optimize and balance the tree. A primary gain is that insertion time can be reduced to $O(\log n)$. Because insertion is so much less frequent than retrieval, this is not a substantial gain. Although tree-structured symbol tables are indeed used in translators, we shall not take the space here to describe them.

An alternative to searching a data structure is to compute the address of the search argument. The process of computing the symbol's address from the symbol itself is known as **hashing**. If the address can be computed directly, the mean time for search or for insertion is independent of n and is in fact $O(1)$. Figure 7.1 summarizes the orders of magnitude of search time and insertion time for the foregoing approaches.

	Search	Insertion
Unsorted array	$O(n)$	$O(n)$
Sorted array	$O(\log n)$	$O(n)$
Tree	$O(\log n)$	$O(\log n)$
Hashing	$O(1)$	$O(1)$

Figure 7.1   Order of Magnitude Time Requirements

Because of the relatively low frequency of insertion, search time predominates. In comparing the time requirements of the different table organizations, it is important to realize that the order of magnitude notation suppresses multiplicative constants. The importance of the unstated coefficients is illustrated by the linear expression n having a smaller value than the logarithmic expression $11 \log_2 n$ for n as large as 64. The availability of table look-up instructions in the computer to be used may indeed make a serial scan faster than a binary search.

Further gains in speed are possible if the symbols to be used are known, and their frequencies of occurrence can be estimated. This occurs, for example, with assembler-language operation codes. A simple technique is to order the symbols by decreasing frequency of occurrence and to scan serially. Although worst-case search time is still $O(n)$, the coefficient can be markedly reduced if a few symbols occur with high probability. It is also possible to use frequency information in balancing a tree probabilistically.

For unknown symbols, however, hashing is often the most effective approach to reducing search time for large n. In computing the table address of a symbol from the symbol, it is fruitful to consider the properties of addresses and those of symbols. The table comprises a fixed, known set A of addresses. No two symbols occupy the same address. The set of addresses is compact, *i.e.*, there are no gaps. In fact, we normally use main storage for speed and consecutive addresses for simplicity and storage economy. The set S of possible symbols is known, being defined by the language to be translated. On the other hand, the set S' of actual symbols that enter a given translation is neither fixed nor known in advance. The symbols are required, however, to be distinct, except in a language with block structure, whose effect upon symbol table management is discussed in Section 7.4.4. The actual symbol set S' is rarely compact, and it is typically very much smaller than the set S of all possible symbols.

Hashing is the application of a **key transformation** $T : S \to A$ that maps each symbol $s \in S$ into an address $a \in A$. We are interested in the behavior of T not so much for the large, known set S of all possible symbols as for the small, unknown set S' of actual symbols. The actual symbols that are mapped into the same address a constitute an equivalence class C_a of symbols. We can define the equivalence class formally, given $a \in A$, as $C_a = \{s \in S' \mid T(s) = a\}$. A particular equivalence class may be empty, or it may contain one symbol, or it may contain several symbols. If it contains more than one, a **collision** is said to have occurred, because only one symbol can occupy a given address. Means must then be provided for distinguishing among the symbols in the equivalence class, and other addresses must be found to hold all but the first symbol destined for the computed address. If the equivalence class is large, considerable extra effort is required. The occurrence of large equivalence classes is known as **clustering**.

An ideal choice of hashing function T would ensure that its restriction $T' : S' \to A$ would have the following three properties. (1) It maps S' onto most of A (provided S' is not much smaller than A), to avoid wasting space in the symbol table. For convenience, we shall describe such a hashing function as **compact**. (2) It has a unique inverse, meaning that only one symbol is mapped into a given address, thus eliminating collisions. (3) It is simple, hence fast to compute. Unfortunately, T' is unknown because S' is unknown, and we are free to choose only T, not T'. Moreover, we cannot in general attain all three of the desired properties simultaneously. We can, however, achieve any pair. We must elect simplicity, or our $O(1)$ search time will in fact be slower than the $O(\log n)$ time of a competing symbol table organization. We can guarantee freedom from collisions among the unknown symbols S' only by so doing for the larger set S. This would require a symbol table as large as S, usually not a practical possibility. The normal choice, therefore, is to design a hashing function that is simple and compact.

A disadvantage is that we must plan for collisions. We design a hashing function for S and hope that it works well for whatever S' we encounter in practice. A convenient standard of comparison for the behavior of T' is the generation of addresses drawn from all of A at random, with replacement. One can easily show for this case that the table size (number of addresses) must substantially exceed the number of symbols in S' to hold the number of collisions down to a reasonable level. A rule of thumb that usually works well in practice is to make the table large enough that symbols will occupy not more than 80% of the addresses. We consider in Section 7.4.3 some techniques for handling the collisions that do occur. First, however, we describe some hashing functions appropriate for symbols.

7.4.2 Hashing Functions

Programmers often refer to related objects by using a group of symbols that differ in as little as a single character position. Any hashing function that does not depend on that character position will map the entire group into a single address. To avoid such clustering, a suitable hashing function must therefore depend on all characters of the symbol.

The symbol is usually alphanumeric, and in some languages can be very long compared to a machine word. Symbol table addresses are numeric, and most computers (and languages) provide a richer assortment of operations on numeric quantities than on character strings. An important component in hashing symbols is therefore to treat the symbol string as though it were purely numeric. The usual approach is to consider the bits of its representation to constitute a binary numeral. This is accomplished almost trivially in assembler languages, and with differing degrees of difficulty in machine-independent languages.

One very simple hashing function divides the symbol by the table size and uses the remainder as a zero-origin address within the table. Poor choice of the divisor, however, can result in substantial clustering. Suppose, for example, that a 512-word table is used, and that addressing is binary. Then the remainder after division of the symbol by 512 is just the original low-order 9 bits of the symbol. The address depends only on the low-order character and on part of its neighbor. This is bad enough in general; for left-justified short symbols, which necessarily have spaces as the low-order characters, it is simply terrible. A much better choice of divisor is a prime number. We can either use a prime slightly smaller than the table size, say 509, or we can make the table size itself a prime, say 509 or 521.

Another hashing function, particularly suitable for long symbols, is known as **folding**. The symbol is split into pieces, each a few characters long, and the pieces are added. Overflow is ignored; it can also be suppressed by using **exclusive or** (modulo 2 addition) if that operation is available.

A third type of function depends on multiplication. One variation is to multiply the symbol by an appropriate constant and take the leading bits of the least significant half of the product. Another is the **mid-square** method, in which the n-bit symbol is squared. The middle n bits of the $2n$-bit product are selected as the address, because they depend on every bit of the symbol.

In some computers, the encodings of characters that are permitted in symbols is highly redundant. For example, alphanumeric characters are represented in the EBCDIC code by 8 bits of which the first two are invariably 11. Another form of redundancy is that variable-length symbols are often represented as fixed-length strings having a fixed character (the space) in all unused positions. A refinement that can be applied to many hashing functions is to ignore redundant bits or redundant characters. If symbols are of varying length, a method appropriate to the length can be chosen at the cost of time to test the length and of space to hold code for more than one method. Another way to invest some extra time and space is to use two or more of the foregoing hashing functions in combination.

Thus a transformation might be preceded by folding to produce a one-word operand, or followed by division to yield addresses in the range of the table size.

7.4.3 Overflow Techniques

If an attempt is made to insert a symbol where there is one already, table **overflow** is said to have occurred and space must be found elsewhere. This can always be done, provided that the table size is as large as the number of symbols to be inserted.

One approach is to reduce the frequency of collisions by providing extra space at each table address. Instead of room for merely one symbol (and its attributes), this yields a **bucket** that can hold more than one symbol. Application of the hashing function is followed by a serial scan within the bucket. If the bucket size is b, then the first b members of an equivalence class to be inserted will fit in the bucket. Overflow does not occur unless $b+1$ members of an equivalence class are to be inserted. It is not necessary that the number of addresses $|A|$ computed by the hashing function be as large as the number of symbols $|S'|$. The requirement is rather $b|A| \geq |S'|$. There is little point, however, in using buckets if the frequency of overflow is not reduced. Consequently, the use of buckets normally entails the provision of some extra storage. Nevertheless, buckets do not eliminate overflow; they only reduce its frequency. Some method of handling overflow is still required.

A second approach to overflow is **open addressing**, which is also known as "scatter storage". If the address computed by the hashing function is occupied by a symbol different from the search argument, another address is computed somehow and the search continues from there. If that new address is occupied, a third address is computed and the search continues until it finds the argument, an empty address, or an address that has already been examined. If the last case arises during an insertion attempt, we consider the table to be full, even if empty unexamined addresses remain. It is always possible to choose an open addressing strategy that guarantees that this will not occur unless the table is full.

Three ways of probing the table after a collision at address a are the following. In **linear** probing, the address examined on the ith attempt is $a + ri$ (modulo the table size), where r is some integer constant. If $r = 1$, as is common, then the entire table is probed before failure is reported. The recomputation is fast, requiring only the addition of r and a test that the new address is within the range of the table. If, however, collisions occur at successive addresses, further collisions are induced by displaced symbols and the resulting congestion can slow down considerably the execution of the symbol table routines. This effect is mitigated by **quadratic** probing, in which the address examined on the ith attempt is $a + si + ti^2$ (modulo the table size). If the table size is prime, quadratic probing will examine fully half the table before reporting failure. If the constants $s + t$ and $2t$ are stored in advance, the recomputation requires one multiplication and two additions. The last example of open addressing is to **rehash** the original address, using it as the argument of a hashing function. This second function is usually different from the function used to transform the symbol because their arguments are of different lengths.

A third approach to overflow is related to open addressing, but seeks to eliminate the repeated computation of the same probe address each time a search is made for the same symbol. Once the probe address has been determined, by whatever means, it is stored with the previous symbol as a pointer in a search **chain**. The price of saving the recomputation time is the provision of storage for all the pointers. A disadvantage of chained overflow is that means are required to prevent chains from becoming tangled when two chains intersect at one address. We shall not treat that problem here.

The foregoing techniques all place overflow symbols at addresses that might otherwise legitimately be occupied by other symbols, thus inducing collisions where none were present. A fourth approach to overflow avoids this problem by using for overflow symbols a table area distinct from the primary symbol table. If collisions are not too frequent, a wholly satisfactory organization of the overflow table is as a linear list that is scanned serially. If the overflow table is expected to be large, time can be saved by appending newly inserted symbols at the end and using one pointer field in each entry to chain together the members of each equivalence class.

7.4.4 Block Structure

In a language with block structure, two or more distinct objects may have the same name. Each of the objects must nevertheless have its own symbol table entry, because its attributes are not shared by its namesakes. Finding the entry that corresponds to the occurrence of a symbol within a given program block requires a conceptual search of the environment. The search starts from the given block and proceeds outward through enclosing blocks until a declaration of the symbol is first encountered. There are three principal approaches to implementing this conceptual search of the environment as an actual search of the symbol table. One is to include the block number as an attribute; a second is to replace nonunique names of distinct objects by unique names; the third is to group together in the symbol table all entries for symbols declared in the same block. We examine each approach in turn.

If the block number is used as an attribute, there will be duplicate symbols whose entries can be distinguished only by examining the block number. This approach diminishes the already low appeal of an unsorted linear table, unless it is very short. The reason is the necessity to scan the entire table to ensure finding the symbol instance associated with the innermost block of the environment. Search by hashing can be readily performed at the cost of a pointer field in each entry, used to link entries for the same symbol in different blocks. Because the duplicated symbols are not necessarily inserted in the table in nesting sequence, merely linking them into a chain in the order of insertion is insufficient for rapid searching. In fact, a chain of pointers is less helpful than a set of pointers that captures the static nesting structure of the program. Each entry for a symbol should point rather to the closest entry for the same symbol in an enclosing block. These pointers are directed upward toward the root of the tree that describes the static nesting. To yield the desired linkage pattern, the pointers can be reset whenever a symbol is inserted or a block is closed.

If a sorted linear table is used, entries for duplicate symbols will necessarily be consecutive. If a given symbol occurs k times, at most k extra probes will be required (or $k - 1$ if the last entry for each symbol is marked as such). We must still accept he disadvantage that search time is $O(\log n)$.

The second approach to block structure is to replace duplicated symbols by distinct symbols. Uniqueness of symbols can be ensured if each duplicated symbol is qualified by the block number. The qualification is most readily accomplished by catenating the block number to the symbol. This approach requires multiple searches, each for a different version of the symbol. When a symbol is first encountered, there is no way of knowing whether it will be duplicated in blocks to be entered later. The name qualification must therefore be applied to all symbols.

Our third approach to implementing block structure in the symbol table is to group entries by block and keep track of which portion of the table corresponds to which block. Figure 7.2 shows the block structure and declarations for two different versions of a program. The blocks are numbered in the sequence in which their openings are encountered. In Figure 7.2(a), declarations are restricted to precede any other text within their block. Once a block is entered, all declarations in every block that encloses it have already been encountered. Because that restriction considerably simplifies symbol table construction, we begin by assuming declarations to be so restricted. Later we shall consider unrestricted declarations, as in Figure 7.2(b).

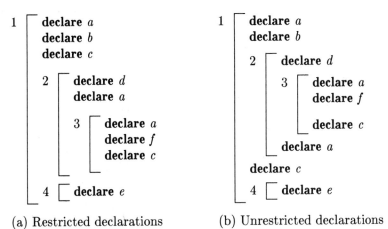

(a) Restricted declarations   (b) Unrestricted declarations

Figure 7.2   Block Structure in Source Text

Dynamic symbol tables. Given the restriction on placement of declarations, we can build a dynamically changing symbol table with the use of two arrays. One array, *table*, holds symbol and attribute entries. They are appended to the array upon encounter and removed from the end of the array as the block in which they are declared is closed. The other array, *level*, holds pointers to those entries in the first array that begin a new block. Figure 7.3 shows four stages in the life of such a symbol table while the program of Figure 7.2(a) is being scanned. The index values for each array element are shown at the left. Symbol attributes have been omitted; they could be placed either together with the symbols or else in an array of the same length in correspondence with *table*. For ease in interpreting the figure, the block number appears in parentheses next to the symbol. It need not actually be stored in *table*.

	table	level	table	level	table	level	table	level
8.			c (3)					
7.			f (3)					
6.			a (3)					
5.			a (2)		a (2)			
4.			d (2)		d (2)		f (4)	
3.	c (1)		c (1)	6	c (1)		c (1)	
2.	b (1)		b (1)	4	b (1)	4	b (1)	4
1.	a (1)	1	a (1)	1	a (1)	1	a (1)	1
	(a) in block 1		(b) in block 3		(c) in block 2		(d) in block 4	

Figure 7.3   Dynamic Symbol Table

Stage (a) holds after the declarations of block 1 have been examined. After scanning has proceeded beyond the declarations of block 3, the symbol table attains stage (b). The pointers 1, 4, 6 in the second array indicate the first symbol declared in each of blocks 1, 2, and 3, which constitute block 3's environment. After the closure of block 3 has been scanned, but before the closure of block 2, stage (c) holds. The symbols declared in block 3 have vanished from the symbol array, and the pointer to the first of them has been removed from the pointer array. Stage (d) holds after scanning has advanced beyond the closure of block 2, the opening of block 4, and the last declaration. The second pointer, 4, points to the first declaration not of the second block in text order but rather of the block nested at the second level. At stages (b) and (c), the second-level block was block 2; now block 4 holds that position. The pointer array is thus a compilation-time analog of the execution-time display. Instead of pointing to activation records of the different blocks, it points to their symbol table entries.

Because the foregoing dynamic symbol table grows and shrinks according to a LIFO discipline, it is sometimes called a **stack symbol table**. Such a designation is not wholly accurate, however, because the pointers allow access to positions other than the top. Once scanning of the text is complete, the dynamic symbol table no longer exists. Its use is restricted, therefore, to one-pass compilation. We shall soon present an alternative organization suitable for multiple-pass translation. First, however, we examine the management of a dynamic symbol table.

The table building process is facilitated by the provision of two pointers, one to the next available position in each of the two arrays. Let the index of the first unused element in the symbol array *table* be *tabletop* and that of the first unused element in the pointer array *level* be *leveltop*. Both pointers are initialized to 1 before scanning begins. When a declaration is encountered, the appropriate entry is placed in *table*[*tabletop*], and *tabletop* is incremented by 1. Entry to a new block causes the execution of

$$level[leveltop] \leftarrow tabletop$$
$$leveltop \leftarrow leveltop + 1$$

Exit from a block undoes the foregoing action by executing

$$leveltop \leftarrow leveltop - 1$$
$$tabletop \leftarrow level[leveltop]$$

Linear search begins at *table*[*tabletop* − 1], precluding the need to delete entries for old blocks, and proceeds toward the first element. The first entry encountered for the desired symbol is the one corresponding to the environment of the current block. Search time is still $O(n)$.

The table of Figure 7.4 shows stages (a) and (b) in the preceding program scan. Using that table, we perform a binary search in an array whose conceptual order is alphabetical

$$a(1) \quad a(2) \quad a(3) \quad b(1) \quad c(1) \quad c(3) \quad d(2) \quad f(3)$$

but whose actual order is by block

$$a(1) \quad b(1) \quad c(1) \quad d(2) \quad a(2) \quad a(3) \quad f(3) \quad c(3).$$

If we had the symbols in the conceptual (alphabetic) order, we would perform the binary search directly, repeatedly bisecting the array of symbols. Instead, we bisect an array of pointers to the symbols. Thus we'd like to begin at the fifth symbol of the 8-element array of symbols. So we begin instead at the fifth pointer in an array of pointers. It should point to $c(1)$, which is actually the third symbol. Hence the value of the fifth pointer is 3. In general, $alpha[i] = k$, where $table[k]$ is the ith symbol in $alpha$betic order. In deciding which half of $alpha$ to discard, we compare values not of pointers, but of symbols pointed to.

	alpha	table	level	alpha	table	level
8.				7	$c\ (3)$	
7.				4	$f\ (3)$	
6.				8	$a\ (3)$	
5.				3	$a\ (2)$	
4.				2	$d\ (2)$	
3.	3	$c\ (1)$		6	$c\ (1)$	6
2.	2	$b\ (1)$		5	$b\ (1)$	4
1.	1	$a\ (1)$	1	1	$a\ (1)$	1

(a) in block 1   (b) in block 3

Figure 7.4   Block Structure with Binary Search

If duplicate entries are encountered in $table$, the one with the highest pointer value in $alpha$ is the one we want. Search thus requires $O(\log n)$ time, but with the constant of proportionality increased by the necessity to make the accesses indirectly. Encounter of a new identifier requires $O(n)$ time to insert the pointer into $alpha$. Block closure also requires $O(n)$ time to purge $alpha$ of pointers not lower than the new value of $tabletop$.

The rapid search provided by hashing is still available with a block-structured table. As for binary search, an auxiliary table of pointers is required, because the position of entries in the symbol table is dictated by the block structure rather than by the value of the hashing function. Instead of open addressing to handle collisions, explicit pointers link symbols in the same equivalence class, including duplicates of the same symbol. Each chain begins with the most recently inserted symbol, thus guaranteeing that the first occurrence of a symbol on an equivalence class chain is the one in the current environment. Let the hashing function transform the symbol a to 3, b to 5, c also to 5, d to 6, and f to 1. The complete symbol table is shown in Figure 7.5 for two stages during the scan. Each element in the array *place* is accessed by hashing a symbol and points to whichever symbol in the associated equivalence class was most recently inserted into *table*. The pointer field in each entry of *table* links the symbol to the preceding entry in the same equivalence class. In both *place* and *table*, 0 serves as a null pointer.

	place	table	level	place	table	level
8.		c (3) 3				
7.		f (3) 0				
6.	4	a (3) 5		4		
5.	8	a (2) 1		3	a (2) 1	
4.	0	d (2) 0		0	d (2) 0	
3.	6	c (1) 2	6	5	c (1) 2	
2.	0	b (1) 0	4	0	b (1) 0	4
1.	7	a (1) 0	1	0	a (1) 0	1

| (a) in block 3 | (b) in block 2 |

Figure 7.5 Block Structure with Hashing

Searching requires one application of the key transformation to access *place*, one stage of indirection to reach *table*, and a linear scan of the equivalence class. For a reasonable key transformation this is still $O(1)$ time. Insertion of a new symbol requires simple chain maintenance with no scan, and block opening requires no special action. Block closure, on the other hand, is complicated by the necessity of resetting the chain head pointers in *place*. Access to the correct entries in *place* requires application of the key transformation to each symbol deleted. The time requirement for this relatively infrequent operation is therefore $O(n)$.

Static symbol tables. The dynamic symbol table organizations we have considered limit the compiler to a single pass, because table entries are deleted as soon as the scanner has finished examining the corresponding block. For multipass compilation, all the symbols must remain available after scanning is complete. Because symbols are not deleted when block closure is encountered, there may be symbols from more than one block at a given nesting level. The pointer array *level* therefore becomes incapable of distinguishing among the various blocks, and must be replaced by a fuller specification of the complete block structure. The array *block* designates for each block both the first (*lo*) and the last (*hi*) symbol table entries associated with the block, and specifies the immediately enclosing block (*enc*). The number of entries in *block* is equal not to the maximum nesting level but to the total number of blocks. The complete symbol table for our example program is shown in Figure 7.6 as it stands at the conclusion of scanning. Pointers for binary searching or for hashing are omitted.

	table	*block*		
9.	f (4)			
8.	c (3)			
7.	f (3)			
6.	a (3)	*lo*	*hi*	*enc*
5.	a (2)			
4.	d (2)	9	9	1
3.	c (1)	6	8	2
2.	b (1)	4	5	1
1.	a (1)	1	3	0

Figure 7.6   Static Symbol Table

Linear search of the static block-structured symbol table is straightforward. For a reference in block i, search begins at *table*[$hi[i]$] and proceeds downward through *table*[$lo[i]$]. If the symbol is not found among these entries for the current block, i is replaced by $enc[i]$ and the search continues. Successively enclosing blocks are searched until either the symbol is found or the outermost block is exhausted without finding the symbol. Each probe now requires two comparisons, one of the desired symbol with the entry and one of the index with $lo[i]$. The construction of *block* is nearly trivial, and of course no action is needed when block closure is encountered.

Binary search and hashing are both less efficient than with a dynamic table. After all, the first occurrence of the desired symbol may lie in a block outside the environment being considered. There is no way to verify its eligibility without a further search of *block*. Hence, use of the block number as an attribute is advisable if either binary search or hashing is contemplated with a static symbol table.

Our symbol table construction methods have thus far assumed that declarations precede embedded blocks. If we remove this restriction, as in Figure 7.2(b), declarations for one block may be encountered before the scan of the surrounding block is complete. If symbols are appended to *table* as they are encountered, the entries for a block will no longer be contiguous, nor will nesting order be related to table order.

Matters are easily set right. Because the proper grouping of table entries is not known until block closure is scanned, symbols are appended to the table only at that time. The blocks are therefore represented in the table in the order of their closures, not in the order of their openings. Each symbol waits, between its declaration and the block closure, in a stack. The symbol is pushed onto the stack when its declaration is encountered and popped from the stack when its block closure is encountered. Elements of the array *block* are created, as before, in the order of block openings. Not until a block is closed, however, does its entry in the array *block* point to the array *table*. Until that time, one of its fields (we have chosen *hi*) specifies how many of its declarations have been stacked. Figure 7.7 illustrates four stages in the table construction process for the program of Figure 7.2(b).

At stage (a), three blocks have been entered, and five entries stacked, but no block closed, as indicated by the value 0 in each field *lo*. After the declaration of c in block 3 is encountered, it is stacked and the *hi* field of *block*[3] incremented to 3, the number of its entries on the stack. When closure of block 3 is encountered, that field is used to control popping the three entries from the stack and appending them to the symbol table. During that process *lo*[3] and *hi*[3] are set to 1 and 3, the lowest and highest indices of the corresponding entries in *table*. By stage (b) the foregoing action has been completed and a second declaration encountered in block 2, whose closure has been encountered by stage (c), as has the last declaration of block 1. Before the closure of block 1, block 4 with its lone declaration is opened. Stage (d) shows the completed table.

Thus far we have assumed that a symbol is entered in the table only when its declaration is encountered. It is often convenient, and in one-pass translation mandatory, to enter a symbol in the table as soon as the first reference to it is encountered. But the association of a symbol with its block is not always possible if symbol reference is permitted to precede symbol declaration. In PL/I, for example,

	table	block lo hi enc	stack
5.			f (3)
4.			a (3)
3.		0 2 2	d (2)
2.		0 1 1	b (1)
1.		0 2 0	a (1)

(a) after **declare** f (3)

	table	block lo hi enc	stack
5.			
4.			a (2)
3.	a (3)	1 3 2	d (2)
2.	f (3)	0 2 1	b (1)
1.	c (3)	0 2 2	a (1)

(b) after **declare** a (2)

	table	block lo hi enc	stack
9.			
8.			
7.			
6.			
5.	d (2)		
4.	a (2)		
3.	a (3)	1 3 2	c (1)
2.	f (3)	4 5 1	b (1)
1.	c (3)	0 3 0	a (1)

(c) after **declare** c (1)

	table	block lo hi enc	stack
9.	a (1)		
8.	b (1)		
7.	c (1)		
6.	f (4)		
5.	d (2)		
4.	a (2)	6 6 1	
3.	a (3)	1 3 2	
2.	f (3)	4 5 1	
1.	c (3)	7 9 0	

(d) after block 1 closure

Figure 7.7   Symbol Table Construction for
Program with Deferred Declarations

goto *L* may be a jump to a label yet to be encountered in the current block, to a label already encountered in an enclosing block, or to a label in an enclosing block but not yet encountered.

The foregoing ambiguity can always be resolved by multiple passes in a compiler, or by an extra scan of the full text by an interpreter. If processing without extra passes is desired, the ambiguity can be prohibited by restricting the source language. An obvious restriction is to require declaration to precede reference. This is good practice anyhow with respect to variables and procedures, but many programmers find it unduly restrictive for labels. An alternative restriction on the use of labels is to prohibit the "unusual return", a jump to a label in an enclosing block. This restriction has the further merit of simplifying the execution-time management of the activation-record stack.

FOR FURTHER STUDY

Waite84 presents a good discussion of source-language features in Chapter 2, and an overview of compiler design in Chapter 14. Other overviews are presented in the tutorial Glass69, Chapter 5 of Beck85, and Section 3.2 of Toy86.

Forms of intermediate code are discussed fully in Section 8.1 of Aho86 and in Chapter 10 of Tremblay85.

A simple introduction to attribute grammars is given in Jazayeri75. A more extensive one is presented in Section 5 of Marcotty76. Their use in compilation is treated in Chapter 8 of Waite84 and Chapter 2 of Hunter85.

Symbol tables in the context of translators are presented briefly by Wegner68 (Section 2.2), and more fully by Hopgood69 (Chapter 4), Gries71 (Chapters 9–10), and Aho86 (Section 7.6). Tree-structured tables are emphasized in Severance74, Davie81 (Sections 10.1–10.5), Horowitz84b (Chapter 9), and Tremblay85 (Chapter 8). Maurer75 offers a good survey of hashing. Block structure in symbol tables is discussed in Gries71 (Section 9.5), Tremblay 85 (Chapter 8), and, for one-pass compilers only, McKeeman74.

REVIEW QUESTIONS

7.1 Can a nonreserved keyword, such as PL/I's **sum**, be used both as a variable and as a built-in function within a single program?

7.2 What effect does backtracking by the parser have on the generation of intermediate code?

7.3 Should A := B always be represented in postfix as A B ASSIGN rather than B A ASSIGN?

7.4 Could an interpreter be written to execute quadruples?

7.5 Does the use of triples, as opposed to quadruples, reduce the need for temporary storage at execution time?

7.6 In indirect triples, why are jump destinations not given as triple numbers?

7.7 To what different source-language constructs can a branch in intermediate code correspond?

7.8 How do source-code and intermediate-code branches differ?

7.9 Under what circumstances might it be better not to replace the tokens of a compiler source language by uniform tokens?

7.10 Give a reason for deferring the generation of constants when they are first encountered.

7.11 What is the chief merit of hashing for a large symbol table?

7.12 One way to build a static symbol table for a language with block structure is to distinguish duplicate names by qualifying each occurrence with the block number. Can this be done by qualifying each name with its nesting level instead of with the block number? Explain.

7.13 If the block number of duplicated symbols is to be incorporated in the search key, why must this be done for *all* symbols?

7.14 What problem arises if symbol reference is permitted to precede symbol declaration in a language with block structure?

7.15 Distinguish a dynamic from a static block-structured symbol table.

7.16 Are the three approaches presented for implementing symbol tables for a block-structured language mutually exclusive?

7.17 At what stage of compilation is it possible to discard source-language names?

PROBLEMS

7.1 What is the general form of **while** *condition* **do** *statement* in postfix?

7.2 Devise a method for the single-pass generation of postfix intermediate code for backward branches in source language.

7.3 Represent the following PASCAL statement in each of the specified forms of intermediate code. Number the symbols or lines, as appropriate, serially from 100.

(**a**) postfix;
(**b**) quadruples;
(**c**) triples;
(**d**) indirect triples.

$$\text{if } X{<}Y \text{ then if } X{>}Z \text{ then } A{:=}B{+}3 \text{ else } A{:=}C$$
$$\text{else if } X{>}Z \text{ then } A{:=}C \qquad \text{else } A{:=}D{-}1$$

7.4 Represent the following PASCAL program segment in each of the specified forms of intermediate code. Number the symbols or lines, as appropriate, serially from 200.

(**a**) postfix;
(**b**) quadruples;
(**c**) triples;
(**d**) indirect triples.

```
while (A < E) do begin
    while (E − A < G) do E := A + F;
    G := A + F
end
```

7.5 A symbol table having the eleven addresses 0–10 is managed with the use of hashing and open addressing. The hashing function in use maps each identifier to its length in characters. The following identifiers arrive for insertion in the order shown: *segment, sector, radius, pi, perim, diameter, circumf, chord, center, area,* and *arc.*

Both for linear probing (with $r = 2$) and for quadratic probing (with $s = 2$ and $t = 2$) show the symbol table and state the number of probes that have been made

(**a**) after the first 8 symbols have arrived;
(**b**) after all 11 symbols have arrived.

For each symbol, count the initial insertion attempt (with $i = 0$) as one probe.

7.6 Consider the implementation of a block-structured symbol table for the following program.

> **procedure** A
>   **declare** w
>   **procedure** B
>   **declare** x
>   **procedure** D
>   **declare** z
>   **end** D
>   **procedure** E
>   **declare** w
>   **end** E
>   **declare** z
>   **end** B
>   **declare** y
>   **procedure** C
>   **declare** x
>   **end** C
>   **declare** z
>   **end** A

(a) Move all declarations ahead of other text in their blocks. Assume the use of a stack symbol table with linear search, as in Figure 7.3. Show the symbol table as it stands just before closure of each block.

(b) Repeat part **a** for a stack symbol table with binary search, as in Figure 7.4.

(c) Repeat part **a** for a stack symbol table with hashing, as in Figure 7.5. Assume that the hashing function transforms w to 4, x and y to 2, and z to 1.

(d) With the declarations moved as in part **a**, assume the use of a static symbol table, as in Figure 7.6. Show the symbol table as it stands at the conclusion of scanning.

(e) Leaving the deferred declarations in place, assume the use of a stack symbol table of the type in Figure 7.7. Show the symbol table as it stands just before closure of each block.

Chapter 8

Compilation

The five basic steps of compilation have already been enumerated: lexical analysis, syntactic analysis, semantic processing, storage allocation, and target code generation. The first two of these, although particularly important to compilers, are encountered in all translators and have already been treated in Chapter 6. This chapter discusses the last three basic steps, which are specific to compilers. It also touches briefly on the important topics of code optimization and error handling.

8.1 SEMANTIC PROCESSING

The parsing algorithms described in Chapter 6 do not merely recognize a string in the programming language, even though they produce no derivation tree explicitly. The algorithms do in fact also parse the string; the derivation tree is implicit in the order in which rules of the grammar are applied. If target code is ultimately to be produced, however, an explicit representation of the tree is indeed required; this is embodied in the intermediate code. The task of semantic processing is to produce this explicit linear representation of the derivation tree, associating with it the semantic information content of the original program. That semantic information resides originally in the tokens that constitute the program text. Semantic processing associates the appropriate semantic information with each nonterminal as it is recognized and thus develops the semantic information required in the intermediate code. Semantic processing incorporates both analytic and synthetic aspects: analysis of semantic content and generation of intermediate code.

To illustrate semantic processing we first show how semantic routines are associated with rules of the grammar in both bottom-up and top-down parsing of expressions. We then consider the semantics of other machine-independent language constructs. Quadruples will be used throughout as the intermediate form. Except for an occasional problem, the generation of postfix or of triples is similar.

The reader should bear in mind that many compilers use parsing methods other than the two presented in Chapter 6. A knowledge of those two alone, however, provides sufficient background for understanding the relation of semantic processing to syntactic analysis, regardless of the choice of parsing method.

We begin with the expression $(X+Y)*Z$ and the grammar of Figure 8.1. This operator precedence grammar differs from that of Figure 6.3 only in having IDENT as a terminal, rather than a choice

1.	*expression*	↔	*expression* '+' *term*
2.	*expression*	↔	*term*
3.	*term*	↔	*term* '*' *factor*
4.	*term*	↔	*factor*
5.	*factor*	↔	'(' *expression* ')'
6.	*factor*	↔	IDENT

(a) Rules

R

L	+	*	(	)	IDENT
+	>	<	<	>	<
*	>	>	<	>	<
(	<	<	<	≐	<
)	>	>		>	
IDENT	>	>		>	

(b) Precedence matrix

Figure 8.1 Grammar for Expressions

among three specific identifiers. The lexical scanner will recognize each of X, Y, and Z as an instance of IDENT.

Bottom-Up Parsing of Expressions. An operator precedence parse, similar to that of Figure 6.12, is shown in the first three columns of Figure 8.2. Here the parenthesized number following the word "reduce" is the number of the grammar rule in Figure 8.1(a) to be applied as a reduction. The intermediate code quadruples

$$
\begin{array}{llll}
+ & X & Y & T1 \\
* & T1 & Z & T2
\end{array}
$$

are to be produced during the bottom-up parsing. The first quadruple should be generated when $n + n$ is reduced to n. This can be accomplished by a semantic routine that is called when reduction 1 of the grammar is applied. Unfortunately, the syntax stack has no information about which identifiers are involved. It is hardly adequate to generate

$$
\begin{array}{llll}
+ & n & n & n
\end{array}
$$

each time reduction 1 is applied. Identifier information must therefore be associated with entries on the syntax stack. Fortunately, the lexical analyzer provides not only the lexical type of each identifier, but also its name or a pointer to the corresponding symbol table entry. If this information is associated first with IDENT and afterwards with the successive nonterminals to which IDENT is reduced, a quadruple can be generated that refers to the specific identifier. This semantic information is shown in the fourth column of Figure 8.2, held on a semantics stack that grows and shrinks in synchronism with the syntax stack. Here we use for clarity the identifier itself. In a practical implementation this might be replaced either by the address of the symbol table entry or by the address of the storage location, if the allocation has already been made.

In writing the semantic routines, we assume the existence of three auxiliary procedures. $QUAD(a,b,c,d)$ writes a quadruple with the four parameters as its fields. It also increments by unity the global variable *quadno*, which holds the number of the next quadruple to be generated. $POP(stack,vbl)$ copies the top element of *stack* to *vbl* and pops the stack. $PUSH(stack,vbl)$ pushes a copy of *vbl* onto *stack*.

We can now write the semantic routine to be associated with reduction 1 as

$$i \leftarrow i + 1$$
$$POP(semantics, opd2)$$
$$POP(semantics, opd1)$$
$$POP(semantics, opd1)$$
$$PUSH(semantics, 'Ti')$$
$$QUAD('+', opd1, opd2, 'Ti')$$

in which the second call of *POP* is required to skip over the null semantic entry that corresponds to the terminal + on the syntax stack. The incrementation of i, which is global to the semantic routine, ensures the generation of distinct temporary variable names. For simplicity, we use the notation 'Ti' to represent the catenation of the character 'T' with the character-string representation of the integer i. A similar semantic routine is provided for reduction 3 (multiplication).

Means are still required for ensuring that the correct identifier information is indeed on the semantics stack when the quadruples are generated. Every time a symbol is shifted onto the syntax stack, the required item is shifted (pushed) onto the semantics stack. For identifiers, the identifier name is pushed; for all other symbols, a

Syntax stack	Current symbol	Shift/reduce decision	Semantics stack	Semantic routine
empty	(	shift	*empty*	0
(	IDENT	shift	null	7
(IDENT	+	reduce (6)	null X	*none*
(n	+	shift	null X	0
(n +	IDENT	shift	null X null	7
(n + IDENT	)	reduce (6)	null X null Y	*none*
(n + n	)	reduce (1)	null X null Y	1
(n	)	shift	null T1	0
(n)	*	reduce (5)	null T1 null	5
n	*	shift	T1	0
n *	IDENT	shift	T1 null	7
n * IDENT		reduce (6)	T1 null Z	*none*
n * n		reduce (3)	T1 null Z	3
n			T2	

Figure 8.2   Parse of (X+Y)*Z with Semantic Actions

null item is pushed. The semantic action for reductions 2, 4, and 6 is merely to continue to associate the same identifier name with the topmost syntax stack element. Those reductions require no semantic routines. Reduction 5, which replaces (n) by n, does not result in any change of identifier, but we must discard the null entries that correspond to the two parentheses. The semantic routine therefore includes three pops and one push. Figure 8.2 is completed by a fifth column, which gives the number of the semantic routine to be called. Numbers between 1 and 6 correspond to the rules of the grammar in Figure 8.1(a), routine 0 stacks a null entry, and routine 7 stacks the identifier name. Of the eight semantic routines, only routines 1 and 3 generate intermediate code.

There may be yet more stacks for different kinds of semantic information. The type of each variable or expression is an obvious candidate. Although the syntax and semantics stacks are conceptually distinct, they may be implemented as a single stack whose entries have multiple fields. If a two-stack implementation is retained, however, some simplification is possible in the semantic routines that have been described. If the semantics stack is pushed only for identifiers, there will never be any null entries on it. Then the semantic routines for reductions 1 and 3 will not need the second pop, and a semantic routine for reduction 5 will not be required at all.

Top-Down Parsing of Expressions. In top-down parsing by recursive descent, no explicit syntax stack is created; the stack of activation records serves instead. Figure 8.3 presents three recursive descent routines for parsing (without semantic processing) the grammar of Figure 8.1.

Semantic processing is most readily performed by incorporating into each routine the semantic action appropriate to the nonterminal that the routine recognizes. The routine must therefore produce the semantic information associated with the nonterminal. Several kinds of semantic information may be required, and it is convenient to provide a parameter for the transmission of each. We shall concern ourselves here only with the name of each variable. This permits us to recast each recognition routine as a procedure with a single parameter. We place in that parameter the name of the original or temporary variable associated with the nonterminal

```
procedure EXPRESSION
    TERM
    while token = '+' do
        SCANNER(token)
        TERM

procedure TERM
    FACTOR
    while token = '*' do
        SCANNER(token)
        FACTOR

procedure FACTOR
    case token of
        IDENT:
        '(:     SCANNER(token)
                EXPRESSION
                if token ≠ ')' then ERROR
        other:  ERROR
    SCANNER(token)
```

Figure 8.3   Recognition Routines for Grammar of Figure 8.1

that has been recognized. Local variables within each routine hold the names delivered by the recognition procedures that it calls.

The procedure *SCANNER* is modified accordingly, and now has two parameters. To the first it delivers, as before, the actual token it has found. To the second parameter it delivers, but only if the token is an identifier, the name of the identifier. The three recognition routines have been recast in Figure 8.4 as one-parameter procedures with semantic processing included. Their use would be invoked by a sequence such as

$$i \leftarrow 1$$
$$SCANNER(token, idname)$$
$$EXPRESSION(name)$$

in which the counter i ensures, as before, that different intermediate results have unique names, and *name* is a character variable that will eventually hold the name associated with the expression being parsed.

```
procedure EXPRESSION(exprname)
   char exprname
   char opd1, opd2
   begin
      TERM(opd1)
      while token = '+' do
         SCANNER(token,idname)
         TERM(opd2)
         QUAD('+',opd1,opd2,'Ti')
         opd1 ← 'Ti'
         i ← i + 1
      exprname ← opd1
   end

procedure TERM(termname)
   char termname
   char opd1, opd2
   begin
      FACTOR(opd1)
      while token = '*' do
         SCANNER(token,idname)
         FACTOR(opd2)
         QUAD('*',opd1,opd2,'Ti')
         opd1 ← 'Ti'
         i ← i + 1
      termname ← opd1
   end

procedure FACTOR(factname)
   char factname
   begin
      case token of
         IDENT: factname ← idname
         '(':   SCANNER(token,idname)
                EXPRESSION(factname)
                if token ≠ ')' then ERROR
         other: ERROR
      SCANNER(token,idname)
   end
```

Figure 8.4   Recognition Routines with Semantic Processing

A brief examination of procedure *TERM* will help to explain how the semantic processing is accomplished. The call to *FACTOR* delivers the name of the factor to local variable *opd1*. That execution of *FACTOR* concluded with a lookahead call of *SCANNER*, which made the next terminal available for examination in the global variable *token*. If that terminal is not an asterisk, then no intermediate code is generated and the name of the factor is delivered as the name of the term. If, on the other hand, that terminal is an asterisk, then a call of *SCANNER* prepares another call of *FACTOR*, and the name of the next factor is placed in the local variable *opd2*. Intermediate code is now generated and the search for more factors continues. Each time, the first operand of the quadruple is given the name of the previously created temporary variable. The name of the last temporary variable is delivered as the name of the term.

Beyond Expressions. We now look beyond the realm of expression evaluation and ask what semantic processing is required by other language constructs. An assignment to an unsubscripted variable results in very simple generation. In reducing

$$stmt \leftrightarrow \text{IDENT} := expression$$

where the name of the identifier is in *opd1* and that of the expression is in *opd2*, it is sufficient to execute $QUAD(`:=`, opd2,, opd1)$. Thus $A := (X * Y) + Z$ might yield

*	X	Y	T1
+	T1	Z	T2
:=	T2		A

where we hope that subsequent optimization would replace the last two quadruples by a single one that delivers the sum to A directly. A more attractive action would be simply to insert the name of the identifier in place of the temporary variable in the destination field of the last quadruple generated for *expression*.

The declaration of an identifier usually does not result in the generation of intermediate code. It does cause the compiler to store semantic information for later use. The identifier's type is entered in the symbol table. If the identifier is an array name, the number of dimensions is entered in the symbol table and the bounds for each dimension, if supplied, are saved for later use in performing address calculations.

A source-language declaration statement may include the specification of an initial value. This is routinely available in ADA, and is also provided by PL/I's **initial** attribute and by the "typed constant" of TURBO PASCAL. The compiler can treat the **initial** specification as it would an assignment statement and generate the code to perform the assignment at execution time. If, however, the variable is of storage class **static** or is declared in the outermost block, execution-time efficiency can be enhanced by generating the specified value during compilation. This may be accomplished either by flagging the symbol table entry and noting the value or by entering the value into the table of constants, together with a pointer to the symbol table entry. The pointer is used to place the generated constant in the storage associated with the identifier rather than in the literal pool.

Branches involving labels and **goto** statements can be processed in a manner that need not distinguish forward from backward references. With each label there is associated in the symbol table the number of the first quadruple in the intermediate code for the statement that follows that label. When the **goto** is recognized, a quadruple is generated that specifies not the target *quadruple* (whose number is not known if the branch is forward) but rather the target *label*. This jump to label quadruple might be generated by the call $QUAD(\text{'JLABEL'},,,labelname)$, where *labelname* contains the name of the label. The quadruple number associated with the label is entered in the symbol table when the label definition is encountered during parsing. When all labels have been processed, it is an easy matter to substitute quadruple numbers or storage addresses and to generate code with jumps to numeric addresses.

The use of JLABEL as an intermediate step can be bypassed by handling forward and backward branches differently. For a backward branch the symbol table yields the quadruple number, and the call $QUAD(\text{'JUMP'},,, labelname.number)$ suffices. For a forward branch, the quadruple JUMP,,,0 is generated and the number of the quadruple is placed with the label in the symbol table. If that label already pointed to a quadruple, the quadruple numbers are chained. When the label definition is eventually encountered, the chain is followed and the jump destination fields are replaced by the number of the quadruple now known to correspond to the label. This chain-following action is similar to that of one-pass assemblers.

Conditional statements involve a bit more work. A convenient form in which to represent their syntax is the following:

1.	ifstmt	↔	ifclause stmt
2.	ifstmt	↔	truepart stmt
3.	truepart	↔	ifclause stmt **else**
4.	ifclause	↔	**if** condition **then** .

The PASCAL text

$$\textbf{if } A{<}B \textbf{ then } C := B{+}D{*}4$$
$$\textbf{else } \; C := A{+}D{*}4$$

should cause quadruples such as the following to be generated, where JFALSE is a jump on result false.

11.	<	A	B	T5
12.	JFALSE	T5		16
13.	*	D	4	T6
14.	+	B	T6	C
15.	JUMP			18
16.	*	D	4	T7
17.	+	A	T7	C

Parsing of *condition* results in the generation of quadruple 11. Reduction 4 is then applied, and it must generate a quadruple with a jump forward to an undetermined destination quadruple. The semantic routine for reduction 4 generates a JFALSE quadruple with no destination address, and saves the address of the generated quadruple as semantic information associated with the nonterminal *ifclause*.

Quadruples 13 and 14 are then generated during the recognition of $C := B{+}D{*}4$ as *stmt*, and reduction 3 is applied next because of the presence of **else**. The associated semantic routine must insert the address 16 in the destination field of quadruple 12, whose number was earlier placed in association with *ifclause*. Before doing so, it must generate the unconditional jump forward as quadruple 15, albeit without a destination, and thereby advance *quadno*.

Quadruples 16 and 17 are subsequently generated during the recognition of $C := A{+}D{*}4$ as *stmt*, and reduction 2 is applied next. The only semantic action required at this time is to enter the destination address in quadruple 15. Processing of the conditional statement is then complete. If, instead of the source text presented, the **else** clause were missing, reduction 1 would be made instead of reductions 3 and 2, and similar semantic action performed.

The four semantic routines are shown in Figure 8.5. The stack *semantics* is to be understood here as holding only the semantic information that pertains to destination quadruple numbers. The quadruples are stored in the two-dimensional array *quadruple*, whose first index is the quadruple number and whose second index selects one of the four fields. Patching the destination field of a previously generated quadruple is not convenient if that quadruple has been written to an external file. In that event, the semantic routine makes a record of the modification, which is applied after the quadruple is next read in. In routine (d), the operand Ti is the temporary variable that holds the result of evaluating *condition*.

$$POP(semantics, origin)$$
$$quadruple[origin, 4] \leftarrow quadno$$

(a) *ifstmt* $\leftrightarrow$ *ifclause stmt*

$$POP(semantics, origin)$$
$$quadruple[origin, 4] \leftarrow quadno$$

(b) *ifstmt* $\leftrightarrow$ *truepart stmt*

$$POP(semantics, origin)$$
$$PUSH(semantics, quadno)$$
$$QUAD(\text{'JUMP'},,,)$$
$$quadruple[origin, 4] \leftarrow quadno$$

(c) *truepart* $\leftrightarrow$ *ifclause stmt* **else**

$$PUSH(semantics, quadno)$$
$$QUAD(\text{'JFALSE'}, \text{'}Ti\text{'},,)$$

(d) *ifclause* $\leftrightarrow$ **if** *condition* **then**

Figure 8.5 Semantic Routines for Conditional Statements

The syntax that we have been using here for conditional statements is ambiguous, as is that of Figure 6.7. Two distinct parse subtrees for the same language construct are shown in Figure 8.6, in which the four rules already introduced are complemented by the rule *stmt* $\leftrightarrow$ *ifstmt*. The example is an instance of the well-known problem of matching each **else** with the correct **then** in PASCAL, C, and similar languages. The correct interpretation of the syntactically ambiguous conditional statement is the one shown in the upper portion of Figure 8.6. Each **else** is to match the nearest preceding unmatched **then**.

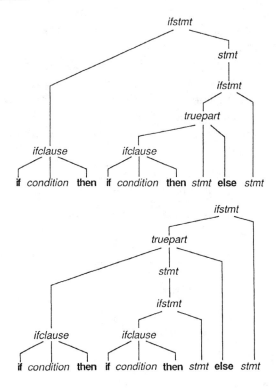

Figure 8.6 Syntactic Ambiguity in Conditional Statement

How can we ensure that the correct semantic interpretation is made? One approach is to rewrite the grammar to remove the ambiguity and admit only the desired interpretation. This is difficult to do in general, and usually results in the introduction of many more rules and nonterminals. An alternative is to write the parser to accept only the desired semantic interpretation. Consider the problem of applying a shift/reduce parser to conditional statements in which an **else** clause is optional. Suppose that the incoming terminal is **else**, the topmost stack terminal is **then**, and there is another **then** lower on the stack. The conventional grammar does not specify which of the two occurrences of **then** is to be matched. No matter. The correct semantic interpretation for most languages results from the simple solution of always shifting **else** onto the stack. The key approach is not to worry excessively about the grammar, but rather to design the parser to do what we want. Consider next a recursive descent parser for the same language. The procedure that recognizes *ifstmt* begins by finding **if** *condition* **then** *statement*. Instead of returning from this point, it proceeds to check whether the next terminal is **else**. If so, the **else** clause is also recognized as part of *ifstmt*. Thus each **else** will be matched with the proper **then**.

As a final example, consider the semantic processing associated with an iterative control structure. The statement **while** $A+B<C$ **do** $A := A*A+B$ should yield the following quadruples.

24.	+	A	B	T12
25.	<	T12	C	T13
26.	JFALSE	T13		30
27.	*	A	A	T14
28.	+	T14	B	A
29.	JUMP			24

A convenient form of syntax is

$$whilestmt \quad \leftrightarrow \quad whilepart \; stmt$$
$$whilepart \quad \leftrightarrow \quad \textbf{while} \; condition \; \textbf{do}$$

For the example text, quadruples 24 and 25 are generated for *condition* after the number 24 has been retained during the recognition of *whilepart*. Further semantic actions in recognizing the latter include the generation of quadruple 26 (with the forward destination reference missing) and retention of its quadruple number, too. During recognition of *whilestmt*, quadruples 27 and 28 are generated for *stmt* and quadruple 29 is generated to close the loop. Finally, the forward reference is inserted in quadruple 26. The two processing routines are shown in Figure 8.7. Variable *first* holds the number (24) of the first quadruple of the **while-do** control structure. Variable *escape* holds the number (26) of the quadruple from which the jump escapes when the condition is no longer met. We assume that *CONDITION* and *STMT* leave the stack *semantics* as they found it. Iterative structures using **repeat-until** are handled similarly.

The indexed loop contains more components than do the simpler iterative structures. The PASCAL statement model

$$\textbf{for} \; ident := expr1 \; \textbf{downto} \; expr2 \; \textbf{do} \; stmt$$

should lead to the quadruples shown in Figure 8.8.

```
procedure WHILEPART
   begin
      if token ≠ 'while' then ERROR
      PUSH(semantics,quadno)              {start of condition}
      SCANNER(token)
      CONDITION                           {generating more quadruples}
      if token ≠ 'do' then ERROR
      PUSH(semantics,quadno)              {forward jump location}
      QUAD('JFALSE','Ti',,)
   end

procedure WHILESTMT
   integer first,escape
   begin
      WHILEPART
      STMT                                {generating more quadruples}
      POP(semantics,escape)
      POP(semantics,first)
      QUAD('JUMP',,,first)                {incrementing quadno}
      quadruple[escape,4] ← quadno
   end
```

Figure 8.7   Parsing and Semantic Routines for **while-do**

$$
\begin{array}{ll}
q+1. & \left.\begin{array}{l}\\ \\ \end{array}\right\} \text{quadruple(s) for } ident := expr1 \\
r-1. & \\
r. & \left.\begin{array}{l}\\ \\ \end{array}\right\} \text{quadruple(s) for } expr2 \\
s-3. & \\
\end{array}
$$

$s-2.$	JUMP			s
$s-1.$	−	$ident$	@1	$ident$
$s.$	<	$ident$	$expr2$	Ti
$s+1.$	JTRUE	Ti		$t+1$

$$
\begin{array}{ll}
s+2. & \left.\begin{array}{l}\\ \\ \end{array}\right\} \text{quadruple(s) for } stmt \\
t-1. & \\
\end{array}
$$

$t.$	JUMP		$s-1$

Figure 8.8   Quadruples for **for** statement

If the statement syntax is defined by

$$forstmt \quad \leftrightarrow \quad \textbf{for } ident := forlist \textbf{ do } stmt$$
$$forlist \quad \leftrightarrow \quad expression \textbf{ downto } expression$$

it is virtually impossible to associate semantic actions with each reduction. A suitable definition is given instead by

$$forstmt \quad \leftrightarrow \quad idxpart \textbf{ do } stmt$$
$$idxpart \quad \leftrightarrow \quad forpart \textbf{ downto } expression$$
$$forpart \quad \leftrightarrow \quad \textbf{for } \text{IDENT} := expression.$$

Semantic actions associated with the second reduction increment i and generate quadruples $s - 2$ through $s + 1$, and semantic actions associated with the first reduction generate quadruple t. The adjustment of the jump destination addresses is straightforward.

This last example illustrates the importance to semantic processing of having the syntactic analysis performed in a suitable manner. In rewriting a grammar to facilitate semantic processing, we must take care not to change the language defined by the grammar.

The present section is illustrative rather than exhaustive. Several important constructs of machine-independent languages have not been considered. A major omission is that of arrays and subscripts, which cause the generation of arithmetic instructions that perform addressing calculations, even in the absence of knowledge at compilation time of the size of an array. Expression lists, which appear not only in subscripting, but also in declarations (as lists of variables) and in input/output statements, have been omitted. The many problems raised by block structure have been ignored. An interesting example is a **goto** naming a label that may be a forward reference (not yet defined) within the same block, a backward reference into an enclosing block, or even a forward reference into an enclosing block.

Semantic Checking. For simplicity in the foregoing presentation, we have assumed correct input. Semantic errors do occur, however, and the compiler must check for them. Although we discuss semantic checking here in a separate section, it is usually not performed as a separate operation. Instead, the code to implement semantic checking is usually combined with the code for processing the constructs being checked.

Semantic checking includes several tasks. One is the detection of structural error. For example, the number of array subscripts must equal the number of dimensions. Procedure calls must agree with the procedure definition in the number and types of parameters.

Another task is the resolution of names. A name may be defined either implicitly through use or explicitly through declaration. Whether a definition is implicit or explicit, each use of a name must be associated with the appropriate definition. This means that the compiler must apply scope rules both to make the correct association, and to detect multiple definitions within a single scope. The symbol table routines, normally called by the semantic analyzer, perform both of these functions. Section 7.4.4 discusses the design of symbol tables to handle block structure. The detection of multiple definitions is straightforward. An attempt to insert a name that has already been defined is flagged as a multiple-definition error. Missing definitions are also readily detected.

A third task is the proper determination and handling of type information. Type requirements are imposed by many different language constructs. Expressions that control conditional branching must be boolean. Addends must be capable of being added. Array subscripts must must be integers or, in languages like PASCAL, scalars of an enumerated type. Branch destinations must be labels. The target and source of an assignment must be compatible.

For some operators, a type requirement is stringent. For example, the expression governed by **while** in PASCAL must be boolean. If it is not, there is an error in the program. For other operators, there is more flexibility. For example, many languages permit the expressions governed by '+' to be of one of several types. This actually results in using a single symbol for different operations, such as the addition of reals and the addition of integers. This association of multiple meanings with a single symbol is known as **overloading**. The compiler must generate code for the correct variant of the operator. Another problem arises when the language permits the two operands of addition to be of *different* types. The sum of a real and an integer is often defined to be a real. Instead of flagging an error, the compiler generates code to call a run-time conversion routine.

Type checking requires the semantic analyzer to associate type information with each language construct. In expression evaluation, for example, this would result in the modification of the recognition routines of Figure 8.4. Each routine would return not only the name of each temporary variable, but also the type of the subexpression it represents. Similar approaches can be used with other language constructs. As the constructs become nested, their types become complicated (*e.g.*, pointer to array of integer). This leads to a language of "type expressions", which can be used to specify a type checker formally.

8.2 STORAGE ALLOCATION

Before target code can be generated, the addresses of variables and constants to be accessed at execution time must be determinable (except, of course, for any relocation factor). The generator must also have a means of producing code that will either incorporate or calculate the necessary addresses. If allocation and access are provided for variables, then constants surely pose no problem. We therefore present storage allocation in terms of variables. Just as a variable has scope, or extent in space, so does it have **life**, or extent in time. Some variables exist only while the block in which they are declared is active. These are called **dynamic variables** and space allocated to them is called **dynamic storage**. Others have life that extends beyond that of the blocks to which they are local. Those are called **static variables** and the space allocated to them is called **static storage**. Be careful to distinguish use of the terms "static" and "dynamic" in this context from their use to describe the nesting of program blocks in the compilation-time text or of activation records in the execution-time stack.

In addition to the distinction between static and dynamic storage, another distinction is important to the compiler. The attributes of a variable may or may not be known at compilation time. To the extent that allocation of storage is dependent upon unknown attributes (*e.g.*, the size of an array or the type of a variable), the task of the storage allocation step becomes more difficult. Before considering either dynamic storage or the execution-time specification of attributes, we consider static storage for variables whose attributes are known at compilation time.

Static variables with known attributes. All storage in FORTRAN, **own** variables in ALGOL (except arrays whose bounds are formal parameters), and **static** storage in several other languages can be allocated by the compiler on the basis of complete information. The compiler can scan the symbol table, allocating to each elementary variable the amount of space it requires, and incrementing a counter appropriately. The amount allocated depends both on the architecture of the target machine and on the desired trade-off between space and time requirements of the target code. A boolean variable may be allocated either an entire word (or byte on a byte-addressed machine), or a single bit in a word that it shares with other boolean variables. Allocating a private word uses more space, but sharing a word requires extra time for packing and unpacking. A character-string variable will be allocated the number of words or bytes appropriate to its length, with some waste perhaps if a nonintegral number of words is required. If the string is of variable length, two approaches are possible.

One approach is to allocate and free space dynamically as the string expands and shrinks; the other is to allocate the maximum amount at all times. In either event, extra space is required to store at least the current length and perhaps the maximum length, although the latter quantity may be embedded instead in the generated target code. A variable declared as **integer** or **fixed** is usually allocated a single word. If a radix point is implied, the generated code must provide for scaling. So-called "variable field length" data, especially decimal numbers (as in the IBM 370), are often used. Despite the name, the length of each item is typically fixed, and enough bytes or words are allocated. A variable declared as **real** or **float** is allocated a word or double word, as appropriate to the stated precision, for a target machine with floating-point instructions. If the floating-point operations are to be performed by subroutines, a more convenient allocation is usually a pair of words, one for the fraction and one for the exponent.

Some machines, particularly those with byte addressing, impose **alignment** restrictions on the addresses at which a datum may be stored. In the IBM 360, for example, the addresses of double words were required to be multiples of 8; those of full words, multiples of 4; and those of half words, multiples of 2. If the next address to be allocated is not an appropriate multiple, one or more bytes must be skipped until a suitable address is reached. The attendant storage waste can be eliminated by first allocating all double words, then all full words, *etc.* This requires multiple scans over the symbol table.

Elementary variables with the same attributes can be collected by the programmer into an array and accessed by the use of a common name qualified by subscripts. A one-dimensional array, or vector, of variables is allocated consecutive units of storage in the amount appropriate to each element. The total required is easily computed as the product of that amount by the number of elements. To access an array element it is necessary to know where the array begins, how long each element is, and which element is desired. The starting or base address B is available from the symbol table, as are the element length N and the lower and upper subscript bounds L and U. The starting address of the ith element is therefore $B+N*(i-L)$. If i is known at compilation time, as in $PAYT[3]$, the compiler can calculate the address in full. Suppose, however, that i will be the result of evaluating an expression at execution time, as in $PAYT[J+1]$. Then the compiler can calculate the constant part $B-N*L$. It can also generate execution-time code to evaluate the subscript expression, multiply it by N, and add it to the constant part, yielding the address of the desired operand.

An arbitrary one-dimensional array maps naturally onto main storage, which is itself essentially a vector (with the address as subscript). A two-dimensional array, or matrix, is not vectorial, and we need a way of mapping it onto the vectorial structure of storage. A one-stage mapping is effected by storing the elements consecutively in a prescribed order. The two obvious orders are one row at a time and one column at a time. Let an array of M rows and N columns be declared as $A[1..M,1..N]$. The sequence in **row-major** order (one row at a time), in which the first index changes least frequently, is

$$A[1,1],A[1,2],..,A[1,N],A[2,1],A[2,2],..,A[2,N],..,A[M,1],A[M,2],..,A[M,N],$$

whereas in **column-major** order it is

$$A[1,1],A[2,1],..,A[M,1],A[1,2],A[2,2],..,A[M,2],..,A[1,N],A[2,N],..,A[M,N].$$

Although standard Fortran uses column-major order, row-major order is more common and will be assumed henceforth.

Let one-word items be declared as the array $X[L1..U1,L2..U2]$, where the number of rows is $R = U1-(L1-1)$ and the number of columns is $C = U2-(L2-1)$. Then if the starting address is B, the address of $X[i,k]$ is $(i-L1)*C+(k-L2)+B$. The constant part $B-(L2+C*L1)$ is calculated once, at compilation time, and can be stored with the entry for X in the symbol table. The remaining part $(i*C)+k$ will in general be calculated at execution time from the index expression values i and k at the cost of one multiplication and one addition. A second addition is needed to add the constant part of the address.

An alternative to linearizing a two-dimensional array is to store each row separately as a vector. An extra vector $P[L1..U1]$ of pointers holds the starting address for each row. Determination of the address of $X[i,k]$ requires first an access to $P[i]$, the value of which is added to $k-L2$ before the desired matrix element can then be accessed. In this two-stage mapping, an extra storage access replaces the multiplication required for a linearized matrix. That multiplication may be costly on some machines. Another advantage is that not all rows need be in main storage simultaneously. This can be of considerable benefit in solving large linear systems by elimination methods, which typically require only two rows at a time during much of the processing. If the entire array is in main storage, then this allocation method requires extra storage space for the vector of pointers.

Either the linearization or the successive access method is easily generalized to multidimensional arrays. Such arrays are most likely to be used on large machines with fast multiplication, and linearization is probably more common. We can view the execution-time address calculation in two dimensions as the evaluation of a first-degree mixed-radix polynomial in R and C. For n dimensions it generalizes to a polynomial of degree $n-1$ in the mixed radices r_i, which are the lengths of the array in each dimension. The calculation requires $n-1$ multiplications and n additions.

An important function in accessing array elements is to ensure that the values of the subscript expressions lie within the bounds of the array. If they do not, access is attempted to the wrong location in a linearized array, or even to some other area in storage. The result may be the reading of invalid data, the writing of incorrect results, modification of the running program, destruction of another user's program or data, or an attempt to address an area protected against the current program. Whether the consequences are the insidious calculation of nearly correct results or abrupt termination of execution, they are undesirable. Intermediate code to check index expressions against the array bounds may or may not be produced. Because bounds checking requires considerable time and space, it is often omitted in compiling programs believed to be correct. In a compiler for debugging, however, it is extremely valuable. In some compilers it is available optionally.

For tree-structured aggregates of elementary variables, storage needs to be allocated only for the elementary variables, which are the leaves of the tree. This is most readily done in leaf order, and is straightforward even if arrays appear either at the leaf level or at higher levels of the tree. The chief complexity introduced by tree-structured variables is due to the use of identifiers to correspond to other nodes than leaves, and to the use of a given identifier for more than one nonroot node. These are problems of symbol table design that do not affect the allocation process.

Dynamic variables with known attributes. We turn now to allocation of storage that is dynamic, but still for variables all of whose attributes are known at compilation time. The easiest such dynamic allocation is for those variables that are created upon activation of the block to which they are local and deleted upon exit from the block. Storage for these variables is allocated in the activation record of that block. Even if activation records are stored consecutively, absolute storage addresses cannot be assigned by the compiler. This is because the sequence of activation records on the execution-time stack is not predictable at compilation time. Instead, the compiler assigns to each variable a two-part address (l,d) composed of the block nesting level l and a displacement d within the block. A variable local to the current block is stored in that block's activation record. It can be accessed by use of d alone, provided that the starting location of the current activation record is made available to the program. This can be done by loading the program and activation record together, relocating addresses in the program to correspond to the location of the activation record. A disadvantage is the necessity to perform relocation every time a block is invoked. An alternative method is particularly suited to machines with base-register addressing. Each time an activation record is allocated, its starting address is provided as a base for use by the program.

Access to nonlocal identifiers requires indirection. Although there may exist several blocks at a given nesting level l in the static text, at most one of them is in the environment of the current block at any given moment during execution time. Let the current block, at level c, include a reference to a variable at location (e,d) in the enclosing block at level e. Assume a numbering convention that assigns nesting level 1 to the outermost block, and successively higher integers for successively deeper nesting. If the nesting structure is represented at execution time by a static chain, then $c - e$ links in that chain must be followed to determine the starting address of the enclosing block. Because the number $c - e$ is known at compilation time, the compiler can generate code for the current block to access the variable. If the nesting structure is represented at execution time by a display, then the eth element of the display is the desired starting address. A single stage of indirect addressing, easily generated at compilation time, provides the desired access.

Whether a static chain or a display is used, it must be adjusted on block entry and exit. For the static chain, block entry requires the setting of one static link. That link points either to the previously current block or to another block in the static chain emanating from the previously current block. In either event, code can be generated for the previously current block to supply the required address. Block exit requires no action. Maintenance of a display is more demanding. On block entry, the starting address of the new current block is appended to the end of the display, after deletion of the addresses, if any, of blocks not in the environment of the current block. The reverse process, which is performed on block exit, may require that addresses of blocks that are inaccessible before exit be appended after deletion of the current block's address. This can be facilitated by providing a stack of displays, which are address vectors of different lengths. An alternative, and rather convenient arrangement, is to store each display in the activation record that uses it.

Maintenance of a display requires more time or space, or both, than does maintenance of a static chain. Use of a display requires less time and space than does use of a static chain. The choice depends on the complexity required to compile the maintenance and access processes and on the expected relative frequencies of access to nonlocal identifiers and of block entry and exit. A compromise made in at least one PASCAL compiler is the use of a static chain together with a pointer to global storage, which usually contains the most frequently accessed nonlocal identifiers. That pointer can be viewed, of course, as a partial display.

The allocation method we have just described is sometimes called **block-level** allocation, because a separate activation record is provided for each block. The convenience of assigning a distinct base register to each block, or at least to each accessible block, is available only if the number of such activation records is not too large. One way to reduce the number of activation records is to provide them only for procedure blocks. Storage associated with the various nonprocedure blocks nested within a procedure is allocated within the activation record for the procedure. In the resulting **procedure-level** allocation, the burden of maintaining displays is reduced, as is the number of base registers needed. This method, like *block-level* allocation, does not require extra space for blocks at the same level of nesting. A certain amount of bookkeeping is necessary, however, to keep track of the allocations.

Storage for some variables is allocated dynamically not on block entry but under programmer control. This is true of pointer-qualified variables in C and PASCAL. Even if the attributes are known, the total storage requirement is not, because the number of allocations of each variable cannot be determined at compilation time. One method for handling such variables is to allocate and free space on top of the activation-record stack as requests are encountered at execution time. Because of the lack of constraints on the order in which allocations are freed, it is not possible to manage that portion of storage purely as a stack. Moreover, a dynamically created variable may have a longer life than the block that created it. Block termination then creates a fragment of storage between the new stack top and the dynamic variable area. The leftover dynamic variables now stand in the way of managing the stack.

To overcome these problems, it has become common to use a different area of storage altogether for dynamically allocated vari-

ables. This area, usually known as the **heap**, is often built at one
end of the program's storage allocation, while the stack is built at
the other end. Execution of the PASCAL statements **new** and **dispose**, for example, would then result in the allocation and release
of space within the heap. Note, incidentally, that this use of the
word "heap" is unrelated to the data structure of the same name.
A compiler's heap is devoid of structure. The heap can be managed
either by one of the compiler's run-time routines, or by the operating
system. We shall not discuss here techniques for managing storage
under arbitrary allocation and release requests.

Dynamic variables with unknown attributes. Identifier attributes
that are not known at compilation time can be handled by compiling a **template** or **descriptor** to be filled in later. One example
is the address of a nonlocal identifier. It is by no means necessary
to recompute the address for accesses after the first, if a location
is reserved in the using activation record to hold the address once
computed. Although the time saving is small compared to use of a
display, it can be substantial relative to use of a long static chain.
The attribute whose lack most seriously affects storage allocation is
the specification of array bounds. If the declaration of array size
can be postponed until execution time, the array is said to be **dynamic**. What is already known at compilation time is the number
of dimensions, hence the nature of the calculation that will be required to access an array element. What is not yet known is the
value of each constant that enters the calculation. Consider again
the declaration $X[L1..U1,L1..U2]$. The required constants are C
and $B-(L2+C*L1)$, where B is the starting address of the array,
and $C = U2 - (L2 - 1)$ is the number of columns. If the declaration
is processed in the absence of values for the four bounds, those constants cannot be compiled. Moreover, storage for the array cannot
be allocated because its size is unknown.

What can be allocated, however, is a descriptor for the array,
called a **dope vector**. The dope vector will ultimately hold B and
the four bounds, and perhaps also the length of an individual element. Because the length of the dope vector depends on the number
of dimensions of the array it describes, the dope vector's own length
must be either specified in the dope vector itself or compiled into the
address-generating code. The dope vector is filled in when the array

bounds are specified at execution time, whether on block entry or even later. Address B is assigned the current stack top value. The stack top is redefined to an address beyond B just far enough to allow for an array of the specified size. Thus the size of the activation record depends on the bounds of its dynamic arrays. Another interpretation is that dynamic arrays are stacked above the activation record, rather than within it. Whatever the interpretation, fixed-size items, including all the dope vectors, must precede any variable-size items. Once B and the bounds are known, code generated at compilation time computes at execution time the constants required to determine addresses of subscripted identifiers. These constants are then stored in activation record locations referenced by the code, also generated at compilation time, which performs the address calculations. A convenient place to store these constants is in the dope vector itself, and they may well be placed there instead of the bounds and the starting address. If subscript checking is to be performed, however, we must also save the bounds. Reference to a dynamic array in an enclosing block is made through its dope vector, whose displacement within the activation record for its block is known (*i.e.*, fixed at compilation time).

A typical layout for an activation record is shown in Figure 8.9. While the block is current, some of the items shown may be held in registers for faster operation. This is particularly true of the instruction counter, environment indicator, and parameters or their addresses. The fourth group (storage allocated at execution time) may, of course, be in the heap rather than the stack.

One item shown has not yet been discussed. Storage must be allocated for the temporary variables ("temporaries") generated into the intermediate code. Their names may be preserved either in the symbol table or in a separate table. In allocating storage for temporaries, it is usually desirable to re-use space once a temporary is no longer needed. To the extent that the use of temporaries is either nested or disjoint, as it is in expression evaluation, locations can be assigned in a execution-time stack. Overlapping use of temporaries can occur, however, perhaps as the result of optimization to remove the redundant computation of common subexpressions. In general, it is necessary then to determine at compilation time the **range** of quadruple numbers over which each temporary must be saved. This range may exceed the span from the numerically first to the numerically last quadruple that references the temporary. For example, the entire body of a loop may lie in the range of a temporary that is used in the test at the start of the loop code. Several methods exist for determining the range of temporaries and for assigning the minimum required number of locations.

Organizational Information
    instruction counter
    back pointer to previous activation record (dynamic link)
    environment indicator [one of the following]
        back pointer to enclosing activation record (static link)
        pointer to start of current display
        entire current display
    save area [if block issues calls]

Nonlocal Addresses
    pointers to actual parameters [if block is called]
    pointers to values of nonlocal identifiers [optional]

Local Storage Allocated at Compilation Time
    values of local identifiers
    values of temporary variables (work area)
    values of arrays with fixed bounds
    dope vectors for arrays with dynamic bounds

Local Storage Allocated at Execution Time
    arrays with dynamic bounds
    pointer-qualified variables

Figure 8.9 Typical Content of Activation Record

8.3 TARGET-CODE GENERATION

The last of the five basic steps in compilation is the generation of target code. A spectrum of target languages is available, ranging from executable machine code (in a load-and-go compiler) through object code, to assembler language, and on to various macro languages. The present section is restricted to the generation of object (or machine) code. Other approaches are discussed in Section 10.3.1.

We can think of the generation of object code as the expansion of macros defined by the compiler writer and called by the intermediate code. The implementation of target code generation in some compilers actually hews rather closely to that model. Code generation is thus conceptually simple, but it can be extremely complicated in practice because of its great dependence on the architecture of the target machine.

The number of central registers may be 0, 1, or many and, if there are many, the function of a given register may be specialized (accumulator, base, index, etc.) or general. If there is only one accumulator, noncommutative arithmetic operations such as subtraction and division must be handled differently from commutative operations. It may even be necessary to remove an operand already being held in the accumulator. Whether there are many registers or only one, it is necessary to keep track at compilation time of what quantities will be in each register at execution time. This information is required to ensure proper utilization of intermediate results and is helpful in such optimizations as elimination of redundant stores and loads. If the target machine uses a stack rather than addressable registers, the code to be generated is quite different.

A peculiar register is the condition register or "condition code" of some computers. Its value is set by execution of various instructions and tested by conditional branches. It can obviate the storage of a temporary value specified in the intermediate code. Recognizing such a situation and using the condition register can be a challenge.

The instruction set of the target machine may offer choices of code generation patterns, and it may impose constraints that must be circumvented. Instructions to copy data from one storage location to another are standard in machines without an accumulator but they may be provided in others as well. The assignment quadruple :=,T2,,A would then normally cause generation of a storage-to-storage copy instruction. If, however, T2 will be in the accumulator at that point during execution, a store instruction needs to be generated instead. Suppose next that the machine has no divide instruction, and the intermediate code specifies a division. This requires generation of either in-line target code to compute the quotient by other means or of a call to a service routine. A similar remark holds for a machine with no multiply instruction.

Relational operators in the intermediate code also raise problems. Many machines do not provide instructions for each of the six common relational operators. If the intermediate code specifies one that is not available, the operator must be synthesized from those that are (*e.g.*, A=B as A$\leq$B **and** B$\geq$A). On some machines, comparisons require the use of arithmetic instructions. If the operands are character strings, serious complications arise if the source-language collating sequence does not match the target-machine encoding sequence. If the operands are arithmetic, different complications may ensue. In evaluating A<B by performing A$-$B followed by a test for negative result, underflow and even overflow are possible.

The boolean operators available in the source language may not all have counterparts in machine language. In some machines, none is provided and arithmetic instructions must be used. Single-bit logical **and** can be replaced by multiplication, and **or** can be replaced by an addition followed by loading unity if the result is nonzero. Logical **not** can be replaced either by subtraction from unity or, if the operand is already in an accumulator, by first subtracting unity from it and then taking the absolute value (if *that* operation is provided). If boolean instructions are available in the machine, the set provided may not be the same as that available in the source language and used in the intermediate code. Although those provided in the machine will normally be capable of generating all 16 boolean functions of two or fewer arguments, the amount of target code required may be substantial. The reader is invited to express **xor** (exclusive or) in terms of **and** and **not** alone. It is simpler to encode **xor** arithmetically (absolute value of difference).

If the machine instruction set is rich, the generation of efficient target code can capitalize on the added instructions. Immediate addressing can save both the storage and the access time for constants. Negation can be performed with a load negative instruction. The load address (LA) instruction of the IBM 370 provides the most efficient addition of a positive integer less than 4096 (provided that both addend and sum are positive integers less than 2^{24}). Exploiting these and similar efficiencies is a real challenge to the compiler writer.

Some of the functions performed in code generation are required whatever the architecture of the target machine. Typical of this class are type conversion and constant generation. Conversion of operand types will usually be performed by calling conversion routines at execution time. Because storage will need to be allocated for the results of conversion, it is usually more convenient to specify type conversion during production of intermediate code than during generation of target code. The generation of constants by a compiler is no different from their generation by an assembler, except that the translator rather than the programmer must ensure that the pool of constants will be addressable.

The code generation routines are concerned with how operands of machine instructions will be addressed. The computation of addresses of operands in storage is intimately associated with the organization of execution-time storage, and has been discussed in Section 8.2. The form that the required addresses take, and the instructions needed to perform indirect addressing, depend on the target machine. Addressing of operands in registers is dependent on the register assignments, which are performed by the code generation routines, and on the target-machine instruction formats.

The generation routines must be appropriate to the form of intermediate code that serves as their input. If postfix notation is used, code generation is similar to the one-pass single-stack evaluation method described at the beginning of Section 7.2.1. A slight modification of that method results not in evaluating an expression, but in generating target code to perform the evaluation. Instead of stacking values of operands, the compiler stacks their tokens. On encountering an operator of degree i, it generates code that embodies the topmost i operand tokens. New tokens, created to represent temporary results, are stacked as required. Nonarithmetic operators, such as assignments and jumps, are handled straightforwardly. Figure 8.10 shows instructions, in the assembler language of Section 2.1, that could be generated in this fashion.

The source text is the PASCAL conditional construct

$$\textbf{if } \text{A} < \text{B} \textbf{ then } C := B + D * 4$$
$$\textbf{else } \quad C := A + D * 4$$

for which the intermediate postfix code is given in Section 7.2.1. Each line of the figure shows the postfix token being examined, the target code (if any) generated as a result of encountering the token, and the stack of tokens (with top to the right) as it stands after the encounter. Note that a line of output code, such as that produced after examination of tokens 51 and 55, is not necessarily generated

	Token	Code		Stack
37.	A			A
38.	B			A B
39.	−	LOAD	A	
		SUB	B	
		STORE	T1	T1
40.	51			T1 51
41.	JPZ	LOAD	T1	
		BRPOS	LABEL51	
		BRZERO	LABEL51	
42.	!C			C
43.	B			C B
44.	D			C B D
45.	4			C B D 4
46.	*	LOAD	@4	
		MULT	D	
		STORE	T2	C B T2
47.	+	LOAD	T2	
		ADD	B	
		STORE	T3	C T3
48.	←	LOAD	T3	
		STORE	C	
49.	58			58
50.	JUMP	BR	LABEL58	
51.	!C	LABEL51		C
52.	A			C A
53.	D			C A D
54.	4			C A D 4
55.	*	LOAD	@4	
		MULT	D	
		STORE	T4	C A T4
56.	+	LOAD	T4	
		ADD	A	
		STORE	T5	C T5
57.	←	LOAD	T5	
		STORE	C	

Figure 8.10   Target-Code Generation from Postfix

all at once. An auxiliary table, not shown, saves forward references
and causes labels such as LABEL51 to be generated. Further improvement of the generated target code is clearly possible, for there

are several redundant STORE/LOAD pairs. Section 8.4 discusses code improvement, and the example in the next paragraph illustrates one way to avoid redundancy in the original generation.

A typical routine for generating from a quadruple the target code to perform an addition is shown in Figure 8.11. A field in the symbol table or list of temporaries stores with each variable a flag *inacc* that has value **true** if that variable will be in the target machine's single accumulator before execution of the next instruction to be generated, and **false** otherwise. The accumulator can hold simultaneously the values of two or more variables, if those values are equal, as they are after executing an assignment such as $I \leftarrow N$. The global list *accvalue* holds the names of all variables whose value will be in the accumulator before execution of the next instruction to be generated.

```
procedure ADD(a,b,c)
    char a,b,c
    begin
            if a.inacc then generate 'ADD      ',b
            else if b.inacc then generate 'ADD      ',a
            else begin
                        generate 'LOAD    ',a
                        generate 'ADD      ',b
            end
        generate 'STORE ',c
        delete all names from accvalue,
            setting the inacc flag of each to false
        insert c on accvalue
        c.inacc ← true
    end
```

Figure 8.11   Code Generation Routine for Quadruple $(+,a,b,c)$

The generation routine tests the flags of the addition operands to determine whether either will already be in the accumulator, thus saving a LOAD instruction. Following code generation, the name of the result is entered on *accvalue* and its flag is set to **true** to indicate that it will be available in the accumulator for the next generation. The names of all other variables are removed from *accvalue* and their flags are set to **false**. Although the flags are designated in the program by qualified names, an actual implementation would probably use a procedure, with the variable's name as parameter, to test or set the flag. Another simplification made in the example is the choice of assembler language as the target code to be generated. Actually, machine representations of operation codes and operand addresses would usually be generated instead.

The generation of target code from triples is a bit different, because an intermediate result is referred to not by name, but by the number of the triple that produced it. Descriptions of temporary values do not need to be maintained throughout the compilation, as they are for quadruples, and this is a major reason for the use of triples in intermediate code. We shall not discuss here the details of code generation from triples.

If the intermediate code is in such a form that target code can be generated from it in a single pass, then target code generation can be performed directly by the semantic routines, with no need for intermediate code. This increases the bulk and complexity of the semantic routines, but permits one-pass compilation.

By and large, target code generation is characterized by the maintenance of much status information, many tests of status, and the consideration of many different cases. It is highly machine dependent and quite complex.

8.4 CODE OPTIMIZATION

Most of the algorithms for generating intermediate code look at one source-language construct in isolation from its neighbors. Most of those for generating target code look at one intermediate-code construct in isolation. Many redundancies result, such as the STORE/ LOAD pairs of Figure 8.10. Other inefficiencies, too, appear. The removal of these inefficiencies is widely known as **code optimization**.

The term "code optimization" is a misnomer. There is no agreed standard for defining optimality nor does it appear likely that there is any guarantee of achieving what might be agreed upon as optimal. What is possible, however, is to make **improvements** to the code generated by the implementation processes discussed in this chapter. These improvements, which may move, remove, or replace code, usually both speed up execution of the compiled program and reduce its size. Code optimization, as we shall continue to call it because the term has become entrenched, may be applied to both the machine-independent and the machine-dependent aspects of the program.

We first examine machine-independent optimization. In generating code for the PASCAL statement

$$\textbf{if } A<B \textbf{ then } C := B+D*4$$
$$\textbf{else } \quad C := A+D*4$$

we saw that the computation of $D*4$ could be performed once rather than twice, as it can for the following pair.

$$R := B+D*4;$$
$$S := A+D*4$$

Yet this saving is precluded if the second statement is labeled, as in

$$R := B+D*4;$$
$$L: S := A+D*4$$

Why must the common subexpression now be computed twice? Because the flow of control may enter the second statement without having passed through the first, with no guarantee that D holds the same value as it does when control flows through both statements. This observation leads to the concept of a **basic block** of a program. A basic block is a portion of a program with a single entry, a single exit, and no internal branching. We can depict the flow of control of a program as a directed graph whose nodes are the basic blocks and whose arcs indicate the possible sequences of execution. The basic blocks are not to be confused with the "blocks" that describe the static nesting in a block-structured language.

The classical approach to machine-independent optimization is to divide the program into its basic blocks, perform **local** optimization upon each block, and then perform **global** optimization upon the program as a whole. In performing local optimization, no information is used from outside the block. In practice, perhaps as much as three-fourths of the speed improvement is due to local optimization. Global optimization, using a description of the interblock flow of control, determines in which blocks values of identifiers and expressions are written or read. This permits the elimination of redundant references. Although more and more attention is being directed to optimization of source code, machine-independent optimization is still usually performed on the intermediate code. This choice allows optimization of address calculation arithmetic, which is explicit in the intermediate code, but only implicit in the source code.

We present next a partial enumeration of types of machine-independent optimizations; descriptions of their implementations are omitted.

(1) Code Motion. One example is moving an invariant computation out of a loop. If the assignment $X \leftarrow Y*Z$ appears within the body of a loop that does not change the values of Y and Z, then it can be replaced by $TEMP \leftarrow Y*Z$ in the initialization and $X \leftarrow TEMP$ within the body. This saves time during each iteration. Another example is **hoisting**, which saves space. In

if *cond* **then** $X[I,J] := expr1$ **else** $X[I,J] := expr2$

the addressing calculation for $X[I,J]$, which would be generated in two locations, can be moved to a position immediately before the test (provided, of course, that evaluation of *cond* leaves I and J unchanged).

(2) Strength Reduction. An arithmetic operation can often be replaced by one of lower "strength". Thus, if N is a small integer, it may be faster to evaluate $X**N$ by repeated multiplication than to call a service routine for exponentiation. An extreme case is the total elimination of an addition or subtraction of zero or of a multiplication or division by unity. An important benefit of strength reduction is that it often permits further optimizations to follow.

(3) Loop Unrolling. Time can be saved at the expense of space by writing out sequentially a set of operations initially coded iteratively. If the number of iterations is a constant known at compilation time, the result can be straight-line code with no tests or branches. This can be applied, for example, to the reduced form of $X**N$ if the integer N is a constant. If the number of iterations is not known at compilation time, it may still be possible to increase the loop size and reduce the number of iterations, hence time for tests and branches.

(4) Constant Propagation. Also known as **folding**, this is the computation of values from constants at compilation time. If no assignments to I intervene between $I \leftarrow 5$ and a subsequent $X[I+1]$, the

entire addressing calculation can be performed at compilation time and eliminated from the generated code.

(5) Elimination of Redundant Expressions. The classic example is the common subexpression, such as $D*4$ in the first example of this section. Another is the repeated addressing calculation, as in $A[I,J]$ $\leftarrow 1-B[I,J]$. Although the former could have been avoided by a careful programmer, the latter could not.

(6) Elimination of Dead Variables. A **dead** variable is one whose value is not used later in the computation. A loop index may be a dead variable; others may occur as the result of previous optimizations. A variable that is not dead is said, of course, to be **live**.

(7) Elimination of Useless Variables. A **useless** variable is one whose value is *never* used. It, too, may result from other optimizations. Not only can any assignment to such a variable be suppressed; even its space allocation can be taken away.

Machine-independent optimization is most conveniently performed on the intermediate code, usually as a separate step before storage allocation. Machine-dependent optimization, on the other hand, must wait for a later stage in the compilation. Although it may be performed as a separate step following the generation of target code, it is usually combined with the code generation. Two machine-dependent optimizations are the following.

(1) Redundant STORE instructions or STORE/LOAD pairs, such as those of Figure 8.10, can be eliminated.

(2) If the machine has several registers, the assignment of registers to hold different temporary values, base addresses, and index amounts can be made in a variety of ways. "Optimizing" these assignments can reduce considerably the need to save and restore register contents. It can also permit the use of register-register machine operations in place of the usually slower register-storage operations.

Depending on the precise architecture of the target machine, a host of other optimizations may be available.

8.5 ERROR HANDLING

The foregoing descriptions of implementation structures and processes have assumed a requirement to perform translation of error-free input and to perform it as simply as possible. The assumption that the source-language program is free of error can never be entirely justified, even if an earlier compilation has failed to detect any errors. Even resubmission of the same program text to the same compiler can be marred by a data transmission error.

The compiler cannot reasonably be expected to deal with such errors as the programmer encoding the wrong algorithm. It may or may not be designed to generate code to cope with such execution-time errors as dividing by zero, reading a record from an empty buffer, or using the value of an uninitialized variable. But it must be concerned with errors that are manifested during compilation. It is those errors that are the concern of the present section.

Compilation-time errors can be classified rather broadly and arbitrarily into three groups: lexical, syntactic, and semantic. Lexical errors involve incorrect *tokens*. One example is the unrecognized word, which may be a misspelled identifier or keyword, or perhaps an identifier left over from an earlier version of the program. Another example is the illegal character, often the result of a keying or transmission error. Syntactic errors involve incorrect *structure*. Examples include missing delimiters, mismatched parentheses, missing keywords, and the like. Semantic errors involve incorrect *use* of identifiers and expressions. Among the examples are use of the wrong number of array subscripts or procedure call parameters, mismatched expression types, and the use of undefined values. An instance of the last may not be detectable at compilation time. The unreferenced variable and inaccessible statement, if considered errors, are also semantic.

What can be done about compilation-time errors? Redundancy in the program can be used (1) to **detect** an error, perhaps also to stop, (2) to **recover** from an error and continue compiling, or (3) to **correct** an error by changing the source program. What *should* be done? Detection is mandatory to prevent the generation of garbage without informing the user. Recovery with continued processing is very useful, because it gives the compiler a chance to detect more errors than just the first. Informative messages should be issued, describing both the error and the recovery. The number of runs needed to identify all compiler-detectable errors can thus be substantially reduced. Attempting not merely to continue the compilation, but to revise the source to make it correct may sound attractive. It is rather dangerous, however, except perhaps for lexical errors, for it requires the compiler to divine the programmer's intent.

Provisions for error recovery can permeate the design of a compiler. Although implementation details will not be considered here, space does permit a brief description of approaches. One general consideration is that it is usually more satisfactory to insert tokens into an incorrect program text than to delete tokens, because of the consequent information loss due to the latter.

Lexical errors, if ignored, will lead to subsequent syntactic or semantic errors. Because a symbol table and a keyword list are available, it is often reasonable to attempt to correct misspellings. Thus an unrecognized identifier can be compared with the known ones, and the closest match selected. This requires either a distance measure on words or the use of information describing the frequency of different types of misspellings.

Most of the error recovery performed by compilers is from syntactic errors. If an error is detected during parsing, the compiler can skip to the next keyword or to the end of the statement (if identifiable). This loses semantic information, however, and is therefore less attractive than trying to repair the local context and resume parsing. Probably the most satisfactory technique is to insert terminal symbols. In top-down parsing, the partial parse indicates what type of terminal is acceptable as the next symbol. In bottom-up parsing, the determination of what terminal symbol to insert is more complex. The detailed requirements of error recovery depend on the parsing method and often on the specific grammar.

The most difficult, and perhaps the most numerous, errors encountered in compilation are semantic. The usual approach to recovery is to generate identifiers whose use is semantically correct and to generate assignments of locally suitable values to them. Unfortunately, what appears locally to be a repair may turn out in a larger program context to be a disruption. The consequence may well be the creation of subsequent errors, often in great number. The extra error messages that result can be very aggravating. This problem arises in recovery from syntactic errors as well as semantic. The suppression of extra or duplicated error messages is a challenging task.

FOR FURTHER STUDY

Overviews of compiler design are presented in the tutorial Glass69, Chapter 9 of Ullman76, Chapter 14 of Waite84, Chapter 5 of Beck85, and Section 3.2 of Toy86. Informative books on compilation include Hopgood69, Gries71, Rohl75, and Hunter85. Particularly full treatments are contained in Tremblay85 and Aho86. Most of the foregoing books cover all the matters discussed in this chapter, as well as lexical and syntactic analysis. Brown79b offers much practical general advice on writing a compiler. Anklam82 is specific to the target machine, whereas Schreiner85 is specific to the UNIX development system, and also very practical.

Semantic processing, often called "intermediate code generation", is well described in Waite84 (Chapter 9), Hunter85 (Chapter 6), and Aho86 (Chapter 8). Type checking is discussed at length in Chapter 6 of Aho86.

Execution-time storage management is carefully considered in Wegner68 (Chapter 4) and Griffiths74. Particularly attractive treatments of storage allocation are in Hopgood69 (Chapter 9), which includes an analysis of the range of temporary variables, Davie81 (Chapter 11), and Waite84 (Section 3.3). Hunter85 (Section 9.2) considers heap management well.

Good surveys of target code generation are those of Hopgood69 (Chapter 8), Waite84 (Chapter 10), Hunter85 (Chapter 10), and Aho86 (Chapter 9). Ammann77 describes in detail the generation of target code in a PASCAL compiler for the CDC 6400.

Two attractive general discussions of optimization are Chapter 9 of Rohl75 and Chapter 10 of Aho86. The discussion of machine-independent optimization in Allen69 includes a clear description of basic blocks. Waite84 (Chapter 13) is particularly informative about machine-dependent optimization. Peephole optimization was first described in McKeeman65, and is discussed also in Section 9.9 of Aho86. Fabri82 is a specialized treatment of storage space optimization.

Error handling is discussed in Waite84 (Chapter 12), Hunter85 (Chapter 12), and Tremblay85 (Chapter 5). The PL/C compiler was one of the first to attempt extensive error correction, presented in Conway73. The correction of misspelling errors is discussed in Freeman64 and Morgan70.

REVIEW QUESTIONS

8.1 How does the choice of grammar affect semantic processing?

8.2 State two syntactic properties of many machine-independent languages that cannot be specified by context-free grammars, but may have to be checked by suitable semantic actions.

8.3 Is there a logical requirement that the semantics stack be physically distinct from the syntax stack?

8.4 What semantic processing does the declaration of an identifier usually require?

8.5 Name two distinctions that are important to the compiler in allocating storage for static variables.

8.6 Why doesn't an assembler have to calculate the addresses of array elements?

8.7 Why are actual storage locations for dynamic variables not fixed even at load time?

8.8 What is the cost of using a linearized form of a multidimensional array?

8.9 What compilation-time saving and what execution-time saving in array accessing result from the use of zero as the index origin (*i.e.*, as the lower bound)?

8.10 What is the chief difficulty in allocating storage for an array with dynamic bounds?

8.11 Instead of using separate stacks for activation record management and for parameter passing, it is possible to use a single stack. Explain how to organize and manage such a single stack. Allow for recursion.

8.12 Give a reason for deferring the generation of constants when they are first encountered.

8.13 How can an optimizer use knowledge of live variables in detecting potentially uninitialized variables?

8.14 How does a code generator use live variables to generate more efficient code?

PROBLEMS

8.1 Write the instructions required for the semantic processing of reductions 3 and 5 in Figure 8.1(a).

8.2 The programs of Figure 8.4 perform recursive descent parsing, with semantic processing, for the grammar of Figure 8.1. Let the grammar be extended by addition of the rules

$$
\begin{array}{lrcl}
\text{1a.} & \textit{expression} & \leftrightarrow & \textit{expression '}-\textit{' term} \\
\text{3a.} & \textit{term} & \leftrightarrow & \textit{term '/' factor .} \\
\end{array}
$$

(a) Modify the programs to accommodate the extension. Do not copy unchanged procedures or unchanged portions of procedures.
(b) Trace the translation of $A/(B-C)$ to verify your design. Show the sequence of invocations and returns, the semantic information delivered by each procedure, and the generated quadruples.

8.3 Augment your recursive descent routines for Problem 6.12 with semantic actions that produce (a) postfix code or (b) quadruples.

8.4 Describe, using examples, the actions taken during lexical analysis, syntactic analysis, and semantic interpretation that permit a compiler to disambiguate an identifier that is both (1) declared implicitly (by use rather than by explicit declaration) and (2) identical to a nonreserved keyword.

8.5 Suppose that you are building, for a compiler, a parser that combines operator precedence parsing of expressions with recursive descent parsing of the language as a whole (but excluding lexical analysis). Explain how the required programs can be made to work together.

8.6 Write the semantic routines for the indexed loop described toward the end of Section 8.1. You need not code the parse, but do indicate with which reduction each piece of semantic code is associated.

8.7 Write a semantic routine for processing a **repeat-until** loop.

8.8 Here is one syntactic form of the **case** statement in PL/I.

$$\begin{aligned}&\textbf{select } `(` \; expr \; `)` \; ; \\ &\quad (\; \textbf{when } `(` \; expr_i \; `)` \; stmt_i \;)^+ \\ &\quad \textbf{otherwise } stmt_n \\ &\textbf{end } ;\end{aligned}$$

The generated code is to perform $stmt_i$ for the least i such that $expr = expr_i$. If there is no such i, then it is to perform $stmt_n$.

(**a**) Show all the quadruples that must be generated during the recognition of the complete **select** statement shown.

(**b**) Write semantic routines to generate the quadruples other than those generated during recognition of an instance of *expr* or *stmt* (with or without subscript). For each of your routines specify the symbol string whose recognition invokes that routine.

8.9 [Ghezzi] The **case** statement of an ALGOL-like language is described by the following grammar.

$$\begin{aligned}selection &\leftrightarrow \textbf{case } expression \textbf{ of } caselist \textbf{ esac} \\ caselist &\leftrightarrow (\; ident : stmtlist \;)^+\end{aligned}$$

where *ident* is either a constant or a variable name.

(**a**) Give a recursive descent implementation of the parsing routines, with output in postfix notation.

(**b**) Suppose that more than one *expression* is matched. Augment your routines with actions that verify (at run time) that *exactly one* choice of the **case** is made.

8.10 [Ghezzi] Design an extension of dynamic arrays that permits the bounds to be modified dynamically at any time. The number of dimensions remains fixed. (The **flexible** array of ALGOL 68 provides an example.) How does your solution differ from the classic implementation of dynamic arrays?

8.11 Design an extension of dynamic arrays that allows the specification, at execution time, not only of the bounds for each dimension but also of the number of dimensions. Consider all relevant aspects of compilation and execution. Impose as few restrictions as possible on the programming language; justify any restrictions you do impose. What extra costs does your implementation incur over those of conventional dynamic arrays?

8.12 Consider the following declaration (written in PASCAL) of a tree-structured variable.

```
type Atype = record
    B : record
        C : integer;
        D : record
            E : string[2];
            F : array [1..4] of boolean;
            G : integer;
            end;
        end;
    H : record
        J : array[1..12] of boolean;
        K : integer;
        end;
    end;

var A : array [1..100] of Atype;
```

Examples of references to the variable include A[45].B.D.F[2], A[23].B.C, and A[99].B. What specific information about the identifiers A through K must the symbol table hold?

8.13 Describe both the compilation-time and the execution-time actions necessary to permit reference to a nonlocal variable declared in an enclosing block. Repeat for both a static chain and a display.

8.14 The static nesting structure of a program is diagrammed below.

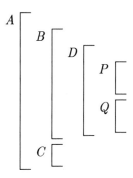

The sequence of invocations is A, C, B, D, Q, P. The definition of P is the following.

> **procedure** $P(s)$
>   **real array** $s[1..10]$
>   **integer** i
>   **do for** i **from** 1 **to** 10
> $s[i] \leftarrow s[i] \times t$
> $s[i] \leftarrow s[i] + i$
> $s[i] \leftarrow s[i] \times s[i]$
>   **end**

Assume that (1) the address of the parameter is passed to P; (2) no code optimization is performed; (3) the subscript calculation is performed by indexing; and (4) you have no register to spare. Determine the total number of address references made by procedure P in accessing the actual parameter

(**a**) by reference;
(**b**) by value result.

The nonlocal variable t is declared in procedure A. Assume that the offset for t is added by indexing. Determine the total number of address references made by procedure P in accessing t by use of

(**c**) a static chain;
(**d**) a display.

8.15 Whether a static chain or a display is used to access the environment, a new pointer must be created upon block entry. Explain, for each of the two representations,
(**a**) how the value of the pointer can be determined;
(**b**) what actions are performed at block entry; and
(**c**) what actions are performed at block exit.

8.16 Describe the activation record management that must occur when the **goto** of the following program is executed. Assume the use of block-level storage allocation.

> **procedure** *A*
>   **call** *B*
>   *mark*: ---
>   **procedure** *B*
>   **call** *C*
>   *mark*: ---
>   **end** *B*
>   **procedure** *C*
>   **block** *D*
>   **goto** *mark*
>   **end** *D*
>   **end** *C*
> **end** *A*

8.17 [Ghezzi] Consider the use of a macro processor to translate from quadruples to assembler language code. One macro is to be provided for each operator. Describe the over-all structure and operation of the translator. In particular, explain how to handle jumps.

8.18 A compiler for a multiple-register computer encounters the program fragment

> **for** $I := 1$ **to** N **do begin**
> $SUM := SUM + R[I,I]$;
> $D := A*B + 16*16 + SIN(B*A)$;
> **end**

in which all the identifiers (except *SIN*) refer to variables. At least five optimizations are possible. Describe each optimization that you find, state the extent to which it is machine-dependent, and explain at what stage of compilation you would perform it.

Chapter 9

Linking and Loading

9.1 FUNCTIONS

An object-code segment produced by a compiler or by a module assembler cannot be executed without modification. As many as five further functions must be performed first. Their logical sequence is the following. (1) If the segment is one of several that have been translated independently but are to be executed together, there will be symbols in one segment that refer to entities defined in another. Establishment of the proper correspondences and use of the correct attributes is called **resolution** of such intersegment symbolic references. (2) A symbol not resolved by comparison with the other segments may be a reference to the execution-time library of system-provided service routines and user-written subroutines. Means are required for managing the library. (3) Storage must be allocated for each segment's private needs, for any area accessed jointly, and for the required library routines. (4) Address fields must be relocated to match the allocation. (5) The segments must be loaded into the allocated storage. We shall now examine these five functions, although in a slightly different order.

9.1.1 Loading

A translator that generates machine code in the locations from which it is to be executed, such as a load-and-go compiler or a load-and-go assembler, performs its own loading function. No separate loader is required. This organization requires the program to be translated each time it is used. Moreover, because there is no provision for modifying the program after translation, it is essentially limited to a single segment. Furthermore, storage space is required not only for the program but for the translator as well. Nevertheless, small programs that are frequently retranslated can be handled conveniently by such a translator.

Two situations exist in which the segment to be loaded is in absolute form ready for execution, but does not occupy the storage locations to which it is destined. One situation arises when the translator, usually an assembler, produces **absolute** machine code, in which all addresses are valid only if the segment is placed in specified locations. The other arises after a program has been copied to backing storage, from which it is later read in to resume execution. An **absolute loader** (or "binary loader") is used to load a machine-code segment. It need only place the code in the specified locations, perhaps checking the accuracy of the information transferred, and then branch to the starting location. Because this function is performed just before execution and does not involve translation, such a loader may quite properly be viewed as a control program rather than a translator.

9.1.2 Relocation

Most translators do not bind the locations that the code they generate must occupy. Instead, they produce one or more relocatable segments, identifying in each which address fields are absolute and which relative. If multiple origins are used, the origin to which each relative address field is relative must also be identified. The task of relocation is to add the applicable relocation constant (address of the segment origin) to each relative address in the segment. Different methods of performing relocation apply to machines with direct addressing and with base addressing. Although relocation can precede loading, this risks binding the execution-time location before storage is allocated. Therefore, relocation is usually performed in conjunction with loading, by a program called a **relocating loader**, which is in part a translator. The actual adjustment of an address field often occurs after the field has been loaded, rather than before. Note that the term "relocation" refers to adjustment of address fields and not to movement of a program segment. Movement of a segment requires relocation, but relocation does not require movement.

9.1.3 Resolution of External References

If a segment is to be executed in combination with others that have been translated separately, the translator prepares for each segment a list of symbols to be resolved. This list includes (1) internal references to externally defined symbols and (2) internally defined symbols that may be referenced externally. The two types of list entries may or may not be segregated. The resolution is usually performed by a program called a **linker**, which performs the following functions. It establishes the correspondences between symbol references and definitions, determines the relocatability attributes of symbols and address expressions, and substitutes addresses for them in the form required by the loader. It typically assumes that symbols still undefined are names of library routines.

The task of a linker is similar to that of an assembler, in that the major accomplishment is the resolution of forward references. For an assembler, the forward scan is over the remaining code of the segment being assembled. For a linker, the forward scan is over segments not yet encountered. Both translators must cope with symbols whose use precedes their definition.

Many systems combine resolution with loading (and usually relocation) in a **linking loader**. If intersegment references are limited to *calls*, whether to library or other routines, their resolution does not require a linker. It can be accomplished simply by use of a **transfer vector** of collected branch instructions to the different segments.

9.1.4 Library Management

Strictly speaking, management of the library of routines available at execution time is not a function of translation, but performing it does affect several aspects of translation. The determination of which library routines are needed and of how much storage to allocate for them is an example. Although library routines used to be in absolute code, it is almost universal practice now to provide them in relocatable form.

The size of the library can often be reduced by replacing similar portions of two or more routines with another routine, which is then called by the routines that it serves. In that event, execution-time calls will be generated not only to the routines named in the user's program but to yet other routines as well. If an index of calls made by library routines is available to the linker, it can determine the entire set of routines that will be needed, and link the references accordingly. If the library is on a linear medium such as paper or magnetic tape, it may be wise to have the copy of each calling routine precede copies of routines that it calls. This is well worth the cost of space for duplicate copies. Then the necessary routines can be loaded in a single pass even if an index of calls is not constructed beforehand, provided that each routine names the others that it needs. If the library routines are on a rotating medium such as disk or drum, a dictionary of their placement should be maintained.

9.1.5 Storage Allocation

Although the translator performs storage allocation within each segment it generates, there remains the problem of ensuring that all the pieces will fit at execution time. Space is required for each of the segments, for the largest of the common data areas used for intersegment communication, and for the library routines that may be called. The linker is the first program in a position to determine the total storage requirement, but it may lack information concerning space needed for library routines. If calls by one library routine to another are not discovered until the former is loaded, space information is not available until loading time. This provides one motive for deferring linking until loading. An important motive for *combining* linking with loading is to reduce the total number of passes over the text. If any of the required library routines is to be generated at execution time rather than merely selected, even loading time is too early to specify the exact size. It may nevertheless be possible to determine an upper bound.

If more space is required than will be available, different segments or routines that need not be present simultaneously can share storage sequentially, each using a given portion of space in turn. This mode of storage use is called **overlaying**. If the writer of the program can predict in what sequence different program segments will be required, the segments can be replaced dynamically in a prede-termined sequence. This **dynamic loading** is programmed in most systems by the user. Some linkers, however, can accept a specifica-tion of what dynamic loading is to be performed and generate the necessary execution-time calls to the loader. Although the loading is dynamic, the overlay structure is static, being unchanged from one execution of the program to the next. The continued increase in main storage sizes, and the increasingly common provision of virtual storage management, have considerably reduced the requirement to manage overlays directly.

Sometimes, however, the selection of required segments cannot be determined before execution, because it is data-dependent. Such dynamic overlay structures are characteristic of transaction-oriented interactive systems, such as airline reservations or banking. The nature of the transaction dictates which processing programs are required, and they are loaded as appropriate and linked with the using programs. Because the translators are no longer available, the control program is called upon to perform this **dynamic linking**.

9.2 IMPLEMENTATIONS

9.2.1 Absolute Loader

The task of an absolute loader is virtually trivial. It reads a stream of bits from a specified source into specified storage locations and transfers control to a designated address. Loader input prepared by an absolute assembler is in the form of records, often card images, each containing the text (instructions, data, or both) to be loaded, the length of the text, and the starting address. The loader reads the record into a fixed location, examines the starting address and length, and copies the text as specified. The last text record is followed by a branch record, which contains the address to which the loader branches. The three main storage accesses required for the text (one for reading, two for copying) can be reduced to one by first reading only the length and starting address. The loader then reads the text directly into its final location.

An absolute loader provided for reloading programs that have been rolled out will surely be designed to effect the foregoing saving.

The length and starting address of the entire program will have been recorded at the beginning of the program. If the program length exceeds the amount that can be fetched in a single read operation, the loader can fetch the program in pieces. As the loader proceeds, it increments the starting address and decrements the remaining length.

9.2.2 Relocating Loader

A translator may generate object code intended to be executed when resident in storage locations whose addresses will be specified only after translation. Address references made by the object code to main storage locations that it will occupy after loading must be adjusted by the addition of a relocation constant before execution. Instruction and data fields that require this adjustment are termed **relative**; those that do not, **absolute**. Within an instruction, the operation code is absolute, as are register addresses. Operand fields may or may not be absolute. Immediate data and shift amounts are absolute; many address fields, although not all, are relative. An address specified numerically in the source program is absolute, but a symbol defined by its appearance in a label field of the same segment is relative. So is a constant literal, and so is the redefinable current-line symbol *. Constants generated by the translator are absolute, except for address constants. The value of an address constant, typically written in source language as A(PLACE), is defined to be the execution-time storage address corresponding to the symbol named. Clearly such an address is relative.

The relocatability attribute of an address expression depends upon those of its components. If an address expression is limited to an algebraic sum of signed symbols (*i.e.*, no products), such as PLACE+7 or HERE-LOOP+STAND, then its relocatability attribute is easily determined. Ignoring each absolute component and replacing each relative component by R reduces the address expression to the form nR, where n is a signed integer. If $n = 1$, the expression is relative; if $n = 0$, the expression is absolute. Thus if HERE and LOOP are relative and STAND is absolute, then we ignore STAND and replace HERE by R and -LOOP by $-$R. This yields zero and the address expression is found to be absolute.

If n has any other value than 0 or 1, the expression is ill-formed. We can see this most readily from an example. The execution-time location A+B, where A and B are relative symbols, cannot be fixed even relative to the origin. Suppose A and B have location counter values 20 and 30, respectively. If the origin is 100, then the execution-time locations A and B are 120 and 130, and A+B is 250, or 150 beyond the origin. But if the origin is 300, then the execution-time location A+B is 650, or 350 beyond the origin. The address expression A+B does not have a reproducible meaning. Similar problems arise if n is greater than 2, or is negative.

If there are no internal references to externally defined symbols, the relocatability attribute of each symbol is known. The translator can therefore determine the relocatability attribute of every field in the object code it generates. Until we discuss linkers, we shall assume that this condition holds.

We examine relocation for a direct-addressing computer first. The relocating loader, having no access to the source text, cannot determine from inspection of the generated text whether a field is absolute or relative. It cannot even distinguish instructions from data. The translator must therefore specify for each field whether it is relative. One way to specify these relocatability attributes, easily implemented in an assembler or in the assembly step of a compiler, is to emit with each line of text one **relocation bit** for each field. In Figure 9.1(a), which shows object code generated for the sample assembler-language program of Figure 2.1, the convention is that bit value unity indicates that the associated field is relative. The relocation constant to be added is the address of the origin of the segment, and is normally specified by the operating system.

The algorithm executed by the relocating loader is simple. It reads lines of object code one at a time. It copies the text of each line to locations formed by adding the relocation constant to the indicated addresses. For each relocation bit equal to unity it also adds the relocation constant to the corresponding text field. This second addition can be performed either before or after the text is copied. If the relocation constant is 40, the resulting content of storage is as shown in Figure 9.1(b). The location counter values can be omitted from the object code if the lines are presented in serial order with no gaps, as they are in the figure. In that event

	Source program				Object code		
Label	Opcode	Opd1	Opd2	Locn	Len	Reloc	Text
	COPY	ZERO	OLDER	00	3	011	13 33 35
	COPY	ONE	OLD	03	3	011	13 34 36
	READ	LIMIT		06	2	011	12 38
	WRITE	OLD		08	2	01	08 36
CALCNEXT	LOAD	OLDER		10	2	01	03 35
	ADD	OLD		12	2	01	02 36
	STORE	NEW		14	2	01	07 37
	SUB	LIMIT		16	2	01	06 38
	BRPOS	FINAL		18	2	01	01 30
	WRITE	NEW		20	2	01	08 37
	COPY	OLD	OLDER	22	3	011	13 36 35
	COPY	NEW	OLD	25	3	011	13 37 36
	BR	CALCNEXT		28	2	01	00 10
FINAL	WRITE	LIMIT		30	2	01	08 38
	STOP			32	1	0	11
ZERO	CONST	0		33	1	0	00
ONE	CONST	1		34	1	0	01
OLDER	SPACE						
OLD	SPACE						
NEW	SPACE						
LIMIT	SPACE						

(a) Before relocation

Locn	Machine code
40	13 73 75
43	13 74 76
46	12 78
48	08 76
50	03 75
52	02 76
54	07 77
56	06 78
58	01 70
60	08 77
62	13 76 75
65	13 77 76
68	00 50
70	08 78
72	11
73	00
74	01

(b) After relocation

Figure 9.1   Use of Relocation Bits

the loader runs an actual location counter initialized to the origin location. If multiple location counters are provided, the object code must include with each relative address a designation of the location counter that applies. The translator must then either indicate the total amount of storage associated with each location counter or segregate the object code associated with each.

Interleaving relocation bits and length fields with the program text precludes reading the text directly into the storage locations it is to occupy. Moreover, it requires that the text be handled in small units, often of variable length. These disadvantages can be avoided by collecting all the relocation bits into a single contiguous **relocation map** that follows the text of the object code. Such a map is readily prepared by the assembler (or other translator), which produces a segment of relocatable text followed immediately by the associated relocation map. The segment and map are read as a unit into storage locations beginning at the segment's assigned origin S, resulting in the status depicted in Figure 9.2(a). The assembler must furnish the lengths of the segment and of the map. The loader determines the location M at which the map begins, scans the map, and adjusts the addresses that correspond to bits that signify relocation. The segment origin S for the first segment is specified by the operating system. The origin of each succeeding segment is defined by performing the assignment S←M before reading. Figure 9.2(b) shows the status after the first segment has been relocated and the second one loaded.

A rather efficient compromise between line relocation and segment relocation is the following. The text is divided into fixed-length chunks having precisely as many potentially relative fields as the machine word has bits. One chunk of relocatable text is loaded, together with one word of relocation bits. The relative addresses in the chunk are relocated before the next chunk is loaded. This approach captures much of the I/O efficiency of the map method, without requiring extra storage for the last segment map, and permits the use of fixed-length units throughout.

For a machine with explicit-base addressing, any program normally incorporates instructions to load appropriate segment origin locations into base registers at execution time. Relocation is then performed even later during execution time by the machine's calcula-

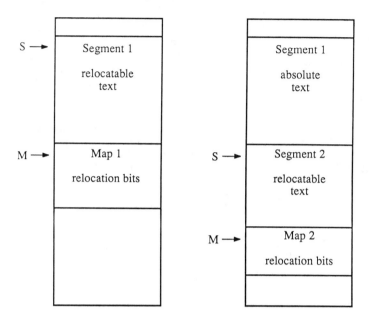

(a) Before relocation of Segment 1   (b) After relocation of Segment 1

Figure 9.2   Use of Relocation Map

tion of effective addresses for each instruction that references storage.
Although this relocation applies to address fields of instructions, it
is not performed upon address constants. These must be relocated
in much the same manner as are *all* addresses in a direct-addressing
machine. Because address constants typically constitute a very small
portion of the text of a program, it is wasteful to supply relocation
bits, all but a few of them zero, for all fields of the program text.
Instead, the assembler appends a **relocation list** that specifies the
adjustments to be made. For the program fragment

```
 0    PROG3     ---    ---
      ---       LOAD   POINTER
      ---       ---    ---
38    LOCN      ---    ---
      ---       ---    ---
71    POINTER   CONST  A(LOCN)
72    TWO       CONST  2
```

(to which the location counter values have been prefixed), the object code assembled at address 71 for the address constant A(LOCN) is the number 38. The relocation list entry specifies the address (71) to be modified and the appropriate location counter (the one whose origin is associated with the symbol PROG3). The loader merely scans the relocation list after loading the text and makes the indicated adjustments. Address constants are normally not used when programming machines with implicit-base addressing.

The foregoing relocation methods all assume that the original program is free of external references. Relocation of addresses that incorporate external references must be postponed until after those references have been resolved.

9.2.3 Transfer Vector

If references to global data are made through a common data area, thus restricting external references to subroutine calls, the translator and loader together can resolve those references by use of a simple mechanism. The translator (say, an assembler) prefixes the program text with a **transfer vector** of symbolic names of the subroutines. After loading the transfer vector and program text, the loader then loads each subroutine specified in the transfer vector. In so doing, it replaces the symbolic name in the transfer vector by the actual address of the subroutine. The assembled code then uses the modified transfer vector in calling the subroutines indirectly. If indirect addressing is available, a call of SUBR can be generated as a branch to the address stored at the transfer vector location associated with SUBR. If only direct addressing is provided, the loader can replace each name in the assembled transfer vector by a branch instruction to the actual subroutine address. In that situation a call of SUBR is generated as a direct branch to the associated transfer vector location, which will branch in turn to the desired subroutine.

Figure 9.3 illustrates the transfer vector mechanism for the direct-addressing machine defined in Chapter 2. The symbols SQRT and SORTFLD are externally defined subroutine names, which appear as branch addresses in (a). The assembler adjoins to the object code a transfer vector, shown at the top of (b), and generates branches to that transfer vector. The loader distinguishes the transfer vector elements from other text by a flag bit, or perhaps a special record to delimit the transfer vector. The result of replacing the transfer vector elements is shown in (c).

			---			---	
		16	SORTFLD		16	BR	376
		18	SQRT		18	BR	200
---			---			---	
BR	SQRT	52	BR	18	52	BR	18
---			---			---	
BRNEG	SORTFLD	93	BRNEG	16	93	BRNEG	16
---			---			---	

(a) Source text	(b) After assembly	(c) After loading

Figure 9.3   Use of a Transfer Vector

If the symbolic names used are longer than the space required to hold the address or complete branch instruction in the transfer vector, space can be wasted. We can eliminate this waste at the cost of extra processing by the assembler, which prepares a separate table of subroutine names and the associated locations within the transfer vector. The loader uses that table rather than the transfer vector itself to determine which subroutines to load and where to insert their addresses.

9.2.4 Linker

If external references are not limited to subroutine calls, then the definition of a symbol in one segment must be applied in translating each instance of its use in another segment. This resolution is performed by a **linker**, using information supplied to it by the assembler (or compiler). In translating a segment of source program, either the assembler assumes that symbols not defined within the segment are defined externally, or the programmer identifies such symbols explicitly. Symbols that are defined and are expected by the programmer to be referenced by other segments cannot be identified as such by the assembler. Some systems do not require the programmer to identify such symbols explicitly. It will then be necessary, whenever an externally defined symbol is encountered in some other segment, to search for its definition over all segments external to that other segment.

The detection of errors is easiest if the source-language program signals both types of external references. Many different syntactic forms occur, some of which use statement fields in a manner that is inconsistent with their use in other statements. For our illustrative assembler language we adopt two assembler directives, INTUSE and INTDEF. The INTUSE directive requires a label, which is a symbol internally used but externally defined. There is no operand. The INTDEF directive, which is not labeled, takes one operand, which is a symbol that must appear as the label on another line. That symbol is internally defined and expected to be externally used. These directives usually precede any other occurrences of the symbols that they contain. Other assembler directives to the linker, all with application to global symbols, may include RENAME and EQU.

The assembler prepares a **definition table** that lists each internally defined global symbol. There is one entry for each symbol, including the name of the program segment. Each entry includes the symbol, its address, and its relocatability mode. The assembler also prepares a **use table** that lists each internally used global symbol. There is one entry for each occurrence, not merely one for each symbol. Each entry includes the symbol itself, the location counter value (i.e., relative address) of the operand field in which it occurs, and the sign with which it occurs. The use table is preferably in address order. The first of two segments to be linked is shown in Figure 9.4, both in source language and as translated independently. The relocatability mode (a for absolute, r for relative) is shown after each word of object code. Although the definition and use tables are shown following the text, either or both can precede the text.

The translation of a symbol defined externally to the segment must necessarily be incomplete. The assembler assigns to it address 0 and mode absolute. This permits uniform processing of address expressions as well as of lone symbols. The address corresponding to each global symbol can later be added or subtracted, as appropriate. Its relocatability mode is also handled straightforwardly, in the manner explained toward the end of this section. Thus PROG2 at address 11 is translated into address 0 and mode absolute. Likewise, TABLE+2 at address 21 is translated into address 2 (zero for TABLE plus the stated 2) and mode absolute (for the sum of two absolute quantities). The second segment, translated similarly, is shown in Figure 9.5.

```
PROG1      START  0
PROG2      INTUSE
TABLE      INTUSE
           INTDEF TEST
           INTDEF RESUMEPT        Addr Word M Word M
           INTDEF HEAD
           ---                    --
TEST       BRPOS  PROG2           10   01   a  00   a
RESUMEPT   LOAD   LIST            12   03   a  30   r
           ---                    14
           ---                    --
           LOAD   TABLE+2         20   03   a  02   a
HEAD       ---                    22
           ---                    --
           STOP                   29   11   a
LIST       CONST  37              30   37   a
           END                    31
```

<table>
<tr><td>(a) Source program</td><td>(b) Object code</td></tr>
</table>

Symbol	Addr	Sign		Symbol	Addr	Mode
PROG2	11	+		PROG1	00	r
TABLE	21	+		TEST	10	r
				RESUMEPT	12	r
				HEAD	22	r

(c) Use table	(d) Definition table

Figure 9.4 First Segment Ready for Linking

Not surprisingly, the implementation of a linker is reminiscent of that of an assembler. A two-pass algorithm collects the global symbol definitions during the first pass and applies them during the second. As in assembly, a symbol table is used, called the **global symbol table** (also "external symbol table" or "linkage symbol table"). During Pass 1 the linker merges the definition tables of the several segments into one, taking appropriate error action if any symbol has more than one definition. For the first segment processed, the definition table entries are copied unchanged into the global symbol table.

The design of the linker is simplified if we assume that the independently translated segments are eventually to be loaded into

```
PROG2     START  O
          INTDEF TABLE
TEST      INTUSE
RESUMEPT  INTUSE                            Addr Word M Word M
HEAD      INTUSE
          ---                               --
          STORE  TABLE+HEAD-TEST            15   07   a  27   r
          ---                               17
          ---                               --
          BR     RESUMEPT                   25   00   a  00   a
TABLE     SPACE                             27   XX   a
          SPACE                             28   XX   a
          SPACE                             29   XX   a
TWO       CONST  2                          30   02   a
ADDRTEST  CONST  A(TEST)                    31   00   a
          END                              32
```

         (a) Source program   (b) Object code

Symbol	Addr	Sign	Symbol	Addr	Mode
HEAD	16	+	PROG2	00	r
TEST	16	−	TABLE	27	r
RESUMEPT	26	+			
TEST	31	+			

        (c) Use table   (d) Definition table

Figure 9.5   Second Segment Ready for Linking

consecutive areas of storage. This will make all segments subject to
a single relocation constant. We shall relax that restriction later. In
processing the second segment under our assumption, the length of
the first segment is added to the address of each relative symbol entered from the second definition table. This ensures that its address
is now relative to the origin of the first segment in the about-to-
be-linked collection of segments. Either during this pass or during
the second, the same adjustment must be made to relative addresses
within the program and to location counter values of entries in the
use table. In processing the third and subsequent segments, the
linker adds the sum of the lengths of the two or more previously
processed segments.

Suppose that the linker now performs Pass 1 processing of the
two segments previously presented, starting with PROG1. The only

change to the first segment is the removal of its definition table, which is copied into the global symbol table. Changes to the second segment are shown in Figure 9.6. We assume that the adjustment of addresses in the program text and use table were performed during Pass 1, although they could have been deferred to Pass 2. Note in particular the adjustment of the operand of the STORE instruction. Figure 9.7 shows the global symbol table produced.

			Addr	Word	M	Word	M
PROG2	START	0					
	INTDEF	TABLE					
TEST	INTUSE						
RESUMEPT	INTUSE						
HEAD	INTUSE						
	---		--				
	STORE	TABLE+HEAD-TEST	46	07	a	58	r
	---		48				
	---		--				
	BR	RESUMEPT	56	00	a	00	a
TABLE	SPACE		58	XX	a		
	SPACE		59	XX	a		
	SPACE		60	XX	a		
TWO	CONST	2	61	02	a		
ADDRTEST	CONST	A(TEST)	62	00	a		
	END						

(a) Source program   (b) Object code

Symbol	Addr	Sign
HEAD	47	+
TEST	47	-
RESUMEPT	57	+
TEST	62	+

(c) Use table

Figure 9.6   Second Segment after Pass 1 of Linker

During Pass 2 the linker updates address fields to reflect the juxtaposition of the segments, unless this was done during Pass 1. Necessarily deferred to Pass 2 is the actual patching of external references. The object code is copied unchanged, except for the updating

Symbol	Addr	Mode
PROG1	00	r
TEST	10	r
RESUMEPT	12	r
HEAD	22	r
PROG2	31	r
TABLE	58	r

Figure 9.7   Global Symbol Table

just described (if it was indeed deferred). This copying continues until the field is reached whose address appears in the next entry of the use table for the segment being copied. The symbol in that entry is looked up in the global symbol table, and its address therefrom added to the object code field. For the programs of Figures 9.4 and 9.6 this first occurs when word 11 is encountered. The symbol PROG2 is looked up in the global symbol table and found to have address 31. This value is added (as directed by the use table sign field) to the 00 in word 11 to yield the correct branch address. The relocation mode indicator of word 11 is also adjusted. The original address is absolute; the address added in is relative. The resulting sum is therefore relative. A similar adjustment occurs in processing word 21, which originally holds the absolute address 02 and is set to the relative address 60.

The processing of word 47 is somewhat more complicated. The original content is the relative address 58. Addition of the value 22 of HEAD yields 80, but HEAD is also relative, and the sum of two relative symbols is illegal. No matter. The linker continues, subtracting the relative address 10 of TEST to yield the legal relative address 70 for the address expression TABLE+HEAD-TEST. During the address adjustment, the linker must count the relative address components algebraically. If the final count is neither 0 nor 1, then an error has occurred. Intermediate values, however, may be other than 0 or 1. The branch address in word 57 and the address constant in word 62 are adjusted without difficulty, and the result of linking the two segments is shown in Figure 9.8.

We imposed earlier a restriction that the linked program be relocated as a single unit. A simple modification suffices to remove this restriction, and also permits the use of multiple location counters within a single segment. The relocation mode indicator of each

			Addr	Word	M	Word	M
PROG1	START	0					
PROG2	INTUSE						
TABLE	INTUSE						
	INTDEF	TEST					
	INTDEF	RESUMEPT					
	INTDEF	HEAD					
	---		--				
TEST	BRPOS	PROG2	10	01	a	31	r
RESUMEPT	LOAD	LIST	12	03	a	30	r
	---		14				
	---		--				
	LOAD	TABLE+2	20	03	a	60	r
HEAD	---		22				
	---		--				
	STOP		29	11	a		
LIST	CONST	37	30	37	a		
	END						
PROG2	START	0					
	INTDEF	TABLE					
TEST	INTUSE						
RESUMEPT	INTUSE						
HEAD	INTUSE						
	---		--				
	STORE	TABLE+HEAD-TEST	46	07	a	70	r
	---		48				
	---		--				
	BR	RESUMEPT	56	00	a	12	r
TABLE	SPACE		58	XX	a		
	SPACE		59	XX	a		
	SPACE		60	XX	a		
TWO	CONST	2	61	02	a		
ADDRTEST	CONST	A(TEST)	62	10	r		
	END						

(a) Source programs adjoined   (b) Object code

Figure 9.8   Program after Pass 2 of Linker

word is not just a bit to indicate relative or absolute, but rather the number of the associated location counter. (Zero can be used if the field is absolute.) This information is included with entries in the global symbol table. The linker verifies during Pass 2 that each field is either absolute or else relative to exactly one location counter.

Although the examples of this section have assumed direct addressing, linking of programs for base-addressed machines is performed similarly. Address constants in different segments are then usually relative to different origins, which are identified in the global symbol table.

Just as assembly can be performed in what is nominally a single pass, so can linking. If there is enough storage to hold the linker and all the segments, the following scheme serves. Each segment is read in, preceded by its definition table and followed by its use table. The definition table of the first segment is copied into the initially empty global symbol table. The use table of the first segment includes references to subsequent segments only. Each symbol in that use table is also entered in the global symbol table, but marked as undefined. The remainder of each entry in the use table (address and sign) is placed on a chain linked with its symbol in the table. As each succeeding definition table is read, each symbol is compared with the global symbol table. If it is not in the table, it is entered as before with its definition and marked as defined. If it is already in the table, marked as undefined, its definition is entered in the table. It is also used to patch the addresses on the associated chain, the space for which can then be released. If the symbol is already in the table, but marked as defined, a duplicate definition error has occurred.

As each succeeding use table entry is read, its symbol is checked against the table. If the symbol is not in the table, it is entered, marked as undefined, and a new reference chain started. If the symbol is indeed in the table, but undefined, an element is appended to the existing chain. If the symbol has already been defined, its table definition is used to patch the specified word in the program, which has already been read in. Alternatively, a true one-pass linker issues to the loader a directive to effect the patch. This organization is not unlike that of the load-and-go assembler, which combines one full pass with a number of mini-passes.

9.2.5 Linking Loader

Although linking is conceptually distinct from relocation, the two functions are often implemented concurrently. This is particularly convenient, because the segments must be read for either linking or loading, and both functions require inspection of the relocation bits. Duplication of these efforts is avoided if linking can be deferred until loading time. A program that loads, links, and relocates segments is called a **linking loader**.

The over-all organization of a linking loader is similar to that of either the two-pass or the one-pass linker previously described. We assume, of course, that enough storage is provided to hold all the segments. The operating system makes a gross allocation of storage, which is known to the linking loader before the first segment is read. The relocation constant associated with each location counter can therefore be established before reading either the definition table or the text of any segment assembled with respect to that location counter. As the definition of each global relative symbol is read into the global symbol table, the appropriate relocation constant is added to its address. The relocation constant for each local relative address is added after the program text has been loaded into its allocated storage.

The object segments read by a linking loader hold relocatable code with interspersed relocation information. This may be in the form of bits with each word, a relocation map for the entire text, or a few words to flag address constants in the code for a machine with explicit-base addressing. Loading must include the separation of each program word from the associated relocation information.

During Pass 1, a two-pass linking loader allocates storage, determines the relocation constants, relocates global relative symbols, and builds the global symbol table. It can defer inspection of program texts and use tables. During Pass 2 it loads the text, relocating local relative symbols as it proceeds, and then adjusts and relocates fields that include externally defined symbols. A one-pass linking loader performs all of these operations in a single pass, augmented by following chains of forward references.

The foregoing descriptions have ignored features such as products of global symbols, which some assembler languages permit, and preparation for execution in the absence of enough storage. Mechanisms for handling the former are rather specialized, and we shall not discuss them here. The latter is the subject of the next two sections.

9.2.6 Static Overlay Generator

A program whose storage requirement exceeds its allocation can still be prepared for execution if not all of its segments need to be resident in main storage concurrently. If a reference is made to a segment that is not in main storage, execution must be delayed to allow that segment to be loaded. The resulting decrease in execution efficiency can often be held to a tolerable level by careful selection of the segments to be resident simultaneously. The translator has no practical way of identifying the groups of segments that should be resident simultaneously to prevent unacceptable loss of efficiency. Consequently, the programmer must specify this information. The specification is customarily a static **overlay structure** in the form of a tree, which may be multiply-rooted. Each node of the tree represents a segment. The tree has the property that two segments that are to be in main storage simultaneously lie either on the same path from a root to a leaf or on disjoint paths from a root to a leaf. Figure 9.9 presents an example.

The unorthodox representation of that tree facilitates the visualization of storage use. Each node is drawn as a vertical line of length proportional to the size of the corresponding segment. The arcs to descendant nodes are drawn as horizontal lines from the bottom end of the parent node. Thus vertical position anywhere in the diagram is in direct correspondence with location in storage. Each segment is labeled by its number and by its storage requirement. Segments 1 and 5 are both root segments; of the others, only segment 3 is not a leaf. Segments 2 and 6 may not be co-resident because they lie on different paths (1,2 and 1,3,6) that are not disjoint. Segments 1, 3, 4, 5, and 8 may be co-resident because segments 1, 3, and 4 lie together on one path, segments 5 and 8 lie together on another path, and the two paths are disjoint. The storage required for those five segments is 78K, the maximum needed for any set of segments that may be co-resident. It would require 132K, on the other hand, to store all nine segments simultaneously.

Segments with a common parent are never co-resident, and in fact are assigned the same origin just beyond the end of their parent's allocation. One such segment **overlays** another when it is loaded. A root segment, of course, is never overlaid.

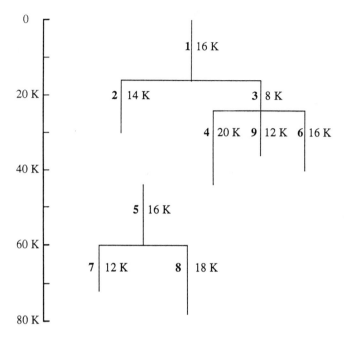

Figure 9.9   Static Overlay Structure

The use of an overlay structure requires the linker and relocating loader (whether they are combined or not) together to ensure that references external to a segment result in the correct execution-time accesses. In examining this requirement it is helpful to distinguish two classes of external references. One is to a segment that is permitted to be co-resident. The other is to a segment that is prohibited from being co-resident. Following IBM parlance, we call the former **inclusive** references and the latter **exclusive** references. For example, an instruction in segment 1 that loads a word from segment 6 makes an inclusive reference; a call of segment 8 by segment 7 is an exclusive reference. An inclusive reference upward in a path presents no problem, because the referenced segment is necessarily in storage. This is true, for example, of a reference from segment 6 to segment 3. Other inclusive references, such as from segment 3 to segment 8, may require prior loading of the referenced segment. This action can be performed at execution time only if a description of the tree structure is available and if the loader can be invoked as needed.

The linker must therefore generate a description of the static overlay structure. This description is often called a **segment table**. To ensure that the segment table will be available at any time during execution, it is placed in a root segment, thereby increasing the length of that segment. The segment table also indicates for each segment whether it is loaded or not. At execution time, a control program called the **overlay supervisor** interrogates the segment table for every external reference other than an upward inclusive reference. The overlay supervisor calls the loader if the referenced segment is not resident. It also updates the segment table entries of the overlaid segment(s) and of each newly loaded segment.

The process of loading a segment is known as **dynamic loading**, because the decision to load is made dynamically at execution time. If a segment about to be overlaid has been modified since its loading, it is normally necessary first to copy that segment to backing storage. An exception occurs if it is known that the segment will never subsequently be reloaded. Such reloading of an overlaid segment is obviated if the segment is serially reusable and the overlaying occurs between successive uses, or if the segment is reenterable.

The linker must generate code for execution-time calls to the overlay supervisor. The moments at which these calls will be issued are, of course, not predictable. It is therefore hardly worth preparing and using an overlay structure if the overlay supervisor is not permanently resident in storage during execution of the overlaid program. This, too, somewhat reduces the space saving.

An exclusive external reference presents the further problem that the segment that makes the reference is overlaid before the segment to which reference is made becomes available. Therefore, some systems do not permit exclusive references. Those that do usually limit them to procedure calls and returns, because unrestricted communication between segments that overlay each other is intolerably inefficient. The linker generates a table of all symbols to which an exclusive reference is made. The overlay supervisor can interrogate this exclusive reference table to discover to which segment an exclusive reference is made, and then consult the segment table as before.

For simplicity, the exclusive reference table can be incorporated in the root segment, to be available at any time. This may waste storage, however, particularly if the tree has several levels and many exclusive references are to nearby nodes. Although the total space required by the table cannot be reduced, the table itself can be overlaid. How low in a singly-rooted tree can the table entry for a symbol be placed? It can be in the lowest common ancestor of the segment that contains the referent and of the segments that refer to it. Thus the exclusive reference table may be distributed among as many as all the nonleaf nodes.

9.2.7 Dynamic Linker

The static linking of an overlay structure is possible only if the programmer is able and willing to specify at linkage time which sets of segments are to be co-resident at execution time. There exist situations, however, in which the programmer may prefer to, or need to, postpone the specification until execution time. An error routine, for example, may very well not be invoked in the course of a particular execution of the program. The programmer knows with which other segments the error routine is to be co-resident if invoked. He or she may nevertheless prefer to allocate storage for it dynamically only if and when it is invoked. This precludes the binding, at linkage time, of references to the error routine. The programmer must choose between allocating a maximum amount of space that *might* be required and deferring the resolution of external references until execution time. In many transaction-oriented systems, the determination of which segments must be co-resident is highly data-dependent. There is often a large collection of processing routines, almost any small subset of which may be needed at a given moment, but hardly enough main storage to hold all. Dependence on a static overlay structure could cause intolerable service delays.

A solution is to perform dynamically not only the loading, but also the linking. The linker does not attempt to resolve external references beyond translating each into an ordered pair (s, d), where s identifies a segment and d is a displacement from the segment origin. As before, a segment table indicates for each segment whether it is in storage and, if so, where its origin is. If segment s is not in main storage when the reference is encountered at execution time, a control program causes the segment to be loaded. Dynamic linking is provided by adding the displacement to the origin to obtain a physical storage address. If no reference is made to a particular segment, no effort is wasted in linking it nor storage in holding it.

Some computers have segmentation hardware to perform the table lookup and addition as part of calculating the effective address. For these computers, all addresses can be provided as segment-displacement pairs, and dynamic linking becomes standard practice rather than a complex expedient.

Program loading is performed just before execution, and storage space is one of the resources managed by the operating system. Therefore, the implementation of linking, loading, and relocation, particularly dynamic loading and linking, is closely tied to that of the control programs. This is a major example of the way in which translators and control programs work cooperatively to provide a programming system.

FOR FURTHER STUDY

Linking and loading are particularly well presented in the brief Section 8.4 of Brooks69, the tutorial Presser72, which is specific to the IBM 360, and in the following book chapters: Graham75 (Chapter 6), Arms76 (Chapter 13), Ullman76 (Chapter 5), Barron78 (Chapter 5), and Beck85 (Chapter 3), which emphasizes overlay management.

REVIEW QUESTIONS

9.1 What is the advantage of considering an undefined external symbol to be the name of a library routine?

9.2 The library routines are usually relocatable. What saving would result from their being made nonrelocatable? What extra burdens and costs would such a restriction impose? Assume a two-pass module assembler, a linker, and a loader.

9.3 An absolute loader is needed for modules of absolute code. List possible sources of such modules.

9.4 Why is "relocation" a misnomer?

9.5 Is there a logical requirement for loading to precede relocation, or *vice versa*?

9.6 Identify each of the following as a relative or absolute field: (**a**) branch address in a machine instruction that specifies a relative branch; (**b**) shift amount; (**c**) address constant; (**d**) literally specified constant; (**e**) other constant; (**f**) reference to a literal.

9.7 Explain the relocation of A(SYM1)-A(SYM2), where the symbol in each of the address constants is internally defined and relative.

9.8 In the source code for a two-pass assembler, is it required that either INTUSE or INTDEF precede all other references to the symbols named therein?

9.9 How does a linker verify, during Pass 2, whether each address expression is valid?

9.10 What advantage results if a one-pass linker processes a segment's internally defined external symbols before its internally used external symbols?

9.11 How can a one-pass linker verify whether each address expression is valid?

9.12 Why is type checking across modules usually not performed by conventional linkers?

9.13 Why does the translator, which can examine the static program text, usually not determine which segments should be co-resident?

9.14 Can an absolute loader handle loading for a static overlay structure?

9.15 If the overlay structure has more than one root, where should the structure description be maintained?

9.16 Why is linking sometimes deferred until execution time?

9.17 In a dynamic loading system, what agent prepares the segment table and what agent updates it?

PROBLEMS

9.1 Explain how the transfer vector mechanism can be extended to other references than subroutine calls.

9.2 Show the changes in Figures 9.4–9.8 under the assumption that PROG*i* uses location counter *i*. You do not need to show unchanged portions.

9.3 Consider the use of an assembler, a linker, and a (separate) loader for a machine with explicit-base addressing. The following modules are to be assembled, linked, and loaded contiguously, starting at 3000 with FIRST, whose length is 800. Trace the steps in producing the final form of the constant in module FIRST, stating the relevant output and actions of each of the three translators, as well as the value of the relocation constant.

(**a**) Assume first that the linker is *not* notified that loading will be contiguous.

(**b**) Assume instead that the linker is so notified.

Address	Label	Opcode	Operand
0	FIRST	START	
	REALIGN	INTUSE	
	OFFSET	SET	240

200	THINK	CONST	A(REALIGN)-OFFSET

		END	
0	SECOND	START	

765	REALIGN	---	

		INTDEF	REALIGN
		END	

9.4 The two assembler-language programs

```
A        START  0              B          START  0
         INTDEF WHISKEY        WHISKEY    INTUSE
ZULU     INTUSE                           INTDEF ZULU
         LOAD   YANKEE                     LOAD   WHISKEY
         STORE  ZULU                       STORE  XRAY
WHISKEY  CONST  15             XRAY        SPACE
YANKEE   CONST  13             ZULU        SPACE
         END                               END
```

have been independently assembled into the following object segments, where "**M**" indicates the relocatability mode.

Definition Table of A			Definition Table of B		
Symbol	Addr	Mode	Symbol	Addr	Mode
A	00	r	B	00	r
WHISKEY	04	r	ZULU	05	r

Text of A				Text of B			
Addr	Word	M	Word	M	Addr	Word	M	Word	M
00	03	a	05	r	00	03	a	00	a
02	07	a	00	a	02	07	a	04	r
04	15	a			04	XX	a		
05	13	a			05	XX	a		

Use Table of A			Use Table of B		
Symbol	Addr	Sign	Symbol	Addr	Sign
ZULU	03	+	WHISKEY	01	+

The external references are to be resolved by a two-pass linker that does *not* assume execution-time contiguity of its input segments. After linking, a separate relocating loader will first load segment A with its origin at location 300 and then segment B with its origin at location 200. Assume that when A is loaded the origin of B is not yet known. Show any changed (or newly created) segments or tables after

(**a**) linker Pass 1;
(**b**) linker Pass 2;
(**c**) loading of segment A;
(**d**) loading of segment B.

9.5 [Ghezzi] A one-pass linker is applied to the two segments of Exercise 9.4. Show the data structures as they stand after reading program A and before reading program B.

9.6 [Donovan] The assembler-linker-loader sequence calculates each of the four address constants in the following program. Explain briefly the method of calculation, stating the actions performed by each of the three translators. Assume that the program is eventually loaded with its origin at location 1000. Where possible, specify numbers for actual locations. Repeat for both (**a**) direct and (**b**) explicit-base addressing.

	0	COMP240	---	
			INTDEF	BRAVO
		OSCAR	INTUSE	

	20	ALFA	---	

	50	BRAVO	---	

	90	CHARLIE	---	

	160	DELTA	SET	3

(i)	201	KILO	CONST	A(OSCAR)
(ii)	202	LIMA	CONST	A(BRAVO)
(iii)	203	METRO	CONST	A(OSCAR)-A(CHARLIE)
(iv)	204	NOVEMBER	CONST	A(CHARLIE)-A(ALFA)+A(DELTA)

9.7 Explain the resolution of symbols defined (as in A EQU B) to be synonyms of externally defined symbols. Show what must appear in the source text, give an example reference, and describe how it is resolved. Assume an assembler-linker sequence.

9.8 Consider a direct-addressing machine for which the translators collect relocatability information into a bit map, which accompanies the program text, definition table, and use table. A two-pass linking loader accepts such object modules and combines them into a single, contiguous unit of machine code in main storage. Describe a suitable organization of the object code, and explain the steps by which the linking loader performs the processing.

Chapter 10

General Issues

We have reserved for this final chapter a number of important issues that are not easily identified with a single type of translator or a single translation technique. First, in Section 10.1, we consider the characteristics of hardware and software that may constrain or facilitate the implementation of translators. In Section 10.2, we view translators not as radically different, but as points on two different spectra. Different design choices, derived either from the hardware and software environment or from different emphases on space and time efficiency, are reviewed in Section 10.3. We discuss the separate translation of modules, independently of each other, in Section 10.4. We treat in Section 10.5 the important issues of program portability and how it is enhanced by suitable translators. Finally, in Section 10.6, we survey briefly some of the accomplishments in harnessing the computer as a tool in writing its own translators.

10.1 SYSTEM ENVIRONMENT

We do not run translators, nor the programs they translate, in a vacuum. Several components of the system environment may influence the design of the translator and that of the code it generates. These include the computer hardware, the operating system, and the other translators available.

10.1.1 Hardware

A major determinant of translator organization and performance is the amount of main storage available. Storage costs are continuing their rapid fall, and ever larger main storage capacities are provided as standard. This suggests that the use of auxiliary files by translators will decline, and that speed can often be obtained in return for the use of greater space. Yet even if the vendor gives the storage away, there remains one potentially significant cost. That cost is the provision of bits in the instruction stream to address the storage. Because those bits themselves require storage and bus bandwidth, economics will continue to dictate a compromise between inadequate storage and unlimited storage.

Stacks are widely used in parsers and in run-time management of activation records, and can often aid in table management. Many computers, such as the Hewlett-Packard 9000 series, provide hardware implementations of stacks. The Burroughs B6700 incorporated a set of hardware Display Registers expressly to point to activation records in the environment. The availability of hardware stacks is an invitation to use stack-based techniques in implementing translators.

Most modern computers offer one or more flavors of indirect addressing. This facilitates the use of linked lists, as in chains of forward references.

10.1.2 Operating Systems

A host of services needed by many programs and helpful to many users have been collected into the modern operating system. These services are available not only to the translator implementer, but also to the program that results from the translation.

I/O Routines. It is not unusual for a mainframe operating system to devote as much as half of its code to the I/O subsystem. The availability of I/O routines spares all programmers the need to write their own versions of these often demanding and complex programs. The translator will normally use operating-system I/O routines. The code it generates will usually do likewise. The input and output operations of the translator and of the programs it translates must therefore conform to the operating system's rules for I/O. Only if there is a substantial space or time advantage in departing from those rules does it pay to deviate. For a cross-translator, of course, the generated code must match the operating system of the *target* computer.

RAM Disks. Many operating systems offer the powerful service known as a **RAM disk**, whose name derives from the acronym for random-access memory. The RAM disk, or "electronic disk", is an electronic simulation of a magnetic disk and its electromechanical disk drive. Implemented in main storage, it offers the function of a disk at the speed of the CPU. The using program accesses the RAM disk by making standard system I/O calls. The programmer need not even be aware whether the disk to be used is real or simulated.

RAM disks are very popular on microcomputers. Not only do they offer speed, but they offer device independence as well. An implementer can test a translator rapidly with small files on a RAM disk, and be assured that the translator will run correctly with large files on real disks. Where disk-based techniques have already been developed for parts of the translator, these can be greatly speeded up without reprogramming. For example, a multi-pass translator with intermediate files on disk can be quickly converted into one that requires more main storage but no disks. Generated code is no different for RAM disks than for real disks; no extra burden is imposed on the translator.

Subroutine Interface. Most operating systems provide a standard subroutine linkage mechanism and calling sequence. Normally, the translator's own subroutine calls should adhere to this standard subroutine interface. Whether the subroutine calls in generated code should adhere to the conventions of the operating system may be an issue of performance. In some operating systems, the standard interface is slow. If the program being translated is not likely to be used in conjunction with other programs, it may be appropriate to enhance its performance by generating nonstandard subroutine calls.

Storage Management. Almost all operating systems allocate storage to the using programs. So-called "virtual storage" systems hide from the programmer the details of storage use. This frees the programmer from needing to know where data and instructions are stored. It also hides this knowledge from the programmer, making it harder to use the computer system efficiently. Of particular concern is the decrease in execution speed due to paging traffic. Careful allocation of translator data structures and code segments to pages can substantially enhance execution speed. To the extent that the translator is itself generated by another translator, the considerations of the following paragraph also apply.

Of perhaps greater importance is the storage efficiency of generated code. To a page-sized or smaller data structure, the translator should allocate storage that does not straddle a page boundary. With the high degree of modularization followed in modern programming, one page is often large enough to accommodate several code modules. The assignment of modules to pages can have a large effect on paging performance of the generated code. Clustering techniques can assign modules to pages in a manner that minimizes the frequency of calling across page boundaries.

10.1.3 Language Systems

The set of translators and their run-time routines should not be a collection of unrelated programs. For example, it is not appropriate for relocation information to be encoded one way by an assembler and interpreted another way by a loader. But it is not really enough that the different programs not disagree. Ideally, they should cooperate harmoniously in a system that, following Habermann76, we shall call "language system".

It is wise to think of each translator as part of the over-all language system. This can lead to several advantages. One is the uniformity of user interfaces; another is the commonality of encodings. The former enhances ease of learning and of use. The latter leads to improved function. For example, if different translators generate the same form of object code, it becomes possible to link modules originally written in different languages. The commonality of encoding also leads to code sharing. For example, a symbol table routine can be provided to serve several translators, such as a compiler and a linker.

The facilities already available in a language system influence the design of new translators. For example, is an assembler available when you write your compiler? If so, you might choose assembler language as the target language of your compiler.

10.2 TRANSLATOR SPECTRA

There are two more-or-less orthogonal spectra, or continua, along which translators can be placed. One, exemplified by compilers v. assemblers, is concerned with degree of complexity. The other, exemplified by compilers v. interpreters, is concerned with choice of binding time.

10.2.1 Compilers *v.* Assemblers

The many source-language features described in Section 7.1.1 result in a number of salient differences between compilers and assemblers. On any one item the distinction may not be clear-cut. Moreover, it may be difficult to distinguish a simple compiler from a powerful macro assembler. Nevertheless, the differences are usually substantial enough that there remains a qualitative distinction between assemblers and compilers.

A compiler usually performs a one-to-many translation, generating many target-language statements from a single source-language statement, whereas an assembler performs a one-to-one translation. There are exceptions, of course. A declaration statement does not result in the generation of any target code (unless it incorporates refinements such as an **initial** attribute). The simple assignment $A \leftarrow B$ may well be translated into a single target statement. An assembler will generate no machine code to correspond to most assembler directives, but may generate substantial amounts of code from a single CONST directive. Moreover, a macro assembler will generate many lines from a one-line call. Nevertheless, the characterization of compilers as one-to-many and of assemblers as one-to-one is reasonably accurate.

An assembler is little concerned with dependence among statements. Except for symbol definition and, on some machines, storage alignment, the translation of one statement is independent of that of other statements. This is not true of the compiler, where there is much greater mutual dependence among source-language statements. Declaration statements are explicitly related to statements that refer to the entities declared, and I/O statements are often explicitly dependent upon format statements. Implicit dependence occurs in loops and other control structures. Another form of implicit dependence is dictated by the target machine rather than by the source language. This is the interstatement competition for such resources as the registers that are to be designated in the code generated from several statements.

An assembler usually faces much simpler lexical and syntactic analysis than does a compiler. This is due in part to the reduced mutual dependence of statements, but also to the simpler forms of individual statements. It is true that an assembler may have to face address expressions and macro calls, both of which can be rather complex. These are rarely as intricate, however, as the statements that may be faced by a compiler.

A compiler usually encounters many more kinds of operands than does an assembler. Not only are there integer, real, boolean, and character types, but there are complex (in the mathematical sense), multidimensional array, tree-structured, label, and entry-name operands. Even for the types that the two may have in common, the compiler must perform type checking and conversion. The assembler, on the other hand, leaves this burden to the programmer.

Another difference is in error handling. Compiler-language programs embody greater redundancy than do assembler-language programs. The compiler is therefore often called upon to check in more detail, to issue elaborate and informative diagnostic messages, and often also to attempt repairs. The modern debugging compiler is a far cry from the sole message "parse failed" of one of the early compilers. Although assemblers are usually no longer that laconic either, they usually perform less extensive error handling than do compilers.

A final difference is that the compiler, unlike the assembler, is concerned with the flow of control at execution time. The assembler-language programmer provides his or her own subroutine linkages, perhaps through use of macro instructions. The assembler really need not distinguish a loop-closing branch from a subroutine call. The compiler, particularly for a block-structured language, may face tasks as complex as allocating storage for the activation records of recursive procedures or evaluating arguments called by name.

10.2.2 Compilers *v.* Interpreters

The distinction between the one-stage process of interpretation and the two-stage process of compilation and later execution is fundamental. The later binding time of translation actions in an interpreter, as compared with a compiler, results in many significant differences. Each approach offers advantages that the other does not. Many translators therefore embody a blend of compilation and interpretation. In this section, we nevertheless contrast pure compilation with pure interpretation, to accentuate their many important differences. In Section 10.3.2, we discuss ways to marry the two approaches.

We can readily distinguish the time to compile a program and the time to execute it. Under interpretation, however, we can observe only the total time. If we ignore compilation time and concentrate on execution time, it is clear that interpretation is slower than execution of machine-language code. One reason is that interpretation not only performs the specified actions, but also determines what they are. A more compelling reason is inherent in the repetitive structure of programs. It is not unusual for a statement in an inner loop to be executed thousands or even millions of times during a single use of a program. A compiler translates that statement once; an interpreter translates the statement each time it is encountered.

Of course, some statements may not be encountered during a particular run. Examples include error routines and branches not taken. The interpreter does not translate such a statement, whereas the compiler must. This saving, however, is rarely significant. What about the effect of including compilation time in our comparison? Even for a program that is executed only once, time to execute interpretively may still exceed that to compile and execute. If we use the program repetitively, the speed advantage of compilation becomes overwhelming.

Translation from machine-independent language to machine language is usually one-to-many. Thus the volume of machine code is often much greater than that of the corresponding source code. For a program of even modest size, the difference in code space required often exceeds the space required by an interpreter for the source language. Hence, interpreter and source code together can occupy less space than compiled machine code alone. This lower space requirement for interpretation than for compilation has led to the popularity of interpreters whenever space is at a premium. Such was very much the case for early microcomputers.

The interpreter is also at an advantage in handling execution-time errors. Examples include nonexistence of a file to be opened, input data of illegal format, and division by zero. The interpreter can check for the foregoing conditions and take corrective action, rather than allow operating-system interrupts or hardware traps to prevail. Because the interpreter has access to the source code, symbol table, and actual values of operands, it can also generate a meaningful error report.

The compiler is not helpless, of course. It can compile code to perform at execution time all the checks that an interpreter can perform. But these cost extra space and time both in the compiler and in the compiled code. Moreover, the lack of source-language information at execution time limits how informative the error reports can be. The degree of execution-time checking provided by a compiler may depend, of course, on the philosophy of the source language. The designer of PASCAL places a high value on checking; the designers of APL and of C subscribe rather to the dictum "*caveat programmer*".

To reuse a program without modification, the compilative approach requires no retranslation. We simply execute the machine-language program as frequently as needed. The interpretive approach, on the other hand, retranslates the program for each reuse. We perform exactly the same translation as previously. This further repetition increases the imbalance in time efficiency between compilation and interpretation. If the program is to be modified, however, compilation bears an extra burden. Unless the program is written in modules, the entire program must be recompiled before execution can begin. If the program is modularized, the changed modules must be recompiled and all modules relinked. There is no extra cost to interpretation, because we must translate the entire program anyway.

A major determinant of efficiency of reuse is how many times the program is to be executed. Some production programs run weekly or even daily for years, with only occasional modifications. Most student programs are changed every time they run. If change is frequent, the inefficiency of interpretation is limited. As a result, and also because of the advantages in error handling, interpreters are often favored for instruction.

We saw in Chapter 5 how easy it is to write an interpreter. If programmer effort or elapsed time to build a running translator is a key resource, write an interpreter. Another area in which compilers and interpreters differ in programmer effort is in debugging. Here, of course, the programmer is the translator's user rather than its implementer. The interpreter has simultaneous access to source-language information and to execution-time attributes. It can report to a programmer who is examining source text the current values of variables at the moment of error detection. Under pure compilation the hapless user is at the mercy of the operating system for information.

10.3 DESIGN CHOICES

10.3.1 Target Language

The target language of a compiler may be either object (or machine) code, almost ready to be interpreted by computer hardware, or else in another form that requires further translation. Figure 10.1 shows three organizations of the over-all translation process. Organization (a) is that of the traditional compiler, which generates either object code ready for relocation (and perhaps linking) or else machine code ready for loading. It is this organization that is implemented in the five steps described in Section 7.1.2.

Under organization (b), a separate assembler program performs the final stages of translation. This organization is attractive when we must build the compiler in a hurry, because the assembler is often already available. The translation is less efficient than in (a), however, because the assembler is not specialized to the restricted form of code produced by the compiler. Moreover, it builds a new symbol table instead of using the one already built by the compiler. Furthermore, the two-stage translation process requires either extra time to load the assembler after the compilation is complete, or space to hold the assembler in main storage during the compilation.

Organization (c) demands even less of the compiler, but requires an interpreter to translate the compiled program further. In organizations (a) and (b) the target-language specification is imposed on the compiler designer. In (c), on the other hand, the compiler and interpreter are designed together and the intermediate language can be specified to suit. In several situations, the relative simplicity of the compiler compensates for the speed loss of the interpreter. One situation occurs for programs with a high ratio of compilations to executions. For programs under development this ratio may approach unity, and for "one-shot" programs it may be nearly as great. Another arises for programs with short execution times. A popular intermediate language for this approach is P-code, developed for use in PASCAL compilers.

A third situation holds when the hardware incorporates features designed to facilitate interpretation of the compiler output. In

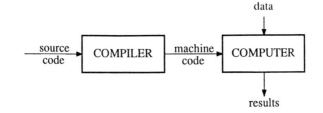

(a) Object or machine code

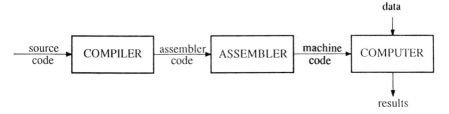

(b) Assembler-language code

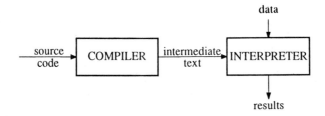

(c) Code for interpretation

Figure 10.1 Translations into Different Compiler Target Languages

other words, if the machine architecture and corresponding machine language are designed to execute intermediate code, organization (c) may be a very efficient approach. This approach was chosen for compilers on the Burroughs B1000 series, whose machine languages can be customized by user microprogramming. Another example is the LILITH computer, which was designed for efficient execution of the intermediate language M-code for MODULA. Another example is provided by the descriptors and stack mechanism of the Burroughs B5000 and its successors, which are highly suited to the direct execution of programs in postfix notation.

10.3.2 Degree of Interpretation

Service Routines. First we review alternatives to generating object code alone. Instead of relying on a hardware interpreter (the computer) to execute the target code, the compiler can make use of a software interpreter. In such interpretive execution, a generalized execution-time **service routine** can be provided for each source-language construct, perhaps for each different operation in the intermediate code. These service routines function as the interpretive subroutines in executing statements in a relatively high-level target language. The interpretive loop prepares the parameters for the service routines and exercises over-all control. The task of code generation is thus greatly simplified at the cost of reduced speed of execution of the program. This is accomplished by deferring part of the translation until more attributes are bound. For some source-language instructions, this deferral is so appealing that service routines are usually used for them even if the bulk of the program is translated into object code. This is particularly true for input and output statements. The space saving of providing a fixed set of specialized routines called at execution time, instead of generating code for each source-program I/O statement, often outweighs the costs of subroutine linkage.

Threaded Code. By the use of what is termed **threaded code**, we can capture in part the advantages of interpretive execution. Instead of relying on an interpretive loop to execute the service routines, the compiler generates a list of the addresses of those routines in the sequence in which they are to be called. Each service routine terminates by loading the next address from the list and branching to it. Actual parameters can be inserted in the list after the address of the service routine that uses them. Execution is faster than for pure interpretation, because subroutine linkage is eliminated. The space requirement is typically smaller than for pure generation, because one instance of a routine plus n instances of its address occupy less space than do n instances of the body of the routine.

Mixed Code. By coding frequently executed portions of a program in machine-language code and infrequently executed portions in interpretive code, we can seek simultaneously the space efficiency of the latter and the time efficiency of the former. The machine-language code can be produced by either an assembler or a compiler. This **mixed-code** approach requires a means of switching control from interpretive code to machine code and *vice versa*, either by calling or by jumping.

At least three methods of implementation are possible. One method, used with jumps, is to enlist the aid of the operating system by trapping. A machine-code segment can use either an illegal machine address or an illegal opcode. An interpretive-code segment can use the latter. Information encoded in the illegal specification tells the operating system what segment to invoke. A second method is for the machine code to issue a subroutine call to interpretive code. The third method is for interpretive code to issue a subroutine call to machine code. This is sometimes referred to as **mode switching** in an interpreter, and we describe it next.

The last interpretive code statement whose execution precedes that of the machine code is a mode-switching statement. Upon recognizing that statement, the interpreter stores enough of its own status to permit it to be resumed later and branches to the machine code. This action, diagrammed in Figure 10.2(a), is easily performed by one of the interpreter's subroutines. The control loop passes to the subroutine as a parameter the address of the start of the machine code segment. The machine code must terminate with restoration of the interpreter's status and a branch back to the interpretive loop, as shown in Figure 10.2(b). The numbers on the arrows in the figure indicate the temporal sequence of the corresponding transfers of control. An alternative to having a special mode switch subroutine

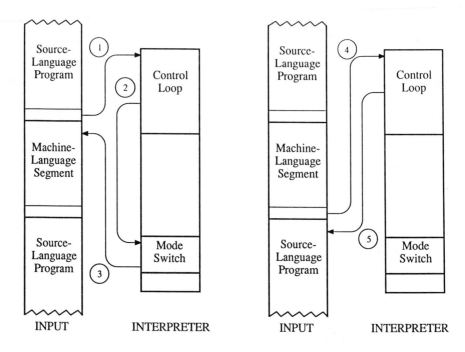

(a) Switching to machine code   (b) Switching from machine code

Figure 10.2   Mode Switching in an Interpreter

in the interpreter is simply to treat the machine-code segment as a user-written subroutine without parameters.

10.3.3 Degree of Recompilation

Pure compilation requires an entire program (or module) to be re-compiled for any change. It also translates code that a particular execution may not reach. Several techniques mitigate the space and time costs incurred by such full compilation.

Incremental Compiling. The object of **incremental compiling** is to offer the user both interactive editing and immediate error detection. As the name indicates, the compiler translates the program in small increments. These are typically single lines in a line-oriented source language, such as FORTRAN or BASIC. The incremental compiler checks each line as it is received and translates it into intermediate code. If the newly entered line has the same number as a previously translated line, code for the new line replaces that for the old. There are two simple ways to implement this replacement. The intermediate code may include source line numbers, or the compiler may maintain a table of line numbers with pointers to the intermediate code.

A major problem, of course, is that source-language lines are not always independent. References may precede declarations, as for the label to which a forward **goto** refers. Moreover, even the **next** statement of BASIC does not include the number of the corresponding **for** statement. Block structure is another complication. It is customary, therefore, to subject the complete program to analysis by a "pre-run module" that performs a global syntax check. It is not evident that this approach is better than the combination of a free-format language, fast compiler, and an editor coupled to the compiler. A good example of such a combination is TURBO PASCAL for the IBM Personal Computer.

Dynamic Compiling. Another approach to reducing the amount of compilation is to generate target code only as needed. Normally performed on a complete intermediate code, this is called **dynamic compiling**. Code that follows branches not taken and code for subroutines not called are not compiled. Compilation and execution are interleaved. Compilation proceeds until a choice must be made, and execution continues until more target code is required. Generated code is saved indefinitely for reuse.

Each time the program runs, however, the choice of branches and of subroutines may be different. The target code generation is therefore repeated. We must pay some degree of recompilation as the price of reducing the total compilation for a particular execution.

Throw-Away Compiling. A variant of dynamic compiling is especially attractive if main storage is limited. Target code is saved as long as possible, but not indefinitely. If more target code is generated than will fit, the code already generated is thrown away to make room for the new. The cost of this **throw-away compiling**, of course, is the recompilation of code thrown away but still needed. It is possible to have storage space and program unit size so badly matched that all code is thrown away after only a single use. With a little luck, or a little planning, this situation does not arise, and a modest amount of recompilation buys a substantial reduction in storage requirement.

10.3.4 Translator Organization

The organization of a translator must provide for a number of data structures. A two-pass assembler, for example, will include the following.

(1) Pass 1 program
(2) Pass 2 program
(3) Source text
(4) Intermediate text
(5) Object text
(6) Listing [if produced]
(7) Symbol table
(8) Global symbol table
(9) Redefinable symbol table [if the function is provided]
(10 Literal table
(11) Machine instruction table
(12) Assembler directive table
(13) Base register table [if explicit base registers are used]

The major differences among translation program organizations are determined by the choice of data structures to keep in main storage. The names of these choices customarily use the word "core" to refer to main storage, because of the once widespread use of coincident-current magnetic cores to implement main storage. For modern machines the term is technically not correct, but its brevity is appealing.

Text-in-Core. The **text-in-core** organization keeps the texts and tables in main storage and the programs in backing storage. Segments of the programs are brought in as needed. This organization is appropriate if the amount of translator program also in core is kept reasonably small. This can be accomplished by subdividing the translator into **phases**, each of which performs a small part of the total function. A compiler might, for example, have separate phases for scanning, parsing expressions, parsing other constructs, converting constants to internal representation, determining when temporary variables can be reused, eliminating redundant STORE/

LOAD pairs from intermediate code, handling storage allocation for dynamic arrays, *etc.* Some compilers have dozens of phases.

There is often no reason to make the entire source-language and target-language texts available continuously. Further space saving results from holding only a portion of these texts in main storage at a given moment. This is the practice in most compilers.

Translator-in-Core. The **translator-in-core** organization retains the translator programs in main storage, along with the tables. The texts reside in backing storage. This organization is particularly suitable for an assembler, because it needs to access the texts only serially.

One-pass translators normally use the translator-in-core organization. A single pass really suffices to perform compilation if the source language is not too rich and if appropriate compiler design decisions are taken. For example, variables should be declared before use. The grammar and parser should be of a type that obviates backtracking. The compiler can embody a one-pass assembler, or the designer can simply decree that the target code will be executed by an interpreter or assembled by a separate assembler.

A variant of this organization makes multiple passes over the program, each one requiring the presence not of the entire compiler, but of a major portion. A typical two-pass organization is to perform the machine-independent functions in Pass 1 and the machine-dependent functions in Pass 2. Additional passes might perform separately any of the five major processing steps described in Section 7.1.2 (except perhaps semantic processing), to perform machine-independent optimization of the intermediate code, or to perform machine-dependent optimization of the target code.

The original compiler for MODULA–2 divided the labor differently. It used Pass 1 for scanning and parsing, Pass 2 to build tables, Pass 3 for type checking, Pass 4 to generate target code, and an optional Pass 5 for listing. A revised version used a single pass with the parser as driver. The original decomposition into tasks was reassigned to modules rather than passes. The principal advantage of multiple passes is reduction in the main storage space required for the compiler. If a macro facility is provided for generating source text to be compiled, it is usually most easily implemented in an extra pass at the beginning.

The design of many popular assemblers dates back to when main storage was much more expensive than it has since become. Consequently, a typical organization for a two-pass assembler combines the translator-in-core approach with the provision of space for only the currently active pass. The texts are maintained in backing storage. The program starts with the Pass 1 program and tables in main storage. After the termination of Pass 1, it overwrites the Pass 1 program with the Pass 2 program, which has been waiting meanwhile in backing storage.

The total main storage requirement for multipass translators is minimized by making the programs for the different passes approximately equal in size. For a two-pass assembler, this is easily accomplished by suitable allocation of those functions that can be performed on either pass.

When extra storage is available that is not being used by an older translator, a RAM disk can speed up the translation. The files that would otherwise be accessed only in backing storage can instead be loaded into a RAM disk and accessed at much higher speed thereafter.

All-in-Core. The **all-in-core** organization is just what its name implies. It is applicable, however, only if there is room for everything. The sharp reduction in the cost of main storage during recent years has made it easier to support this organization.

The all-in-core organization is typical of load-and-go assemblers. Given enough space, it is appropriate also for a two-pass assembler. A full compiler requires yet more space than does a mere assembler, or else limits the source program size more severely. The all-in-core organization is indeed used, however, particularly in compilers designed for debugging small programs. At the cost of over-all translation time, space can often be saved by compiling to intermediate code that is then executed interpretively.

Neither-in-Core. We should perhaps name also the **neither-in-core** organization. The program may be long, the language rich, and the space limited. If so, the program for each pass will have to be brought into main storage in pieces, overlaying pieces loaded earlier. If a paging system is used, paging traffic produced by a compiler can be reduced by carefully laying out the compiler code in pages with a high degree of localness of reference. This process is more easily described, of course, than performed. *Any* program will run more efficiently on a paging system if most references from within a page are to the same page. It is therefore also attractive to have the compiler attempt to produce target code with this property.

10.4 SEPARATE COMPILATION

How much of a source-language program should be translated at one time? Translating the entire program as a single unit gives maximum information to the translator. Although this may appear to be the most efficient choice, it may not always be the best. There are two compelling reasons for translating only a subset of a program. One reason is a different kind of efficiency that follows from dealing with smaller units. The other reason is to make use of the walls that can be built between program units. Sometimes both reasons apply.

Confinement. The principal arguments favoring modules that are smaller than the complete program are discussed in Section 1.6. These are primarily the parallel development of programs and the confinement of the effects of errors and of changes. There is an obvious cost benefit, too, when retranslation becomes necessary.

These advantages of modules have been known for a long time. The earliest assemblers provided for separate translation of different modules of a program. Even FORTRAN allows separate compilation of subroutines. Except for parameters, their external references are to a **common** block that is global to all subroutines. For PASCAL, on the other hand, neither the original nor the ISO standard version offers separate compilation. This lack has proved serious enough to PASCAL devotees that separate compilation of program units is nevertheless provided in many implementations.

Figure 1.1 shows the organization of the translation process when program units are translated separately. The primary burdens on implementation are type checking across module boundaries and the resolution of external references. The former is the responsibility of the compiler; the latter is accomplished by the means discussed in Chapter 9.

If the translator is an assembler, the name given to a unit that can be assembled separately is often language-specific. If the translator is a compiler, the separately compilable unit is a **compilation unit**. Although we have been calling either of these units simply a "module", that term is sometimes given a slightly different meaning in some languages.

Containment. The second major reason for dividing a program into compilation units is to emphasize the boundaries between the units. Controls on the transmission of information across those boundaries serve several purposes.

A classic reason for such containment is **information hiding**, in the software engineering sense of the phrase. This hides the internal implementation of a function, separating it from its external definition. By preventing access to details of implementation, information hiding makes interfaces explicit. It also allows the improvement of an implementation without changing the corresponding interface. In fact, the users of a module may be totally unaware that it has changed. Most significantly, separate compilation units provide concrete realizations of abstract data types.

Another reason for containment is information hiding in the more mundane sense of security. Separate modules can prevent access to proprietary code and to sensitive data such as passwords. The distribution of modules in object code form only also prevents proliferation of versions by multiple users.

The phrase "separate compilation" has come to mean primarily the explicit provision of walls to separate the compilation units. Notable among languages designed to support separate compilation are MODULA-2 and ADA. They provide two constructs for information hiding.

One construct is the explicit declaration of which identifiers are available to other modules and which are expected to be made available by other modules. Type information should be included in the declaration of identifiers even in this second category. This is necessary if the compiler is to perform type checking across module boundaries. Such checking is normally undertaken by the compiler rather than by the linker. MODULA-2's **import** and **export** are examples of this construct. They are analogous to the INTUSE and INTDEF directives of Chapter 2.

The other construct is the **module** in MODULA–2 or the **package** in ADA. Each distinguishes a public interface from a private implementation. MODULA–2 defines the interface in a **definition** module and the implementation in a corresponding **implementation** module. ADA defines the interface in a **package** and the implementation in a corresponding package **body**. Either language allows more than one implementation of a definition, although only one may be used in a given program. Both languages require the definition to be compiled before any implementation.

Reusability. We can view separate compilation, in its second sense, as offering a new form of reusability of program modules. This reusability is one of implementation rather than of execution, and lies at a higher level of granularity than the degrees of reusability discussed in Section 3.1. When two or more implementation modules correspond to one definition module, they are both using that definition. The definition module is therefore being reused, whether concurrently or sequentially, by the different implementations.

10.5 PORTABILITY

It is costly to develop new translators for existing machines whenever a new language is developed or an old one revised, or for an existing language whenever a new machine is developed or an old one modified. This has led to a desire to reuse substantial portions of existing translators, and to the application of generative techniques in writing translators. Before looking in the next section at translator generators, we examine here the issues in harnessing existing translators in the quest for new ones.

10.5.1 Translator Development

Input to a generative translator is written in source language and output is produced in target language. The translator itself is written in an implementation language, which may or may not be executable by hardware (a machine) or software (an interpreter). If it is executable, we refer to it also as the host language for that execution. A translator written in machine language runs on that machine as host.

Most translators are not written directly in machine language, but are translated to it from a different implementation language. That previous translation process has its own source, target, and implementation languages. An excellent device for keeping the roles of the various languages straight is the **T-diagram**, introduced in Bratman61, and illustrated here with three examples. In the "T" of a T-diagram, the left arm of the cross bar indicates the source language, the right arm indicates the target language, and the base of the upright indicates the implementation language.

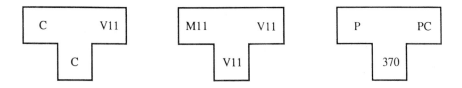

The left T-diagram represents a compiler from C to VAX-11 machine language, implemented in C. The middle T-diagram represents an assembler from MACRO-11 to VAX-11 machine language with the VAX as host. The right T-diagram represents a cross-compiler implemented on a IBM 370, translating from PASCAL to IBM PC machine language.

A common form of compiler produces machine language for its host. If we have one such compiler, we can use its source language as the implementation language for other compilers for the same host. For example, we may already have a PASCAL compiler on an IBM PC. We can write a C compiler in PASCAL, then compile it to obtain a C compiler whose host is the PC. The following combination of T-diagrams represents that translation.

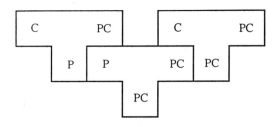

The original compiler appears in the center, with its input program to the left of the left arm and its output program to the right of the right arm. Those input and output programs are translators that accept the same source language and produce the same target language. The implementation language of each matches the source or target language in the adjacent arm of the compiler in the center. Combining T-diagrams in the foregoing manner is purely mechanical.

Suppose next that we have a PASCAL compiler whose host and target are the IBM 370. We need a PASCAL compiler for the VAX. If we write that PASCAL to VAX compiler in PASCAL, two compilations yield the desired result. We first compile the new compiler on the 370, yielding a cross-compiler to the VAX. We then use that cross-compiler to recompile our new compiler. The key is to implement the new compiler in its own source language. The following diagram, which superposes the two compilations, illustrates the process.

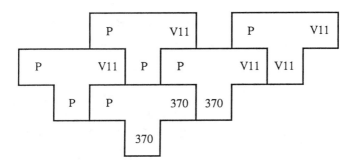

But how is our first compiler written? One approach, known as **bootstrapping**, creates compilers for increasingly larger subsets of the source language. We first implement in the host language H a small compiler for subset S_1 of the source language. We then write, in language S_1, a compiler for larger subset S_2. Using the former to compile the latter yields a compiler for S_2 that runs on our host. In tackling the yet larger subset S_3, the added features of S_2 simplify our task. A second compilation yields a compiler for S_3 that runs on our host. The process continues until the final subset is the full language. We illustrate the first two steps.

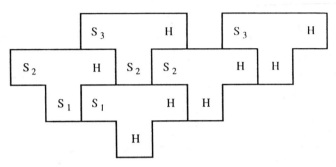

Program portability is the ability to use a program in different hardware and software environments. Modification of the translators that produce a program can lead to different choices of environment. In the next three sections, we consider the modification of each of the three languages that characterize a generative translator.

10.5.2 Source-Language Substitution

If we have a program written in language A but a translator only for language D, an A-to-D converter will allow us to translate and use that program. A classic problem is the source program written in a language for which we have no compiler. Our converter is then a translator from the source language outside our repertory to a source language inside. If we choose our machine language as the target, we have elected to write the missing compiler. Often less onerous is to write a compiler that produces assembler language. That permits us to use our existing assembler. Translation from one machine-independent language to another is rarely feasible.

Substitution of one source language for another is more often performed, not *ex post facto*, however, but with forethought. The introduction of a new language might appear to require the implementation of full translators for that language on various computers. An alternative is to design that language with the goal of implementing preprocessors to translate from it to another language for which translators are already available. This approach is followed in extending the capabilities of an existing language. The language RATFOR offers a FORTRAN-oriented user the ability to use control structures more modern than those available in FORTRAN. It is implemented by a preprocessor that generates FORTRAN code for subsequent compilation.

Application-specific languages are another fruitful class for pre-processing to a general-purpose language. The constructs of the application language can be defined as macros. The preprocessor becomes essentially a macroprocessor that expands macro definitions into strings in the source language of the subsequent translation.

The foregoing reduction of a new language to an existing one by macro processing has been termed **cascading** (Brown79). Although cascading into assembler language is possible, it usually requires considerably more effort than if the target is FORTRAN or PASCAL. The total translation time may also be longer. Another disadvantage is that assembler languages are much less portable than most machine-independent languages. Cascading endows the new languages with the portability of their underlying target languages.

10.5.3 Target-Language Substitution

Sometimes called "retargetability", the substitution of one target language for another enhances the portability of the program to be compiled. A classic problem is the program written in a language for which our only compiler translates to a target language we cannot run. If our translator produces target language T but we can execute only language A, a T-to-A converter will allow us to use that program. If both A and T are machine languages, the high degree of machine dependence of both usually makes it unprofitable to write such a converter. It may be necessary to undo storage allocations performed especially for T. It is also possible that the two instruction sets are quite different. Translation from one machine-dependent language to another is rarely feasible.

An approach that is always available is to write in A an interpreter for language T. If the latter is a machine language, the result is, of course, a simulator of the underlying machine. This simulation is straightforward, but the interpretive overhead results in very slow execution of the original program on the desired machine.

The most reasonable approach, short of writing a new compiler, is to change target code generators in the existing compiler. We replace the generator for language T by a generator for language A. This approach, although simple to describe, is not necessarily simple to implement. If, however, a code-generator generator (*cf.* Section 10.6.3) is available, generator replacement may be quite suitable.

10.5.4 Host-Language Substitution

Sometimes called "rehostability", the substitution of one implementation language for another enhances the portability of the translators themselves. The classic problem here is the program translatable by a compiler C_1 that doesn't run on our machine. If compiler C_1 is available in source-language form, this reduces to retargetability of the compiler C_2 used to translate it. The methods of Section 10.5.3 apply. Another possibility is the use of a simulator for the implementation language of C_1. Manual recoding of C_1 is also possible as a last resort.

10.6 TRANSLATOR GENERATORS

As the art of compiler writing has progressed, so has our understanding of compilation. This has been reflected in the development of formalisms to describe not only procedural languages, but also the processes of translation. We used to consider much of compilation, especially its machine-dependent aspects, to be ad hoc and unsystematic. Yet we now have systematic, formal descriptions of more and more of the compilation process. From such a description it is often possible to generate the corresponding part of the compiler. An important tool for the translator writer is thus seen to be the computer itself. The resulting **translator generators** are often called "compiler-writing systems" or "compiler compilers", although the claim implied by those terms is a bit extravagant.

The earliest generators were for parsers. This was a logical consequence of the importance of efficient parsing and of the existence of a vast body of parsing theory. Scanner generators, although less demanding, appeared quickly and proved very convenient. Work then turned to the incorporation of increasing semantic information in parsing and to the machine-dependent parts of compilers. In recent years, we have seen generators also for cross-assemblers, cross-compilers, cross-linkers, interpreters, and even optimizers. In this section, however, we focus on generators of scanners and parsers, and of target code generators.

10.6.1 Scanner Generators

The rules for recognizing tokens in most programming languages are given by grammar productions of the type known as **regular expressions**. The rules given in Section 6.3.2 for recognizing unsigned numbers are an example. It has long been known that the recognition of regular expressions can be performed by an abstract machine known as a **finite-state automaton**. The state diagrams of Section 6.3.2 are in fact representations of such automata. From a set of regular expressions, it is a straightforward process to generate a state-transition table of the sort shown in Figure 6.20. This table can be used by a program such as that of Figure 6.21 to perform the scanning.

One of the best known scanner generators is *LEX*, which is widely used under UNIX. It accepts as input a sequence of regular expressions and produces in the C language a state-transition table and a program for recognizing tokens. Subsequent compilation of the C program yields a scanner particularized to the language described by the regular expressions.

10.6.2 Parser Generators

The rules for recognizing almost all syntactic constructs in procedural languages are given by grammars of the type known as **context-free**. Intuitively, this phrase means that a production considers only the symbols being replaced, and not the symbols that surround them. Many forms of context-free grammars and parsing methods have been developed. In Section 6.2, we considered two methods, recursive descent and operator precedence. More commonly used in compilers is the method known as **LR** parsing. This is the most general shift/reduce parsing method that does not backtrack. It is applicable to almost all procedural-language constructs, and it can be implemented efficiently.

Unfortunately, manual construction of an LR parser is very tedious. This makes a generator of LR parsers particularly attractive. As with other shift/reduce parsers, at the heart of the parser is a table of parsing actions: shift, reduce, accept, and error. From most procedural-language grammars, it is possible to generate the corresponding LR parsing table. Although the process may be tedious, it is straightforward. An LR parsing program can use the parsing table to carry out the parse.

One of the earliest and still most widely used parser generators is *YACC*. Denoting "yet another compiler-compiler", it is available as a command under UNIX. *YACC* is based on a variant of LR parsing known as "lookahead-LR" or "LALR" parsing. It accepts as input a list of token declarations, and a set of productions each accompanied by a description of the corresponding semantic action. It produces in the C language a LALR parsing table that can be used with an existing table-driven parser. Subsequent compilation of the table and general parser yields a parser specialized to the source language described in the input to *YACC*.

A context-free grammar can be generalized by associating with each symbol of the grammar a set of attributes and with each production a set of semantic rules. Each rule specifies the value of an attribute at the parse-tree node corresponding to that production. Typical attributes are the type of an identifier, the storage allocated for it, and the types of the arguments and result of a function. If the semantic rules that specify attribute values have no side effects, the grammar that results from this generalization is called an **attribute grammar**.

Most rules specify the value of an attribute in terms of the values of other attributes in the parse tree. Values of some attributes are derived from the values of attributes at child nodes. Such an attribute is said to be **synthesized**. For example, the value of an expression is synthesized from the values of its components. Values of other attributes are derived from the values of attributes of parent or sibling nodes. Such an attribute is said to be **inherited**. For example, the type attribute of an identifier is inherited from the type specified in the declaration of the identifier.

A parse tree with all its attributes evaluated is called a **decorated** (or "annotated") parse tree. A tree is decorated (its attributes are evaluated) by sweeping up and down the tree, propagating synthesized attribute values upward and inherited attribute values downward. When the tree is fully decorated, a single traversal suffices to generate intermediate code. Parsers generated from an attribute grammar thus yield not merely a parser, but a complete semantic analyzer.

10.6.3 Code-Generator Generators

Automatic generation of code generators requires a description of the target machine. This may be a set of templates specifying the machine code that corresponds to each construct in intermediate code. It may be a more formal specification in some machine description language. Thus a code-generator generator (CGG), like scanner generators and parser generators, is table-driven.

The most successful CGGs express target-language instructions as productions in a grammar. The right-hand side represents an operation and the left-hand side the result of that operation. Parsing theory is used to construct the code generation algorithm. Because of alternate ways to effect many operations, the grammar is usually ambiguous. This requires appropriate parsing techniques, and a means of selecting choices. Early CGGs built using this approach have been efficient and the generators they produce have been provably correct.

Nevertheless, with ordinary context-free grammars there have been a number of problems. The required target-machine grammar may be very large. The intermediate code language is at so low a level that it, too, may need to be changed to make a compiler portable. Global information about the program is often difficult to use effectively. As a result, the quality of the generated code may be disappointing. For these reasons, CGG development has turned to attribute grammars. CGGs based on attribute grammars have been implemented that rapidly generate target code of excellent quality.

FOR FURTHER STUDY

Tanenbaum84 presents a good general introduction to hardware issues that bear on translation. Calingaert82 is an elementary exposition of operating systems.

The use of interpretation in code generation is discussed in Gries71 (Chapter 16) and in Ganapathi82. Threaded code is described in Bell73. Dawson73 presents three methods for combining interpretive code and compilative code in the mixed-code approach. Klint81 presents a good comparison of pure interpretation with compilation, and with both direct and indirect threaded code. Gros78 offers quantitative comparisons of interpretation and compilation. P-code is described in Nori76. Chung78 presents details of converting from P-code to Intel 8080 machine language.

Brown79b discusses incremental compiling in Chapter 2.4 and dynamic compiling in Chapter 8.2. Incremental compiling is also treated in Gros78. Throw-away compiling was introduced in the book Brown76, and is also mentioned in Chapter 8.2 of Brown79b, and well summarized in Robson83.

Section 11.1 of Ford85 explains briefly the benefits of separate compilation.

Brown77 is a course of lectures on portability. Both the classic paper McIlroy60 and the book Brown74 discuss macro processing for programming languages. Munn80, Hayashi83, and Semakin84 illustrate the achievement of portability through preprocessors. A good account of the history of this activity is presented in Layzell85. An interesting technique for target-language substitution is indirect threaded code, introduced in Dewar75. The survey article Ganapathi82 presents an excellent overview of techniques for retargetable code generation.

Johnson78 presents a lucid discussion of translator generators. The ideas underlying scanner generators go back at least to Johnson68. *LEX* was presented in Lesk75, and is described in Section 3.5 of Aho86. Evans78 states clearly the issues in parser generation and describes a particular system. *YACC* was presented in Johnson75, and is described in Section 4.9 of Aho86. A simple introduction to attribute grammars is given in Jazayeri75. A more extensive one is presented in Section 5 of Marcotty76. Their use in compilers is treated in Waite84 (Chapter 8) and Hunter85 (Chapter 2).

Williams79 presents a good early description of a real code-generator generator. Several approaches to code-generator generation are discussed in Ganapathi82. The interdependence of intermediate code and code generation is considered in Ganapathi84. Branquart84 presents an intermediate language designed for portable code generators.

Generators of cross assemblers are described in VanBuer78 and Ancona85, of cross compilers in Tanenbaum83, of cross-linkers in Fraser82, of interpreters in Hoffman79, and of optimizers in Davidson84a.

REVIEW QUESTIONS

10.1 Why is it desirable to minimize the frequency of calling across page boundaries?

10.2 Checking the syntax of source-language statements as they are entered into a interactive system provides helpful feedback to a programmer. Are the relative costs and benefits of this action different for interpreters than for compilers?

10.3 State briefly the principal advantages and disadvantages of using assembler language, rather than object (or machine) language, as the target language of a compiler.

10.4 What does threaded code save over straight interpretation? Over object code generation?

10.5 The indirect branch instruction of a certain computer uses the computer's only register. Explain why threaded code is not satisfactory as the output of a cross-compiler of programs to be executed by that computer.

10.6 Explain briefly why dynamic compiling can require less time than does pure interpretation of intermediate code and less space than pure compilation from intermediate code.

10.7 In the mixed-code approach, can we give a compiler the ability to decide which portions of a program to leave in source language for interpretive execution?

10.8 Identify one parameter that *must* be passed to the mode-switch subroutine.

10.9 In the mixed-code approach, describe an implementation of machine code calling an interpretive-code subroutine.

10.10 State the advantages of a load-and-go compiler over other compilers.

10.11 Type checking and target code generation were performed by independent passes in Wirth's first MODULA–2 compiler. The second version of the compiler combined both functions in a single module. Why?

10.12 In what sense does bootstrapping illustrate portability?

PROBLEMS

10.1 Describe in detail a scheme for passing an arbitrary number of parameters between a source-language program being interpreted and a host-language segment.

10.2 Write a mode-switch subroutine to accompany the interpretive loop of Figure 5.3. State any assumptions you make about the source-language program.

10.3 Using T-diagrams, show the use of an optimizing assembler (e.g., SOAP for the IBM 650) to optimize itself.

10.4 [Ghezzi] Consider the use of a macro processor to translate from quadruples to assembler language code. One macro is to be provided for each operator. Describe the over-all structure and operation of the translator. In particular, explain how to handle jumps.

10.5 Describe how you could modify each of the following to obtain a cross-compiler to run on the UNIVAC 1110, translating from standard FORTRAN to CDC 6500 code. Assume that standard FORTRAN really is standard.

(a) only a UNIVAC 1110 standard FORTRAN compiler, written in UNIVAC 1110 assembler language;
(b) only a CDC 6500 standard FORTRAN compiler, written in CDC 6500 assembler language;
(c) both of the foregoing compilers [use both].

BIBLIOGRAPHY

Aho74

A. V. Aho and S. C. Johnson. LR Parsing. *Computing Surveys* **6**(2): 99–124; June 1974.

Aho86

Alfred V. Aho, Ravi Sethi, and Jeffrey D. Ullman. *Compilers: Principles, Techniques, and Tools.* Addison-Wesley, Reading, MA; 1986.

Allen69

F. E. Allen. *Program Optimization. Annual Review in Automatic Programming* **5**: 239–307; 1969.

Ammann77

Urs Ammann. On Code Generation in a Pascal Compiler. *Softw. Pract. Exp.* **7**(3): 391–423; June/July 1977.

Ancona85

M. Ancona, A. Clematis, G. Dodero, and A. Pino. A High Level Language Based System for Cross-Assembler Definition. *Softw. Pract. Exp.* **15**(12): 1159–1184; December 1985.

Anklam82

Patricia Anklam, David Cutler, Roger Heinem, Jr., and M. Donald MacLaren. *Engineering a Compiler: VAX-11 Code Generation and Optimization.* Digital Press, Bedford, MA; 1982.

Anonymous79

Anonymous. *UNIX Programmer's Manual: Supplementary Documents.* Computer Science Division, Department of Electrical Engineering and Computer Science, University of California, Berkeley; 1979.

Arms76

W. Y. Arms, J. E. Baker, and R. M. Pengelly. *A Practical Approach to Computing.* Wiley, London; 1976.

Bailes85
Paul A. Bailes. A Low-Cost Implementation of Coroutines for C. *Softw. Pract. Exp.* **15**(4): 379–395; April 1985.

Barrett86
William A. Barrett, Rodney M. Bates, David A. Gustafson, and John D. Couch. *Compiler Construction: Theory and Practice, 2nd ed.* Science Research Associates, Chicago; 1986.

Barron77
D. W. Barron. *An Introduction to the Study of Programming Languages.* Cambridge University Press, Cambridge; 1977.

Barron78
D. W. Barron. *Assemblers and Loaders, 3rd ed.* Elsevier North-Holland, New York; 1978.

Bauer74
F. L. Bauer and J. Eickel (eds.). *Compiler Construction — An Advanced Course.* Springer-Verlag, Berlin; 1974.

Beck85
Leland L. Beck. *System Software: an Introduction to Systems Programming.* Addison-Wesley, Reading, MA; 1985.

Bell73
James R. Bell. Threaded Code. *Comm. ACM* **16**(6): 370–372; June 1973.

Berthaud73
M. Berthaud and M. Griffiths. Incremental Compilation and Conversational Interpretation. *Annual Review in Automatic Programming* **7**(2): 95–114; 1973.

Blaauw66
G. A. Blaauw. Door de Vingers Zien (*inaugural lecture*). Technische Hogeschool Twente, Enschede (The Netherlands), 3 March 1966.

Blaauw70
Gerrit A. Blaauw. *Hardware Requirements for the Fourth Generation.* In Fred Gruenberger (ed.). *Fourth Generation Computers: User Requirements and Transition*: 155–168. Prentice-Hall, Englewood Cliffs, NJ; 1970.

Branquart84
P. Branquart. A High Level Intermediate Code. Pages 317–343 of Lorho84.

Bratman61
Harvey Bratman. An Alternate Form of the "UNCOL diagram". *Comm. ACM* **4**(3): 142; March 1961.

Brooks69
Frederick P. Brooks, Jr., and Kenneth E. Iverson. *Automatic Data Processing, System/360 edition.* Wiley, New York; 1969.

Brooks75
Frederick P. Brooks, Jr. *The Mythical Man-Month.* Addison-Wesley, Reading, MA; 1975.

Brown74
P. J. Brown. *Macro Processors and Techniques for Portable Software.* Wiley, London; 1974.

Brown76
P. J. Brown. Throw-Away Compiling. *Softw. Pract. Exp.* **6**(3): 423–434; July–Sept. 1976.

Brown77
P. J. Brown (ed.). *Software Portability.* Cambridge University Press, Cambridge; 1977.

Brown79a
P. J. Brown. Macros Without Tears. *Softw. Pract. Exp.* **9**(6): 433–437; June 1979.

Brown79b
P. J. Brown. *Writing Interactive Compilers and Interpreters.* Wiley, Chichester (U.K.); 1979.

Brown81
Frank M. Brown. Design of a MUMPS Interpreter. *Softw. Pract. Exp.* **11**(12): 1293–1297; December 1981.

Brown84
Cynthia A. Brown and Paul W. Purdom, Jr. A Methodology and Notation for Compiler Front End Design. *Softw. Pract. Exp.* **14**(4): 335–346; April 1984.

Calingaert79
Peter Calingaert. *Assemblers, Compilers, and Program Translation.* Computer Science Press, Potomac, MD; 1979.

Calingaert82
Peter Calingaert. *Operating System Elements: A User Perspective.* Prentice-Hall, Englewood Cliffs, NJ; 1982.

Campbell73
M. Campbell-Kelly. *An Introduction to Macros.* Macdonald, London; 1973.

Cattell79
Roderick G. G. Cattell, Joseph M. Newcomer, and Bruce W. Leverett. Code Generation in a Machine-Independent Compiler. *SIGPLAN Notices* **14**(8): 65–75; August 1979.

Celentano80
Augusto Celentano, Pierluigi Della Vigna, Carlo Ghezzi, and Dino Mandrioli. Separate Compilation and Partial Specification in Pascal. *IEEE Trans. Softw. Eng.* **SE–6**(4): 320–328; July 1980.

Chung78
Kim-Man Chung and Herbert Yuen. A "Tiny" Pascal Compiler, Part 3: P-Code to 8080 Conversion. *BYTE* **3**(11): 182–192; November 1978.

Cole81
A. J. Cole. *Macro Processors, 2nd ed.* Cambridge University Press, Cambridge; 1981.

Conway63
Melvin E. Conway. Design of a Separable Transition-Diagram Compiler. *Comm. ACM* **6**(7): 396–408; July 1963.

Conway73
Richard W. Conway and Thomas R. Wilcox. Design and Implementation of a Diagnostic Compiler for PL/I. *Comm. ACM* **16**(3): 169–179; March 1973.

Cook83
Robert P. Cook and Thomas J. LeBlanc. A Symbol Table Abstraction to Implement Languages with Explicit Scope Control. *IEEE Trans. Softw. Eng.* **SE–9**(1): 8–12; January 1983.

Dakin73
R. J. Dakin and P. C. Poole. A Mixed Code Approach. *Computer J.* **16**(3): 219–222; August 1973.

Davidson80
J. W. Davidson and C. W. Fraser. The Design and Application of a Retargetable Peephole Optimizer. *ACM Trans. Prog. Lang. Syst.* **2**(2): 191–202; April 1980. *Corrigendum in* **3**(1): 110; January 1981.

Davidson84a
Jack W. Davidson and Christopher W. Fraser. Automatic Generation of Peephole Optimizers. *SIGPLAN Notices* **19**(6): 111–116; June 1984.

Davidson84b
Jack W. Davidson and Christopher W. Fraser. Code Selection through Object Code Optimization. *ACM Trans. Prog. Lang. Syst.* **6**(4): 505–526; October 1984.

Davie81
A. J. T. Davie and R. Morrison. *Recursive Descent Compiling.* Ellis Horwood, Chichester (U.K.); 1981.

Davis81

Henry Davis. Compiler or Interpreter? *Interface Age* **6**(1): 90–91; January 1981.

Dawson73

J. L. Dawson. Combining Interpretive Code with Machine Code. *Computer J.* **16**(3): 216–219; August 1973.

Dedourek80

John M. Dedourek, Uday G. Gujar, and Marion E. McIntyre. Scanner Design. *Softw. Pract. Exp.* **10**(12): 959–972; December 1980.

Dewar75

Robert B. K. Dewar. Indirect Threaded Code. *Comm. ACM* **18**(6): 330–331; June 1975.

Dijkstra65

E. W. Dijkstra. Cooperating Sequential Processes. EWD123, Mathematics Department, Technological University, Eindhoven (The Netherlands); September 1965. *Reprinted in* F. Genuys (ed.). *Programming Languages.* Academic Press, London; 1968.

Donovan72

John J. Donovan. *Systems Programming.* McGraw-Hill, New York; 1972.

Elson72

M. Elson and S. T. Rake. Code-Generation Technique for Large-Language Compilers. *IBM Syst. J.* **9**(3): 166–188; 1970. *Reprinted in* Pollack72.

Elson73

Mark Elson. *Concepts of Programming Languages.* Science Research Associates, Palo Alto, CA; 1973.

Evans78

R. V. Evans, G. S. Lockington, and T. N. Reid. A Compiler Compiler and Methodology for Problem Oriented Language Compiler Implementors. *Computer J.* **21**(2): 117–121; May 1978.

Fabri82

Janet Fabri. *Automatic Storage Optimization.* UMI Research Press, Ann Arbor, MI; 1982.

Faiman80

R. Neil Faiman, Jr., and Alan A. Kortesoja. An Optimizing Pascal Compiler. *IEEE Trans. Softw. Eng.* **SE-6**(6): 512–519; November 1980.

Ferguson66

David E. Ferguson. Evolution of the Meta-Assembly Program. *Comm. ACM* **9**(3): 190–196; March 1966.

Fisher84

A. J. Fisher. Guarded and Unguarded Coroutines: an Implementation in BCPL. *Softw. Pract. Exp.* **14**(4): 369–376; April 1984.

Floyd63

Robert W. Floyd. Syntactic Analysis and Operator Precedence. *J. ACM* **10**(3): 316–333; July 1963. *Reprinted in* Pollack72.

Ford85

Gary Ford and Richard Weiner. *Modula-2: a Software Development Approach.* Wiley, New York; 1985.

Foster86

David G. Foster. Separate Compilation in a Modula–2 Compiler. *Softw. Pract. Exp.* **16**(2): 101–106; February 1986.

Fraser77

C. W. Fraser. A Knowledge-Based Code Generator Generator. *SIG-PLAN Notices* **12**(8): 126–129; August 1977.

Fraser79

Christopher W. Fraser. A Compact, Machine-Independent Peephole Optimizer. *Conference Record of the 6th Annual ACM Symposium on Principles of Programming Languages*: 1–6. ACM, New York; 1979.

Fraser82

Christopher W. Fraser and David R. Hanson. A Machine-Independent Linker. *Softw. Pract. Exp.* **12**(4): 351–366; April 1982.

Freeman64

David N. Freeman. Error Correction in CORC, the Cornell Computing Language. *Proc. AFIPS Conf. (FJCC)* **26**: 15–34; 1964. *Reprinted in* Pollack72.

Freeman75

Peter Freeman. *Software System Principles.* Science Research Associates, Palo Alto, CA; 1975.

Gale81

W. A. Gale. Write Your Own Compiler. *Dr. Dobb's J.* **6**(8): 6–14; August 1981.

Ganapathi82

Mahadevan Ganapathi, Charles N. Fischer, and John L. Hennessy. Retargetable Compiler Code Generation. *Computing Surveys* **14**(4): 573–592; December 1982.

Ganapathi84

Mahadevan Ganapathi and Charles N. Fischer. Attributed Linear Intermediate Representations for Retargetable Code Generators. *Softw. Pract. Exp.* **14**(4): 347–364; April 1984.

Gear80

C. William Gear. *Computer Organization and Programming, 3rd ed.* McGraw-Hill, New York; 1980.

Ghezzi82

Carlo Ghezzi and Mehdi Jazayeri. *Programming Language Concepts.* Wiley, New York; 1982.

Glanville78

R. Steven Glanville and Susan L. Graham. A New Method for Compiler Code Generation. *Conference Record of the 5th ACM Symposium on Principles of Programming Languages*: 231–240. ACM, New York; 1978.

Glass69

Robert L. Glass. An Elementary Discussion of Compiler/Interpreter Writing. *Computing Surveys* **1**(1): 55–77; March 1969.

Gorczynski82

E. W. Gorczynski. Development of Chemical Engineering Software Using a FORTRAN Preprocessor. *Advances in Engineering Software* **4**(3): 107–111; July 1982.

Graham75

Robert M. Graham. *Principles of Systems Programming.* Wiley, New York; 1975.

Graham79

S. L. Graham, W. N. Joy, and O. Roubine. Hashed Symbol Tables for Languages with Explicit Scope Control. *SIGPLAN Notices* **14**(8): 50–57; August 1979.

Graham84

S. L. Graham. Code Generation and Optimization. *Pages 251–288 of* Lorho84.

Gries71

David Gries. *Compiler Construction for Digital Computers.* Wiley, New York; 1971.

Griffiths74

M. Griffiths. Run-Time Storage Management. *Chapter 3.B of* Bauer74.

Gros78

Rick Gros. Interpreters vs. Compilers. *Interface Age* **3**(3): 152–155; March 1978.

Guida81

Giovanni Guida. An Effective Preprocessor for structured FORTRAN: the HENTRAN System. *Intl. J. Comput. Inf. Sci.* **10**(4): 283–297; August 1981.

Habermann76

A. N. Habermann. *Introduction to Operating System Design.* Science Research Associates, Palo Alto, CA; 1976.

Hanson83

David R. Hanson. Simple Code Optimizations. *Softw. Pract. Exp.* **13**(8): 745–763; August 1983.

Hanson85

David R. Hanson. Compact Recursive-Descent Parsing of Expressions. *Softw. Pract. Exp.* **15**(12): 1205–1212; December 1985.

Hayashi83

Tsunetoshi Hayashi. A Program Structuring Preprocessor for a Macro Assembly Language. *Softw. Pract. Exp.* **13**(6): 487–494; June 1983.

Heliard84

J. C. Heliard. Compiling Ada. *Pages 371–398 of* Lorho84.

Hennessy82

John L. Hennessy and Noah Mendelsohn. Compilation of the Pascal Case Statement. *Softw. Pract. Exp.* **12**(9): 879–882; September 1982.

Hoffman79

Christoph M. Hoffman and Michael J. O'Donnell. An Interpreter Generator Using Tree Pattern Matching. *Conference Record of the 6th Annual ACM Symposium on Principles of Programming Languages*: 169–179. ACM, New York; 1979.

Hopgood69

F. R. A. Hopgood. *Compiling Techniques.* Macdonald, London; 1969.

Horowitz84a

Ellis Horowitz. *Fundamentals of Programming Languages, 2nd ed.* Computer Science Press, Rockville, MD; 1984.

Horowitz84b

Ellis Horowitz and Sartaj Sahni. *Fundamentals of Data Structures in Pascal.* Computer Science Press, Rockville, MD; 1984.

Horspool85

R. Nigel Horspool and André Scheunemann. Automating the Selection of Code Templates. *Softw. Pract. Exp.* **15**(5): 503–514; May 1985.

Horton86

I. A. Horton and S. J. Turner. Using Coroutines in Pascal. *Softw. Pract. Exp.* **16**(1): 45–61; January 1986.

Hunter85

Robin Hunter. *Compilers: Their Design and Construction Using Pascal.* Wiley, Chichester (U.K.); 1985.

Ingerman61
P. Z. Ingerman. Thunks. *Comm. ACM* **4**(1): 55–58; January 1961. *Reprinted in* Pollack72.

Inman81
Don Inman and Kurt Inman. *The Atari Assembler*. Reston, Reston, VA; 1981.

Jazayeri75
Mehdi Jazayeri and Kenneth G. Walter. Alternating Semantic Evaluator. *Proc. ACM Annual Conf.*: 230–234. October 1975.

Johnson68
Walter L. Johnson, James H. Porter, Stephanie I. Ackley, and Douglas T. Ross. Automatic Generation of Efficient Lexical Processors Using Finite State Techniques. *Comm. ACM* **11**(12): 805–813; December 1968.

Johnson75
Stephen C. Johnson. Yacc: Yet Another Compiler-Compiler. *Computing Science Technical Report No. 32*. Bell Laboratories, Murray Hill, NJ; 1975. *Reprinted in* Anonymous79.

Johnson78
S. C. Johnson. A Portable Compiler: Theory and Practice. *Conference Record of the 5th Annual ACM Symposium on Principles of Programming Languages*: 97–104. ACM, New York; 1978.

Jones83
Douglas W. Jones. Assembly Language as Object Code. *Softw. Pract. Exp.* **13**(8): 715–725; August 1983.

Klint81
Paul Klint. Interpretation Techniques. *Softw. Pract. Exp.* **11**(9): 963–973; September 1981.

Knuth62
Donald E. Knuth. A History of Writing Compilers. *Computers and Automation* **11**(12): 8–14; December 1962. *Reprinted in* Pollack72.

Knuth64
Donald E. Knuth. Backus Normal Form vs. Backus Naur Form. *Comm. ACM* **7**(12): 735–736; December 1964.

Knuth65
Donald E. Knuth. On the Translation of Languages from Left to Right. *Information and Control* **8**(6): 607–639; December 1965.

Knuth73
Donald E. Knuth. *The Art of Computer Programming, vol. 1: Fundamental Algorithms, 2nd ed.* Addison-Wesley, Reading, MA; 1973.

Layzell85

P. J. Layzell. The History of Macro Processors in Programming Language Extensibility. *Computer J.* **28**(1): 29–33; February 1985.

LeBlanc84

Richard J. LeBlanc and Charles N. Fischer. A Simple Separate Compilation Mechanism for Block-Structured Languages. *IEEE Trans. Softw. Eng.* **SE–10**(3): 221–227; May 1984.

Lee74

John A. N. Lee. *The Anatomy of a Compiler, 2nd ed.* Van Nostrand Reinhold, New York; 1974.

Lesk75

M. E. Lesk and E. Schmidt. Lex — a Lexical Analyzer Generator. *Computing Science Technical Report No. 39.* Bell Laboratories, Murray Hill, NJ; 1975. *Reprinted in* Anonymous79.

Leverett80

Bruce Leverett and Thomas G. Szymanski. Chaining Span-Dependent Jump Instructions. *ACM Trans. Prog. Lang. Syst.* **2**(3): 274–289; July 1980.

Lorho84

B. Lorho (ed.). *Methods and Tools for Compiler Construction.* Cambridge University Press, Cambridge; 1984.

Lucas61

P. Lucas. Die Strukturanalyse von Formelübersetzern. *Elektronische Rechenanlagen* **3**: 159–167; 1961.

Lukasiewicz29

Jan Łukasiewicz. *Elementy Logiki Matematycznej.* Association of Mathematics and Physics Students in Warsaw University, Warsaw; 1929. *Translated as Elements of Mathematical Logic*: 24. Pergamon Press, Oxford; 1963.

Marcotty76

Michael Marcotty, Henry F. Ledgard, and Gregor V. Bochmann. A Sampler of Formal Definitions. *Computing Surveys* **8**(2): 191–276; June 1976.

Marti83

Jed Marti. The Little META Translator Writing System. *Softw. Pract. Exp.* **13**(10): 941–959; October 1983.

Maurer75

W. D. Maurer and T. G. Lewis. Hash Table Methods. *Computing Surveys* **7**(1): 6–19; March 1975.

McIlroy60
M. Douglas McIlroy. Macro Instruction Extensions of Compiler Languages. *Comm. ACM* **3**(4): 214–220; April 1960. *Reprinted in* Rosen-67b *and in* Pollack72.

McKeeman65
W. M. McKeeman. Peephole Optimization. *Comm. ACM* **8**(7): 443–444; July 1965. *Reprinted in* Pollack72.

McKeeman74
W. M. McKeeman. Symbol Table Access. *Chapter 3.D of* Bauer74.

Morgan70
Howard L. Morgan. Spelling Correction in Systems Programs. *Comm. ACM* **13**(2): 90–94; February 1970.

Morris83
Derrick Morris. *An Introduction to System Programming — Based on the PDP11.* Macmillan, London; 1983.

Munn80
R. J. Munn and J. M. Stewart. RATMAC: a Preprocessor for Writing Portable Scientific Software. *Softw. Pract. Exp.* **10**(9): 743–749; September 1980.

Nori76
K. V. Nori *et al.* The Pascal <P> Compiler; Implementation Notes. Eidgenössische Technische Hochschule, Zürich; 1976. *Reprinted as* Pascal-P Implementation Notes *in* D. W. Barron (ed.). *Pascal — The Language and its Implementation*: 125–170. Wiley, Chichester (U.K.); 1981.

Pollack72
Bary W. Pollack (ed.). *Compiler Techniques.* Auerbach, Princeton, NJ; 1972.

Pratt75
Terence W. Pratt. *Programming Languages: Design and Implementation.* Prentice-Hall, Englewood Cliffs, NJ; 1975.

Presser72
Leon Presser and John R. White. Linkers and Loaders. *Computing Surveys* **4**(3): 149–167; September 1972.

Prywes83
N. S. Prywes and A. Pnueli. Compilation of Nonprocedural Specifications into Computer Programs. *IEEE Trans. Softw. Eng.* **SE–9**(3): 267–279; May 1983.

Randell75
Brian Randell (ed.). *The Origins of Digital Computers.* Springer-Verlag, Berlin; 1975.

Reiser81

J. F. Reiser. Compiling Three-Address Code for C Programs. *Bell Syst. Tech. J.* **60**(2): 159–166; February 1981.

Revesz85

Gyorgy Revesz. A Note on Macro Generation. *Softw. Pract. Exp.* **15**(5): 423–426; May 1985.

Rice65

H. Gordon Rice. Recursion and Iteration. *Comm. ACM* **8**(2): 114–115; February 1965.

Rice84

John R. Rice, Calvin Ribbens, and William A. Ward. Algorithm 622. A Simple Macroprocessor. *ACM Trans. Math. Softw.* **10**(4): 410–416; December 1984.

Roberts85

M. L. Roberts and P. D. Griffiths. Design Considerations for IBM Personal Computer Professional FORTRAN, an Optimizing Compiler. *IBM Syst. J.* **24**(1): 49–60; 1985.

Robson83

D. J. Robson. An Evaluation of Throw-Away Compiling. *Softw. Pract. Exp.* **13**(3): 241–249; March 1983.

Rohl75

J. S. Rohl. *An Introduction to Compiler Writing.* Macdonald, London; 1975.

Rosen64

Saul Rosen. Programming Systems and Languages — a Historical Survey. *Proc. AFIPS Conf. (SJCC)* **25**: 1–15; 1964. *Reprinted in* Rosen67b.

Rosen67a

Saul Rosen. Programming Systems and Languages — Some Recent Developments. *Part* 1B *of* Rosen67b.

Rosen67b

Saul Rosen (ed.). *Programming Systems and Languages.* McGraw-Hill, New York; 1967.

Rosen69

Saul Rosen. Electronic Computers: A Historical Survey. *Computing Surveys* **1**(1): 7–36; March 1969.

Samet80

Hanan Samet. A Coroutine Approach to Parsing. *ACM Trans. Prog. Lang. Syst.* **2**(3): 290–306; July 1980.

Samet85

Hanan Samet. Bidirectional Coroutines. *Info. Process. Lett.* **21**(1): 1–6; 10 July 1985.

Schreiner85
Axel T. Schreiner and H. George Friedman, Jr. *Introduction to Compiler Construction with UNIX*. Prentice-Hall, Englewood Cliffs, NJ; 1985.

Semakin84
I. S. Semakin. PL/I Preprocessor-Based Macroprocessor. *Programming and Computer Software*: 64–67; July 1985.

Severance74
Dennis G. Severance. Identifier Search Mechanisms: A Survey and Generalized Model. *Computing Surveys* **6**(3): 175–194; September 1974.

Shammas84
Namir Shammas. NBASIC: a Structured Preprocessor for MBASIC. *Dr. Dobb's J.* **9**(1): 24–34; January 1984.

Sippu83
Seppo Sippu and Eljas Soisalou-Soininen. A Syntax-Error-Handling Technique and its Experimental Analysis. *ACM Trans. Prog. Lang. Syst.* **5**(4): 656–679; October 1983.

Steel61
Thomas B. Steel, Jr. UNCOL: the Myth and the Fact. *Annual Review in Automatic Programming* **2**: 325–344; 1961.

Strong58
J. Strong *et al*. The Problem of Programming Communication with Changing Machines: a Proposed Solution. *Comm. ACM* **1**(8): 12–18, August 1958, *and* (9): 9–15, September 1958.

Tanenbaum82
Andrew S. Tanenbaum, Hans van Staveren, and Johan W. Stevenson. Using Peephole Optimization on Intermediate Code. *ACM Trans. Prog. Lang. Syst.* **4**(1): 21–36; January 1982.

Tanenbaum83
Andrew S. Tanenbaum *et al*. A Practical Tool Kit for Making Portable Compilers. *Comm. ACM* **26**(9): 654–660; September 1983.

Tanenbaum84
Andrew S. Tanenbaum. *Structured Computer Organization, 2nd ed.* Prentice-Hall, Englewood Cliffs, NJ; 1984.

Tavernier80
Karel R. Tavernier and Paul H. Notredame. Macro-Based Cross Assemblers. *IEEE Trans. Softw. Eng.* **SE–6**(4): 334–340; July 1980.

Toy86
Wing Toy and Benjamin Zee. *Computer Hardware/Software Architecture*. Prentice-Hall, Englewood Cliffs, NJ; 1986.

Tremblay85
Jean-Paul Tremblay and Paul G. Sorenson. *The Theory and Practice of Compiler Writing.* McGraw-Hill, New York; 1985.

Triance85a
J. M. Triance and P. J. Layzell. Macro Processors for Enhancing High-Level Languages — Some Design Principles. *Computer J.* **28**(1): 34–43; February 1985.

Triance85b
J. M. Triance and P. J. Layzell. A Language Enhancement Facility for COBOL — its Design and Implementation. *Computer J.* **28**(2): 128–133; May 1985.

Ullman76
Jeffrey D. Ullman. *Fundamental Concepts of Programming Systems.* Addison-Wesley, Reading, MA; 1976.

VanBuer78
Darrell Van Buer. A LISP Interpreter for the 8080. *Dr. Dobb's J.* **3**(10): 4–11; Nov.–Dec. 1978.

VanBuer80
D. J. Van Buer. A Table Driven Assembler on CP/M. *Dr. Dobb's J.* **5**(2): 18–25; February 1980.

Waite84
William M. Waite and Gerhard Goos. *Compiler Construction.* Springer-Verlag, New York; 1984.

Wallis81
Peter J. L. Wallis. Handling Type Information when Compiling a Language with User-Defined Types. *Softw. Pract. Exp.* **11**(2): 167–173; February 1981.

Wegner68
Peter Wegner. *Programming Languages, Information Structures, and Machine Organization.* McGraw-Hill, New York; 1968.

Williams79
M. H. Williams and A. R. Bulmer. A Transportable Code Generator Generator System. *Info. Process. Lett.* **9**(3): 122–125; 5 October 1979.

Williams82
M. Howard Williams. A Flexible Notation for Syntactic Definitions. *ACM Trans. Prog. Lang. Syst.* **4**(1): 113–119; January 1982.

Wirth77
Niklaus Wirth. What Can We Do about the Unnecessary Diversity of Notation for Syntactic Definitions? *Comm. ACM* **20**(11): 822-823; November 1977.

INDEX

DATE DUE

MAY 2 7 1989		
OCT 1 7 1991		
NOV 1 1 1991		
APR 1 1 1994		
JUL 2 2 1995		
OCT 1 2 1995		